Practical Software Measurement

Objective Information for Decision Makers

John McGarry

David Card

Cheryl Jones

Beth Layman

Elizabeth Clark

Joseph Dean

Fred Hall

✦Addison-Wesley

Boston • San Francisco • New York • Toronto • Montreal
London • Munich • Paris • Madrid • Capetown
Sydney • Tokyo • Singapore • Mexico City

The publisher offers discounts on this book when ordered in quantity for special sales. For more information, please contact:

Pearson Education Corporate Sales Division
201 W. 103rd Street
Indianapolis, IN 46290
(800) 428-5331
corpsales@pearsontechgroup.com

Visit AW on the Web: www.aw.com/cseng/

Library of Congress Cataloging-in-Publication Data

Practical software measurement : objective information for decision makers / John McGarry . . . [et al.].
    p.   cm.
  Includes bibliographical references.
  ISBN 0-201-71516-3 (alk. paper)
   1. Computer software—Quality control. 2. Computer software—Development—Management. I. McGarry, John.

QA76.76.Q35 P73   2001
005.1'0685—dc.21   2001045064

Pearson Education, Inc.
Rights and Contracts Department
75 Arlington Street, Suite 300
Boston, MA 02116
Fax: (617) 848-7047

ISBN 0-201-71516-3
Text printed on recycled paper
1 2 3 4 5 6 7 8 9 10—MA—0504030201
First printing, October 2001

CONTENTS

FOREWORD

The future world of software engineering will be very different from the past or the present. Our systems will be much more complex. Most likely, they will be systems of systems—systems that once marched to different drummers but were ultimately compelled to interoperate smoothly and evolve together.

The safest assumption about systems of systems is that everything will eventually be interconnected. Even this, however, is not a given. Mobile systems can lose contact when they enter a tunnel or their batteries run out. Added to these complexities are the opportunities for chaos introduced by mobile, autonomous agents making deals for you in cyberspace.

Unfortunately, as the complexity of software systems increases, controllability decreases. More and more of a software system's content is driven by commercial off-the-shelf (COTS) products. Vendors may listen to your needs, but their COTS features and evolution ultimately will respond to the overall market demand. In addition to this, your requirements, architecture, process, and resource decisions will have to be made in shorter and shorter time spans, driven by competitive, time-to-market pressures. Further, the rapid pace of change in information technology means that your project commitments must adapt to midcourse changes in technology, in the marketplace, and in your corporate structure.

Of course, all of these challenges are matched by tremendous opportunities for major success—if you can figure out how to best adapt your organization to new modes of operation.

The organizations that have been most successful in doing this are those that have engaged in a thoughtful software measurement program. That is, they have been collecting and analyzing data on where they are, what problems they have encountered, and how well various strategies will improve their situation. Some particularly good success stories are documented on Hewlett-Packard's experience by Bob Grady (1992) and on TRW's CCPDS-R experience by Walker Royce (1998).

However, jumping blindly into a software measurement program carries a high risk of failure. These are some common mistakes.

- *Overkill*—collecting too much data, resulting in wasted effort and reduced morale

- *Measurement dysfunction*— tying measurement to personnel evaluation, resulting in "tell-them-what-they-want-to-hear" data

- *Measurement mismatch*—picking wrong, ambiguous, or inconsistent measures, resulting in inconclusive data analysis

- *Process mismatch*—picking measures that reinforce the wrong processes (e.g., minimizing average problem report closure time will induce people to work the easy problems first)

Fortunately, you don't need to jump blindly into a measurement program for your organization. This book provides both principles and practices for developing, operating, and continuously improving an organization's measurement program. The following are some important points about the Practical Software Measurement (PSM) approach.

- PSM is based on decades of experience of dozens of organizations in learning how to best implement a successful software measurement program. Its principles and practices have been successfully used on a wide variety of software-intensive projects.

- PSM is not a "one-size-fits-all" approach. It includes guidelines for tailoring the measurement framework and practices to fit your organizational and project situations.

- PSM is not merely a set of abstract guidelines but is illustrated by case studies that demonstrate which guidelines to apply to particular projects in the embedded systems and business systems domains.

The case studies not only provide "how to" information but also provide "why" motivation as well as showing practitioners and managers the value of visibility into the state of a complex software project and the value of diagnostic information for identifying and controlling problem situations.

- PSM is compatible with and helps implement recent initiatives such as the Integrated Capability Maturity Model (CMMI^SM^), ISO/IEC 15939 (Software Measurement Process), and the software-intensive, systems-level Experience Factory initiative being piloted by the USC/UMD Center for Empirically Based Software Engineering (CeBASE).

- PSM is complemented by a set of tools, training courses, workshops, and conferences where PSM experiences are shared and discussed.

With all of these supporting advantages, PSM provides you with a way to appreciate the significant benefits of a software measurement program, while at the same time understanding and avoiding the risks involved with a "blind jump." You'll find this book a worthwhile starting point for your future software measurement initiatives, as well as a source of continuing guidance as you chart your way through the sea of complex opportunities ahead.

Barry Boehm, USC
May 2001

PREFACE

Management by fact has become an increasingly popular concept in the software engineering and information technology communities. Organizations are focusing attention on measurement and the use of objective information to make decisions. Quantitative performance information is essential to fact-based management. *Practical Software Measurement: Objective Information for Decision Makers* describes an approach to management by fact for software project managers based on integrating the concepts of a Measurement Information Model and a Measurement Process Model. While these concepts apply to non-software activities as well, the examples and terminology presented in this book focus primarily on software.

The **information needs** of the decision maker drive the selection of software measures and associated analysis techniques. This is the premise behind the widely accepted approaches to software measurement, including goal/question/metric (Basili and Weiss, 1984) and issue/category/measure (McGarry et al., 1997). Information needs result from the efforts of managers to influence the outcomes of projects, processes, and initiatives toward defined objectives. Information needs are usually derived from two sources: (1) goals that the manager seeks to achieve and (2) obstacles that hinder the achievement of these goals. Obstacles, also referred to as issues, include risks, problems, and a lack of information in a goal-related area. Unless there is a manager or other decision maker with an information need, measurement serves no purpose. The issues faced by a software project manager are numerous. Typically they include estimating and allocating project resources, tracking progress, and delivering products that meet customer specifications and expectations.

A **Measurement Information Model** defines the relationship between the information needs of the manager and the objective data to be collected, commonly called **measures**. It also establishes a consistent terminology for basic measurement ideas and concepts, which is critical to communicating the measurement information to decision makers. The information model in Practical Software Measurement (PSM) defines three levels of measures, or quantities: (1) base measures, (2) derived measures, and (3) indicators. It is interesting to note that the three levels of measurement defined in the PSM information model roughly correspond to the three-level structures advocated by many existing measurement approaches. Examples include the goal/question/metric (Basili and Weiss, 1984), factor/criteria/metric (Walters and McCall, 1977), and issue/category/measure (McGarry et al., 1997) approaches already in use within the software community. A similar approach for defining a generic data structure for measurement was developed by Kitchenham et al., who defined their structure as an Entity Relationship Diagram (1995).

An effective measurement process must address the selection of appropriate measures as well as provide for effective analysis of the data collected. The **Measurement Process Model** describes a set of related measurement activities that are generally applicable in all circumstances, regardless of the specific information needs of any particular situation. The process consists of four iterative measurement activities: establish, plan, perform, and evaluate. This process is similar to the commonly seen Plan-Do-Check-Act cycle (Deming, 1986).

Recognition of a need for fact-based, objective information leads to the establishment of a measurement process for a project or an organization. The specific information needs of the decision makers and measurement users drive the selection and definition of appropriate measures during measurement planning. The resulting measurement approach instantiates a project-specific information model identifies the base measures, derived measures, and indicators to be employed, and the analysis techniques to be applied in order to address the project's prioritized information needs.

As the measurement plan is implemented, or performed, the required measurement data is collected and analyzed. The information product that results from the perform measurement activity is provided to the decision makers. Feedback from these measurement users helps in the evaluation of the effectiveness of the measures and measurement process so that they can be improved on a continuing basis.

The basic concepts presented in this book evolved from extensive measurement experience and prior research. They were previously introduced in sequentially released versions of *Practical Software Measurement* (McGarry et al., 1997) and were formalized in ISO/IEC Standard 15939—Software Measurement Process (2001). The measurement process model and measurement terminology from ISO/IEC 15939 have also been adopted as the basis of a new Measurement and Analysis Process Area in the Software Engineering Institute's Capability Maturity Model Integration (CMMI) project (CMMI Development Team, 2000). This book explains how software development and maintenance organizations can implement a viable measurement process based on the proven measurement concepts of ISO/IEC 15939 and the CMMI in a practical and understandable manner.

In simplistic terms, implementing an objective measurement-by-fact process for a software-intensive project encompasses defining and prioritizing the information needs of the project decision makers through the development of a project-specific information model and then tailoring and executing a project-specific set of measurement process activities. The PSM approach to accomplishing this integrates prior experience and research from many sources across many application domains.

How to Use This Book

Practical Software Measurement is structured to provide progressive guidance for implementing a software measurement process. It provides comprehensive descriptions of the Measurement Information Model and the Measurement Process Model, as well as experience-based guidance for applying these models in an actual project environment. No book could ever capture all of the pertinent information and practical examples related to software measurement. As such, the Practical Software Measurement Web site at **www.psmsc.com** contains additional information, guidance, examples, and tools to augment *Practical Software Measurement*.

To enhance readability, the authors have limited most of the in-text references to suggestions for further reading on specific topics. Additional references are provided in the bibliography.

The following topics are addressed in this book:

Chapter 1: Measurement: Key Concepts and Practices. Chapter 1 provides an overview of software measurement, explaining how measurement supports today's information-oriented business models and how measurement can become a corporate resource. It describes the relationships between project- and organizational-level measurement, and introduces the two primary concepts of PSM: the Measurement Information Model and the Measurement Process Model.

Chapter 2: Measurement Information Model. Chapter 2 presents an in-depth discussion of the Measurement Information Model and its measurement components. It relates the Measurement Information Model to measurement planning and implementation activities.

Chapter 3: Plan Measurement. Chapter 3 is the first of five chapters that look at the individual measurement process activities in detail. Chapter 3 focuses on the Plan Measurement activity and describes what is required to define an information-driven, project-specific measurement plan.

Chapter 4: Perform Measurement. Chapter 4 addresses the Perform Measurement activity and discusses how to collect and analyze measurement data. It introduces several concepts related to measurement analysis, including the types of analysis and how to relate information needs and associated issues in terms of cause and effect.

Chapter 5: Analysis Techniques. Chapter 5 provides an in-depth treatment of the three primary types of measurement analysis: estimation, feasibility analysis, and performance analysis.

Chapter 6: Evaluate Measurement. Chapter 6 describes the Evaluate Measurement activity. It focuses on the assessment, evaluation, and improvement of applied project measures and the implemented project measurement processes.

Chapter 7: Establish and Sustain Commitment. Chapter 7 explains the final measurement activity, Establish and Sustain Commitment, which addresses the organizational requirements related to implementing a viable project measurement process. Chapter 7 also addresses measurement "lessons learned."

Chapter 8: Measure for Success. Chapter 8 reviews some of the major concepts presented in this book and identifies key measurement success factors.

Appendix A: Measurement Construct Examples. Appendix A provides detailed examples of measurement constructs typically applied to software-intensive projects.

Appendix B: Information System Case Study. Appendix B provides a comprehensive case study that addresses the implementation of a measurement process for a typical information system.

Appendix C: Synergy Integrated Copier Case Study. Appendix C is a second case study that describes how measurement can be applied to a major software-intensive upgrade project.

1

Measurement: Key Concepts and Practices

All successful software organizations implement measurement as part of their day-to-day management and technical activities. Measurement provides the objective information they need to make informed decisions that positively impact their business and engineering performance. In successful software organizations, measurement-derived information is treated as an important resource and is made available to decision makers throughout all levels of management.

Software measurement has evolved into a key software engineering discipline. In the past, many software organizations treated measurement as an additional, non-value-added task, or just "another thing to do." Measurement is now considered to be a basic software engineering practice, as evidenced by its inclusion in the Level 2 maturity requirements of the Software Engineering Institute's Capability Maturity Model Integration (CMMI) products and related commercial software process standards.

The way measurement is actually implemented and used in a software organization determines how much value is realized in terms of business and engineering performance. Measurement is most effective when implemented in support of an organization's business and technical objectives and when integrated with the existing technical and management activities that define a software project. Measurement works best when it provides objective information related to the risks and problems that may impact a project's defined objectives. In other words, measurement works best when it is considered a significant, integral part of project management.

Top-performing organizations design their technical and management processes to make use of objective measurement data. Measurement data and associated analysis results support both short and long-term decision making. A mature software development organization typically uses measurement to help plan and evaluate a proposed software project, to objectively track actual performance against planned objectives, to guide software process improvement decisions and investments, and to help assess overall business and technical performance against market-driven requirements. A top-performing organization uses measurement across the entire life cycle of a software project, from inception to retirement. Measurement is implemented as a proactive discipline, and measurement-derived information is considered to be a strategic resource.

1.1 Motivation for Measurement

Why measure software? To begin, software has become a major factor in corporate investment and business strategies, even for "non-software-intensive" organizations. It is a key component in an organization's ability to maintain pace with rapidly changing information technology in an increasingly competitive environment. Given the large corporate investment in developing and maintaining critical information assets, there is a growing demand for more objective assessment and management of software-intensive projects.

Measurement is most important at the project level. Software measurement helps the project manager do a better job. It helps to define and implement more realistic plans, to properly allocate scarce resources to put those plans into place, and to accurately monitor progress and performance against those plans. Software measurement provides the information required to make key project decisions and to take appropriate action. Measurement helps to relate and integrate the information derived from other project and technical management disciplines. In effect, it allows the software project manager to make decisions using objective information.

Specifically, software measurement provides objective information to help the project manager do the following:

- *Communicate Effectively:* Measurement provides objective information throughout the software organization. This reduces the ambiguity that often surrounds complex and constrained software projects. Measurement helps managers to identify, prioritize, track, and communicate objectives and associated issues at all levels within the organization. It also is important to communicating between supplier and acquirer organizations.

- *Track Specific Project Objectives:*   Measurement can accurately describe the status of software project processes and products. It is key to objectively representing the progress of project activities and the quality of associated software products across the project life cycle. Measurement helps to answer crucial questions such as: "Is the project on schedule?" and "Is the software ready to be delivered to the user?"

- *Identify and Correct Problems Early:* Measurement facilitates a proactive management strategy. Potential problems are objectively identified as risks to be assessed and managed. Existing problems can be better evaluated and prioritized. Measurement fosters the early discovery and correction of technical and management problems that can be more difficult and costly to resolve later. Managers use measurement as a resource to anticipate problems and to avoid being forced into a reactive, fix-on-fail approach.

- *Make Key Trade-off Decisions:* Every software project is subject to constraints. Cost, schedule, capability, technical quality, and performance must be traded off against each other as well as managed together to meet established project objectives. Decisions in one area almost always impact other areas, even if they seem unrelated. Measurement helps the decision maker to assess these impacts objectively and make informed trade-offs to best meet project objectives and to optimize software project and product performance.

- *Justify Decisions:* The current software and information technology business environments demand successful project performance. Business, technical, and project managers must be able to *defend* the basis of their estimates and plans with historical performance data. Then, they must be able to justify changes to plans with current performance data. Measurement provides an effective rationale for selecting the best alternatives.

Like any management or technical tool, measurement cannot guarantee that a project will be successful. However, it does help the decision maker take a proactive approach in dealing with the critical issues inherent in software- intensive projects. Measurement helps the project, and consequently the organization, to succeed.

1.2   Measurement as an Organizational Discriminator

The current software business environment is characterized by rapidly changing technology within an extremely competitive market. In both the shrink-wrapped and unique-application software marketplace, customers demand more functionality at a lower price and rapid implementation of any new capability to satisfy their changing business demands. In today's environment, it is becoming increasingly difficult to establish a software organization as an information technology market leader and even more difficult to maintain it as a top-performing organization—an organization that performs better than its competitors from both technical and business perspectives.

Experience has shown that almost every top-performing organization can be described as follows:

- Accurate, objective information is available to all decision makers, and its use is an integral part of the corporate culture.

- Past, present, and future business and technical perspectives are taken into account to help define project objectives and performance expectations.

- Organizational processes and procedures are designed to identify, characterize, and manage change. Dealing with change is part of how the organization does business.

- Both good and bad news are freely communicated within the organization. Issues are openly identified and addressed.

- There is a cultural bias for informed decision making and taking action.

These characteristics are all information-related and, therefore, measurement-related. To be a top performer in its sector, an organization needs the right kind of information, on a regular basis, to make the right decisions. It uses information to become more efficient and to produce better-quality products. Measurement facilitates and accelerates organizational learning and supports corporate adaptation within the marketplace. Measurement provides a structure for learning from each project, whether or not it was a good experience. Measurement also helps an organization understand the gaps between how it is performing and the performance levels demanded by the marketplace. It allows an organization to optimize within its business and technical constraints. In effect, measurement information becomes a competitive resource, and an effective measurement process becomes an organizational discriminator.

1.3 The Foundation—Project Measurement

Given measurement's strong relationship to software organizational performance, the key challenge is to implement it in a manner that has the most positive impact on each of the projects within the organization. The foundation of any organizational software measurement program is established at the project level. An organization's performance is essentially based on the success of its projects. To be successful, project and technical managers must make critical decisions related to project resources, schedule, and functional capability on a continual basis. These decisions must result in optimization of the business and technical performance of the software product within organizational and market-driven constraints. There is little room for project rework and restarts.

The software project manager must integrate all of the diverse aspects of software to be successful. Decisions are made daily, if not hourly, on how the technical product will be developed and managed, how resources will be allocated, and which issues will be addressed in what priority. The more effective these decisions are, the more successful the project. The more objective the available data and information, the better the decisions. The project manager usually must guide the project toward planned project objectives, while operating within established constraints.

The project environment is generally one of multiple and diverse cost, schedule, and technical considerations. Experience shows that even in relatively small information technology organizations, each project is unique in terms of domain application, implemented technical processes, operational interdependencies with other systems, and various constraints. Add in the usual and sometimes constant technical and management changes, and each project emerges with distinct process and product characteristics.

The organizational measurement approach must be adaptable to effectively address the unique information needs and characteristics of each project. *Practical Software Measurement* focuses on project-level measurement and shows how measurement can be tailored to satisfy the needs of each project.

Although the project level is the primary level for implementing measurement within an organization, there are valid information needs at higher organizational management levels. In almost all cases, objective organizational-level information is derived from the projects. You need good project data to analyze overall organization. Organizational software measurement can be viewed as measurement across many projects, validly combining the measurement data generated by each project and using different analysis techniques to satisfy different information needs. For example, managers at many different organizational levels may be concerned with how long it takes to develop and field a given software product. The project manager is concerned with the time it takes to implement product capability and reliability and with developing the software product within cost objectives. The marketing or business manager may be concerned with the time it takes to market a new capability and the potential impact of a possible delay on market share. The process manager may be concerned with an overall increase or decrease of the average software-development time line for all of the organization's products and the related impacts from organizational process changes. In all cases, the key variable is the availability of quality data at the project level, and, in fact, most corporate measurement activities take place at the project level.

1.4 What Makes Measurement Work

Many different approaches have been used to implement software measurement on a software-intensive project. Not all of them have been effective, and many have not even outlived the project itself. Some of these approaches have been based on the detailed definition of the "best" set of measures equally applicable to every project in the organization. Others have relied on automated measurement and analysis tools purchased from a vendor with little regard for the organization's processes or business practices already in place. In both of these cases, measurement became just "something else to do" and did not materially help the project achieve its objectives. What makes measurement work in an already challenging project environment? Experience across a wide range of software development and maintenance projects suggests two key characteristics of a successful measurement program:

- The collection, analysis, and reporting of measurement data that relates directly to the **information needs** of the project decision makers. This can be characterized as an information-driven measurement approach, where measures are defined and implemented to address the specific information needs of the project on a prioritized basis, as defined by established project objectives and associated issues. As the project progresses and the information needs change, so do the applied measures. Inherent to the information-driven measurement approach is a clear understanding of the relationships between what information is needed, what is actually measured, and how the measures are defined and combined into usable results.

- A structured and repeatable **measurement process** that defines project measurement activities and related information interfaces. This process must be flexible and adaptable to support existing software technical and management processes and environments already in place, as well as to support the characteristics of the specific application domain. The measurement process must be iterative, continually focusing measurement efforts on the most critical issues. The measurement process is in place throughout the existence of the project. It supports the measurement of evolving process and product attributes as project information needs, and related objectives and issues, change.

The information-driven measurement approach and the measurement process work together on a continual basis during the project life cycle, providing different information to the project managers as their needs change. Both are tailored to meet the specific characteristics of each project. Together they provide a basis for measurement tasks and procedures that support successful project completion and improved business and engineering performance.

To be effective, measurement must be implemented within a project or organization as a supporting software engineering process. As such, measurement must include all of the activities associated with planning, performing, and evaluating measurement-related tasks within an overall project or organizational structure. Measurement does not stand alone. It is implemented within the project environment to define what information the decision makers need and how this information is collected, analyzed, presented, and used. The measurement process combines diverse subjective and objective data into integrated information products that directly address defined project information needs.

Practical Software Measurement provides experience-based guidance on how to define and implement a viable information-driven measurement process for a software-intensive project. PSM addresses the development of a project measurement information structure using the **Measurement Information Model,** and it describes measurement activities and tasks using the **Measurement Process Model.**

1.5   Measurement Information Model

The Measurement Information Model described here is one of the fundamental concepts inherent to a successful, information-driven measurement program. The Measurement Information Model is a mechanism for linking defined information needs to the project software processes and products, the entities that can actually be measured. It establishes a defined structure for relating measurement concepts and, as such, provides a basis for accurately communicating measurement results within the organization.

The Measurement Information Model is a primary resource within the measurement process. It provides a structure that defines specific project measures and relates them to the needs of project decision makers. It provides a well-defined analysis path that supports recommendations derived

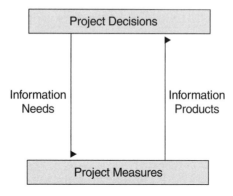

Figure 1-1 Measurement Information Model Relationships

from the analysis of the collected data. The Measurement Information Model directly supports both measurement planning and analysis activities.

In their most basic form, the relationships defined by the Measurement Information Model are depicted in Figure 1-1. During the planning and execution phases of a software project, technical and management decisions addressing many different areas must be made on a continuing basis. Decision makers must make trade-off decisions involving cost, schedule, capability, and quality. As a result, there is a definitive need for information to support the decision-making process. The Measurement Information Model helps to define the information needs of the project decision makers and focuses measurement planning activities on the selection and specification of the most appropriate software measures to address those needs. As the measures are implemented and data is collected, the Measurement Information Model structures the measurement data and associated analysis into structured **information products.** These information products integrate the measurement results with established decision criteria and present recommendations to project decision makers on alternative courses of action.

In a typical software project, there are many information needs defined at any point in time. These information needs tend to change significantly during the course of the project, based on changing project objectives, assumptions, and constraints.

Chapter 2 fully describes the Measurement Information Model and all of its components.

1.6 Measurement Process Model

The Measurement Information Model provides a structure for relating information needs, measures, and information products. The Measurement Process Model works in conjunction with the Measurement Information Model to provide an application framework for implementing measurement on a project. Both models work together to define a measurement program appropriate for each particular, and unique, project.

Figure 1-2 depicts the Measurement Process Model. The model is built around a typical "Plan-Do-Check-Act" management sequence, adapted to support measurement-specific activities and tasks. The Measurement Process Model includes four primary activities, each of which is essential to successful measurement implementation. These activities include

- Plan Measurement

- Perform Measurement

- Evaluate Measurement

- Establish and Sustain Commitment

The Plan Measurement activity encompasses the identification of project information needs and the selection of appropriate measures to address these needs using the Measurement Information Model. Plan Measurement also includes tasks related to the definition of data collection, analysis, and reporting procedures; tasks related to planning for evaluating the measurement results in the form of various information products; and tasks for assessing the measurement process itself. Most significantly, the Plan Measurement activity provides for the integration of the measures into existing project technical and management processes. Rather than force a project to implement a predefined measure, PSM, through this integration task, ensures that the selected measures will be effective within the context of the project. The Plan Measurement activity also addresses the resources and technologies required to implement a project measure-

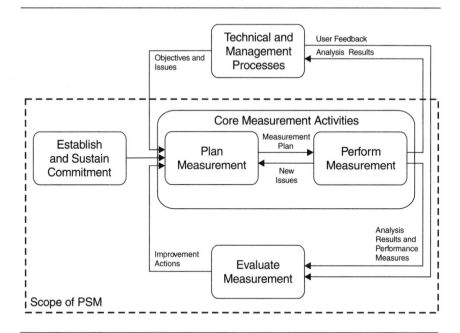

Figure 1-2   Measurement Process Model

ment program. The output of the Plan Measurement activity is a well-defined measurement approach that directly supports the project's information needs.

The Perform Measurement activity, along with Plan Measurement, is one of the core activities that directly address the requirements of the measurement user. Perform Measurement encompasses the collecting and processing of measurement data; the use of the data to analyze both individual information needs and how the information needs and associated issues inter-relate; and the generation of information products to present the analysis results, alternative courses of action, and recommendations to the project decision makers. Perform Measurement implements the measurement plan and produces the information products necessary for effective measurement-based decision making.

The Evaluate Measurement activity applies measurement and analysis techniques to the measurement process itself. It assesses both the applied measures and the capability of the measurement process, and it helps identify associated improvement actions. The Evaluate Measurement activity ensures that the project measurement approach is continually updated to address current information needs and promotes an increasing maturity of the project and organizational measurement process.

The Establish and Sustain Commitment activity ensures that measurement is supported both at the project and organizational levels. It provides the resources and organizational infrastructure required to implement a viable measurement program.

A fifth activity, Technical and Management Processes, is also depicted in the Measurement Process Model. Although technically not a measurement- specific activity the technical and management processes interface directly with the measurement process. The project decision makers operate within these processes, defining information needs and using the measurement information products to make decisions.

The Measurement Process Model is iterative by design. It is defined to be tailored to the characteristics and context of a particular project and to be adaptable to changing project information and decision requirements. Both the Measurement Information Model and the Measurement Process Model establish a measurement approach that captures the experience of and principles learned from previous software measurement applications. Together they provide the basis for an effective software measurement program.

2

Measurement
Information Model

This chapter describes one of the fundamental measurement concepts of *Practical Software Measurement*, the Measurement Information Model. The Measurement Information Model provides a formal mechanism for linking defined information needs to software engineering processes and products that can be measured. Developing a measurement plan for a particular project requires an instantiation of the Measurement Information Model that is specific to the project's information needs. The model serves as a primary resource throughout the measurement process, as it guides the planning and implementation of data collection and analysis activities.

The Measurement Information Model establishes a defined structure for relating different measurement concepts and terms. As such, it establishes a foundation for the consistent definition of measurement terminology. Many terms used by the software measurement community lack widely agreed-on definitions. The term *metric* is probably the best example, as it is commonly misused to describe many different measurement concepts. Because defining and implementing a measurement program involves making many choices with respect to collecting, organizing, and analyzing data, success requires a systematic approach to considering and describing those choices. Without concise and consistent terminology, effective communication among measurement analysts, data providers, and measurement users is impossible. Because decision makers need to understand measurement information, consistent measurement terminology is mandatory. Some of the key terms are addressed below.

Figure 2-1 is an overview of how an information need evolves into a plan for generating the project's measurement products. Measurement planning begins with the recognition that a manager or engineer has a specific **information need** required to support project decision making. Project decisions are usually related to project planning and execution in an operational sense, but may also address strategic and organizational-level requirements. Data that helps to satisfy the defined information need can be obtained by measuring many different software process elements and product characteristics, called *software entities.* The **measurable concept** is an idea about the entities that should be measured in order to satisfy an information need. For example, a decision maker concerned with allocating budget and associated resources to a software task may believe that productivity is related to the type of software task that will be performed. Productivity is therefore the measurable concept that addresses the defined information need. Determining productivity requires that entities such as the software product and process be measured. There are many ways that productivity can be computed, so, at this stage productivity is still only a measurable concept. Eventually, the measurable concept will be formalized as a **measurement construct** that specifies exactly what will be measured and how the data will be combined to produce results that satisfy the information need. Two applicable measures in this example could be software size and effort. A **measurement procedure** defines the mechanics of collecting and organizing the data required to instantiate a measurement construct.

All of the applicable information needs, measurement constructs, and measurement procedures are combined into a **measurement plan**. Execution of the measurement plan produces the **information products** that respond to the project information needs. The information products are the collection of indicators, interpretations, and recommendations provided to the decision maker as an output of the measurement process.

A measurement plan can address a single information need. In most cases, however, it addresses multiple information needs. The plan defines which information needs are applicable to a particular project, how the software will be measured to satisfy those information needs, and how the measurement process will be resourced and managed.

As Figure 2-1 suggests, developing an effective measurement program requires a thorough understanding of the project's software information

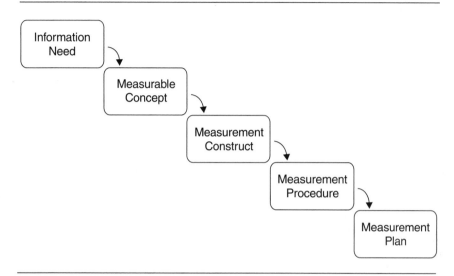

Figure 2-1   Evolution of an information need into a measurement plan

needs, a defined set of related measurable concepts, and knowledge of which software entities are available to be measured within the project.

The terms defined in PSM are derived from the Measurement Information Model documented in the international standard ISO/IEC 15939, "Software Measurement Process." The ISO/IEC 15939 standard describes in a general sense how data is collected and organized to satisfy defined information needs. The reader's knowledge of the software entities is presumed. However, the following sections explain the concepts of information needs and measurement constructs in more detail.

2.1   Information Needs

Information needs result from the efforts of engineers and managers to influence the outcomes of software engineering processes and activities. These technical and management processes may be defined and may operate at either the project or organizational levels. The desired outcomes of such processes usually are defined in terms of objectives. The information needs relate directly to both the established objectives and to the areas of concern that may impact the achievement of these objectives. These areas of concern are often referred to as **issues.** There are three types of issues:

- *Problems*—areas of concern that a project is currently experiencing or is relatively certain to experience

- *Risks*—areas of concern that could occur, but are not certain to occur

- *Lack of information*—areas of concern where the available information is inadequate to reliably predict project impact

Identifying something as an issue does not necessarily mean that it is a problem. In fact, thorough and continual identification and careful tracking of project risks minimize the potential for the emergence of serious problems that could negatively impact project success.

Most projects work toward achieving fixed objectives in terms of budget, schedule, quality, and functionality. Consequently, measurement at the project level tends to focus on providing information related to issues in these areas. While every project involves unique issues, experience shows that most software project information needs can be organized into common information categories. These categories directly relate to project issues that the project manager must manage on a day-to-day basis.

PSM is an issue-based approach to software measurement for project management. PSM defines seven common software information categories:

- *Schedule and Progress:* This information category addresses the achievement of project milestones and the completion of individual work units. A project that falls behind schedule can usually meet its delivery objectives only by eliminating functionality or sacrificing product quality.

- *Resources and Cost:* This information category relates to the balance between the work to be performed and personnel resources assigned to the project. A project that exceeds the budgeted effort usually can recover only by reducing software functionality or by sacrificing product quality.

- *Product Size and Stability:* This information category addresses the stability of the functionality or capability required of the software. It also relates to the volume of software delivered to provide the required capability. Stability includes changes in functional scope or quantity. An increase in software size usually requires increasing the applied resources or extending the project schedule.

- *Product Quality*: This information category addresses the ability of the delivered software product to support the user's needs without failure. If a poor-quality product is delivered, the burden of making it work usually falls on the assigned maintenance organization.

- *Process Performance*: This information category relates to the capability of the supplier relative to project needs. A supplier with a poor software development process or low productivity may have difficulty meeting aggressive project schedule and cost objectives.

- *Technology Effectiveness*: This information category addresses the viability of the proposed technical approach. It addresses engineering approaches such as software reuse, use of commercial software components, reliance on advanced software development processes, and implementation of common software architectures. Cost increases and schedule delays may result if key elements of the proposed technical approach are not achieved.

- *Customer Satisfaction*: This information category addresses the degree to which products and services delivered by the project meet the customer's expectations. Indications of satisfaction may be obtained from customer feedback and the levels of customer support required.

Practical Software Measurement makes use of these common information categories to facilitate the identification and prioritization of a project's specific information needs. In practice, information related to similar information needs often can be addressed using similar measurable concepts, thus reducing the number of resources that must be applied to implement a viable measurement program.

2.2   Measurement Construct

A measurement construct is a detailed structure that links the things that can be measured to a specified information need. Figure 2-2 outlines the

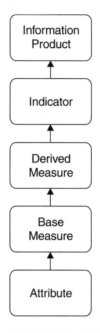

Figure 2-2   Levels of a measurement construct

basic structure of a measurement construct. The things that can actually be
measured include specific attributes of software processes and products,
such as size, effort, and number of defects. The measurement construct
describes how the relevant software attributes are quantified and converted
to indicators that provide a basis for decision making. A single measurement construct may involve three types, or levels, of measures: base measures, derived measures, and indicators. The measurement planner needs to
specify the details of the measurement constructs to be used, as well
as the procedures for data collection, analysis, and reporting, in the measurement plan. The better the design of the measurement construct and
the better it relates the measured attributes of the software to the identified information need, the easier it is for the project manager to make
informed, objective decisions.

At each of the three levels of measures—base measures, derived measures,
and indicators—additional information content is added in the form of
rules, models, and decision criteria. Figure 2-3 illustrates the structure of a
measurement construct in more detail. Specific rules for assigning values,

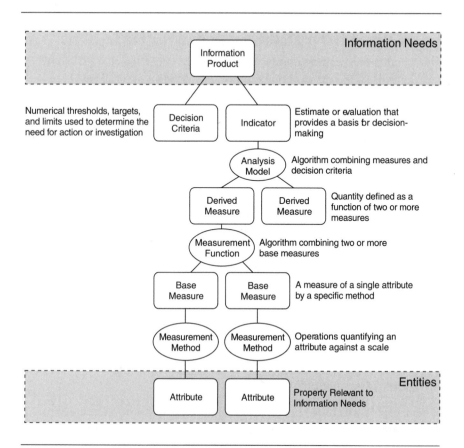

Figure 2-3   Details of a measurement construct

and defining the measurement methods, measurement functions, and analysis models are associated with each level of measure. In formalizing a measurable concept as a measurement construct, the details of the actual processes and products of the software project must be considered, as well as the detailed description of the associated information need. The measurement construct must be able to be practically implemented given the project's characteristics, and it must satisfy the defined information need.

While the complexity implied in Figure 2-3 may seem intimidating, these details help ensure the implementation of an effective and efficient measurement program. The most important benefits of using well-defined measurement constructs include:

- Reducing redundancy by helping to identify a core set of base measures (or *data primitives*) that can serve many purposes

- Increasing accuracy and repeatability by ensuring that all essential aspects of the measurement approach are adequately defined

- Maximizing the value of the base measures by creating patterns of derived measures and indicators that can easily be recognized, reused, and adapted

- Documenting the link between the information need and how is it satisfied

Although Figure 2-3 is organized hierarchically, the process of defining a measurement construct is actually iterative. Chapter 3 describes the measurement planning process in more detail. Section 2.3 and Appendix A provide examples of measurement constructs that address specific information needs.

The individual components of the measurement construct as depicted in Figure 2-3 are described in the following sections.

Attribute (Measurable)

A measurable **attribute** is a distinguishable property or characteristic of a software **entity**. Entities include processes, products, projects, and resources. An entity may have many attributes, only some of which may be suitable to be measured. A measurable attribute is distinguishable either quantitatively or qualitatively by human or automated means. The first step in defining a specific instantiation of the Measurement Information Model is to select the software attributes most relevant to the measurement user's information needs. A given attribute may be incorporated in multiple measurement constructs supporting the same or different information needs.

Base Measure

A **base measure** is a measure of a single attribute defined by a specified measurement method. Executing the method produces a value for the measure. A base measure is functionally independent of all other measures and captures information about a single attribute. Data collection involves assigning values to base measures. Specifying the range and/or type of values that a base measure is expected to take on helps to verify the quality of the data collected. (Data verification is discussed in more detail in Chapter 4.) Each base measure is defined with the following characteristics:

Measurement Method

This is a logical sequence of operations, described generically, used in quantifying an attribute with respect to a specified scale. The operations may involve activities such as counting occurrences or observing the passage of time. The same measurement method may be applied to multiple attributes. However, each unique combination of an attribute and a method produces a different base measure. A measurement method may be implemented in two ways—either automated or manual. A **measurement procedure** describes the specific implementation of a measurement method within a given organizational context. Procedures may be documented either in the measurement plan or separately (see Chapter 3).

Type of Method   The type of measurement method depends on the nature of the operations used to quantify a particular attribute. There are two types of methods:

- *Subjective*—quantification involving human judgment or rating. For example, relying on an expert to rate the complexity of functions as high, medium, or low is a subjective method of measurement.

- *Objective*—quantification based on numerical rules such as counting. These rules may be implemented by human or automated means. For example, lines of Ada code may be quantified by counting semicolons.

Objective measures typically provide more accuracy and repeatability than subjective methods. Where possible, objective methods of measurement are preferable

Scale

A scale is an ordered set of values, continuous or discrete, or a set of categories to which an attribute is mapped. The scale defines the range of possible values that can be produced by executing the measurement method.

The measurement method maps the magnitude of the measured attribute to a value on a scale. A unit of measurement often is associated with a scale.

Type of Scale   The type of scale depends on the nature of the relationship between values on the scale. Four types of scales are commonly defined:

- *Ratio*—numeric data for which equal distances correspond to equal quantities of the attribute, where the value of 0 corresponds to none of the attribute. Counting lines of code produces a ratio scale with values ranging from 0 to (potentially) positive infinity.

- *Interval*—numeric data for which equal distances correspond to equal quantities of the attribute without the use of 0 values. Cyclomatic complexity (the number of logical paths through a software component) provides an interval scale because the minimum value possible is 1.

- *Ordinal*—discrete rankings. For example, a set of software units might be ordered in terms of the expected difficulty of implementing them: most difficult, second most difficult, and so forth.

- *Nominal*—categorical data. For example, a set of problem reports might be classified in terms of the origin of the problem: requirements, design, and so forth.

The type of measurement method usually affects the type of scale that can be used reliably with a given attribute. For example, subjective methods of measurement usually support only ordinal or nominal scales.

Unit of Measurement   A unit of measurement is a particular quantity, defined and adopted by convention, with which other quantities of the same kind are compared in order to express their magnitude relative to that quantity. Only quantities expressed in the same units of measurement are directly comparable. Examples of units include the *hour* and the *meter.* Units of measurement often are not defined for measures determined by subjective methods or incorporating ordinal or nominal scales.

Derived Measure

A derived measure is a measure, or quantity, that is defined as a function of two or more base and/or derived measures. A derived measure captures information about more than one attribute. An example of a derived measure is a calculated value of productivity that is derived by dividing the base measure of hours of effort by the base measure of lines of code. Simple transformations of base measures (for example, taking the square root of a base measure) do not add information, thus do not produce derived measures. Normalization of data often involves converting base measures into derived measures that can be used to compare different entities. Derived measures are defined with the following characteristics:

Measurement Function

A measurement function is an algorithm or calculation performed to combine two or more values of base and/or derived measures. The scale and unit of the derived measure depend on the scales and units of the base measures from which it is composed, as well as how they are combined by the function. Division is the function used to produce the derived measure of productivity. The amount of product produced is divided by the amount of effort used to produce it.

Indicator

An indicator is a measure that provides an estimate or evaluation of specified attributes derived from an analysis model with respect to defined information needs. Indicators are the basis for measurement analysis and decision making. Indicators are, therefore, what should be presented to measurement users. Measurement is always based on imperfect information, so quantifying the uncertainty, accuracy, or importance of indicators is an essential component of presenting the actual indicator value. Indicators often are given the name of the measurable concept they implement. Indicators are defined with the following characteristics:

Analysis Model

This is an algorithm or calculation involving two or more base and/or derived measures with associated decision criteria. An analysis model is based on an understanding of, or assumptions about, the expected relationship between the component measures and their behavior over time. Analysis models produce estimates or evaluations relevant to defined information needs. The scale and method of measurement affect the choice of analysis techniques or models used to produce indicators. As an extreme example, computing the average of categorical data does not make sense.

Decision Criteria

These are numerical thresholds, targets, and limits used to determine the need for action or further investigation or to describe the level of confidence in a given result. Decision criteria help to interpret the measurement results. Decision criteria may be based on a conceptual understanding of expected behavior or calculated from data. Decision criteria may be derived from historical data, plans, and heuristics or computed as statistical control limits or statistical confidence limits.

Other Terminology

A few other issues related to terminology should be addressed before leaving the discussion of a measurement construct. The term **measures** may be used collectively to refer to base measures, derived measures, and/or indicators. The term **data** may be used collectively to refer to the values assigned to base measures and derived measures. Data collection refers to the assignment of values to base measures. In contrast, values of derived measures and indicators are computed from base and/or derived measures. Corresponding measurable concepts, measurement constructs, and indicators often are given the same name. Care must be used to distinguish between them as they are applied.

The measurement information model suggests two general principles for dealing with the question of how much measurement should be standardized within a project or organization. These principles are as follows:

- Standardize on base measures rather than indicators. The same set of base measures can be combined in many ways to produce different indicators that address different information needs. Base measures are tied to specific entities—which tend to be relatively persistent.

- Promote flexibility in the indicators. No single view of the data can effectively serve all levels and types of potential decision makers at all times throughout the project's life cycle. Indicators are tied to information needs—which tend to change frequently.

Measurement constructs are central to the measurement process. During the Plan Measurement activity, the necessary measurement constructs are designed, and specific procedures for collecting and analyzing the data are defined. During the Perform Measurement activity, these procedures are executed to collect data, assign values to the measurement constructs, and develop the information product. Careful attention to the Measurement Information Model throughout these steps helps obtain the maximum benefit from a project's or organization's measurement investment.

The key components of a measurement construct include measurement methods, base measures, measurement functions, derived measures, analysis models, and indicators. Figure 2-4 depicts the relationship between these components mathematically.

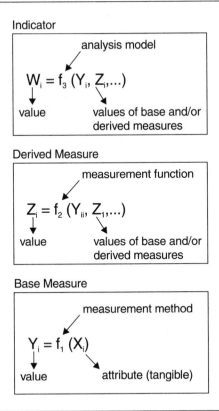

Figure 2-4   Mathematical depiction of a measurement construct

2.3   Measurement Construct Examples

For any given measurable concept, many different measurement constructs can be devised. Several examples of measurement constructs that address common project information needs are provided in the following sections. Bear in mind that these are generic examples. Moreover, these examples illustrate the variety of options supported by the Measurement Information Model and are not necessarily examples of universally recommended measurement constructs.

Productivity Example

The decision maker in the example depicted in Figure 2-5 needs to identify an expected software productivity level as the basis for project planning. The measurable concepts are that productivity from past projects can be used to validly estimate future projects and that productivity is related to the

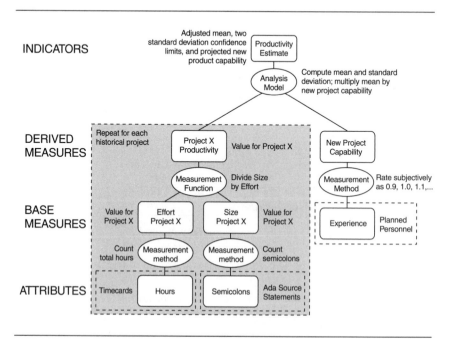

Figure 2-5   Measurement construct—Productivity example

effort expended and amount of software produced. Thus, effort and code are the measurable software entities of concern. Specific attributes of those entities must be selected for quantification and a function designated for combining them into a derived measure for each project in the database.

Regardless of how the productivity number is determined, the uncertainty inherent in software engineering means that there is a high probability the estimated productivity will not be exactly what is achieved. Estimating productivity based on historical data, however, enables the computation of confidence limits that help to assess how close actual results are likely to come to the estimated value.

Quality Example

The decision maker in the example depicted in Figure 2-6 needs to evaluate detailed design quality during the implementation of the software design activity. The measurable concept is that design quality is related to

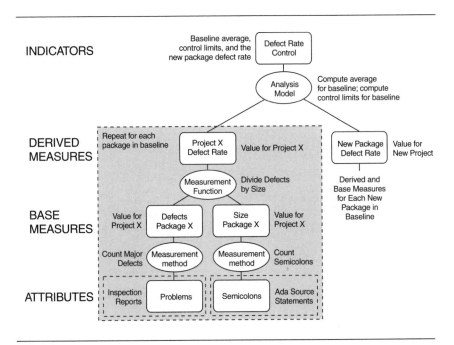

Figure 2-6 Measurement construct—Quality example

the amount of design produced and the number of defects found. Thus, the design packages and the lists of defects are the entities of concern. Computing the defect rate can normalize the quality of the design packages allowing a basic comparison. Thus, data for the base measures must be collected and the derived measure computed for each package as it is reviewed.

Since the defect rate is expected to be somewhat different for every package, control limits can be computed from a baseline set of packages to determine if the defect rate on a new package is different enough from the average to warrant concern.

Coding Progress Example

The decision maker in the example depicted in Figure 2-7 needs to evaluate whether or not the rate of code generation on a project is sufficient to meet projected schedule objectives. The measurable concept is that

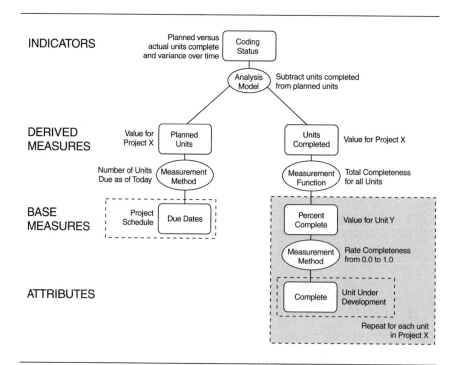

Figure 2-7   Measurement construct—Coding progress example

progress is related to the amount of work planned and the amount of work completed. Planned work items and completed work items are the entities of concern. This example assumes that the degree of completion of each software unit is reported by the developer assigned to it. Thus, data for the base measures must be collected, and the derived measure computed for each work item in the plan. A simple numerical threshold is used as a decision criterion rather than statistical limits.

Since the status of units is a subjective assessment, the indicator is subject to the influence of wishful thinking on the part of the programmers. A more reliable approach would be to count only units completed as defined by explicit exit criteria.

3

Plan Measurement

This chapter describes the first of the activities of the measurement process, Plan Measurement. The Plan Measurement activity provides a consistent method for identifying project information needs, selecting and specifying measures, and integrating them into the project's technical and management processes. Measurement constructs that address the information needs of the decision makers and that can be implemented within the characteristics and constraints of the software project are defined as part of the planning tasks. The objective of the Plan Measurement activity is to select and define the measures that provide the greatest insight into the identified project information needs. In the planning process, the highest-priority information needs are addressed first.

Figure 3-1 illustrates the Plan Measurement activity. The first task in planning is the identification and prioritization of information needs. Information needs, as explained in Chapter 2, drive the entire measurement process. Information needs can be derived from many sources. They are specifically defined within the context of project objectives, issues, and the characteristics of the project environment.

The second planning task is the selection and specification of appropriate measures to address the identified information needs. The selection task employs an experience-based framework that maps identified project information needs to both measurable concepts and specific measures.

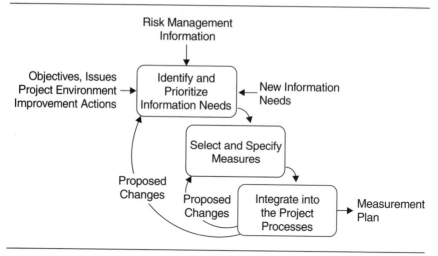

Figure 3-1   Plan Measurement activity

The third and final planning task involves integrating the measures into the project processes. This involves examining the suitability of the selected measures in the context of the actual project processes and the overall technical approach, as well as developing procedures for collecting and analyzing the desired data within the project environment. Measurement requirements should not be used to change the project or organization's technical and management processes, but rather to gain insight into issues related to these processes and associated software products.

The results of the planning process are documented in a project measurement plan. The plan may be formal or informal, and it may be incorporated into another plan, such as the software development plan or the overall project plan. Figure 3-1 indicates that the planning activity is iterative. New information needs may emerge or refinements may be proposed during the course of the project. Alternative measures may be proposed to better satisfy the project manager's information needs or to minimize measurement costs. The priority of the previously identified information needs may change. Essentially, a project's measurement plan continually evolves to address new information needs, changing processes, maturing software products, and the availability of new measurement data.

This chapter focuses on selecting the *best* measures to address the identified information needs. Keep in mind that many measures support multiple information needs and categories. The use of multiple measures and the relationships among them are discussed in Chapter 4.

The following three sections describe each of the measurement planning tasks in more detail.

3.1   Identify and Prioritize Information Needs

All software projects are chartered with specific *objectives*. Objectives may be directed downward by executive management or defined by the project manager in conjunction with the prospective system user. These objectives are typically defined in terms of overall system capability, resource budgets, milestones, quality levels, and business or system performance targets. Project success depends largely on achieving these objectives. **Issues** are areas of concern that may impact the achievement of a project objective and may include risks, problems, and lack of information.

In addition to the information needs identified at the start of the project, new information needs may arise as the project progresses. New or evolving requirements, changes in technology, available resources, and other factors often result in the identification of additional information needs.

Identification of Information Needs

Multiple sources of information should be considered to ensure that all project information needs are identified. Useful sources include the following:

- *Risk assessments*: The results of technical and management risk assessments should always be considered when identifying project information needs. Risk assessments may point to information needs related to requirements, technology, process, cost, or schedule. Risks may also be identified informally in the absence of a structured risk management process.

- *Project constraints and assumptions:* The project plan is usually based on many assumptions, such as the performance of the supplier or the availability of test facilities. Lack of information that impacts effort, schedule, and quality estimates should be treated as an information need. Moreover, schedules and budgets may have inflexible or conflicting constraints. If deviations from these constraints can threaten project success, identify these areas as information needs.

- *Leveraged technologies*: Project success may depend on leveraging certain technologies such as the use of nondeveloped components (commercial, off-the-shelf components; purchased software packages; reused components; etc.), common domain architectures, or advanced programming languages. If project objectives depend on utilizing specific technologies, the effectiveness of these technologies is an information need.

- *Product acceptance criteria*: Customers may impose stringent milestone or acceptance criteria on the deliverable software product. If there is significant doubt about the organization's ability to meet defined acceptance criteria, advertised objectives, or other external criteria, identify the degree of satisfaction of these criteria as an information need.

- *External requirements:* Many project information needs are related to requirements and concerns external to the project. For example, the need to make decisions concerning readiness for test or product delivery may necessitate that certain external customer-derived information needs be identified and tracked within a project. The probability of fulfilling aggressive or unrealistic organizational goals may also be treated as a project information need.

- *Experience:* A project team with experience on similar projects may be able to identify potential problem areas as information needs.

Each information need should be stated in appropriate project terminology. The focus should be on those aspects of the information need most important to the project. For example, a schedule-related information need for a new development project might be whether or not productivity is sufficient to make delivery on the planned completion date. A similar information need for a maintenance project may be whether the number of change requests implemented per staff-month is sufficient to support the planned completion date.

A project's information needs are more likely to be completely identified if those organizations with a significant stake in the project's outcome are included in the identification process. A joint identification process, with representation from all affected organizations, is an effective way to elicit information needs and to reach consensus on measurement priorities. Broad participation also helps promote commitment to the measurement process.

In the absence of other information, the PSM information categories (discussed in Chapter 2) can stimulate thinking about project information needs. While these information categories apply to most projects, their exact nature and priority are usually specific to each project.

Measurement and risk management are synergistic. Both disciplines emphasize the prevention and early detection of problems rather than waiting for problems to become critical. The risk management process helps to identify and prioritize project information needs. The measurement process plays a role in risk management by indicating whether risks are becoming problems and if risk mitigation steps are having the desired effect. However, risk management may address concerns that cannot be quantified easily. For example, environmental and political risks may be covered by the risk management process, but may not be directly measurable. On the other hand, because not all information needs are risks, risk management techniques alone may not be adequate to plan an effective measurement program.

Mapping Information Needs to Information Categories

Experience shows that most project information needs can be grouped into general areas, called **information categories,** that are basic to almost all projects. Information categories represent key concerns that must be managed on a day-to-day basis by the project manager. Once the project information needs have been identified, the next step is to map them to defined information categories.

The seven information categories defined in PSM are

- Schedule and progress

- Resources and cost

- Product size and stability

- Product quality

- Process performance

- Technology effectiveness

- Customer satisfaction

The PSM information categories help in selecting appropriate measures. This is accomplished by allocating each identified project information need to one or more of the seven information categories, as illustrated in Figure 3-2. In this figure, common information categories are mapped to associated measurable concepts and prospective measures. This helps to create the links between identified information needs and prospective measures.

Some project information needs may not map to an existing PSM information category. In these cases, appropriate measures may be defined by applying the general principles outlined in this book.

Prioritizing Information Needs

Managers of software-intensive system projects typically have many information needs. These must be prioritized in order to ensure that the measurement program addresses the information needs that have the greatest potential impact on defined project objectives. For example, a project that plans to make extensive use of nondeveloped or off-the-shelf components may be more concerned with the schedule and progress of integration than with the quality or the size of the nondeveloped components (assuming that the nondeveloped components were selected because they met user requirements). On the other hand, a safety-critical system might have nondeveloped component quality at the top of its priority list.

There are several ways to establish priorities. Using well-defined criteria helps to achieve consensus among project participants on priorities. One approach involves numerically ranking each identified information need based on project impact and probability of occurrence. Figure 3-3 is an example of this approach. In this example, 12 project information needs have been identified, in order of priority. The information needs that have the greatest project exposure (derived by multiplying the probability of

Information Categories	Measurable Concepts	Prospective Measures
Schedule and Progress	Milestone Completion Critical Path Performance Work Unit Progress Incremental Capability	Milestone Dates Slack Time Requirements Traced Requirements Tested Problem Reports Opened Problem Reports Closed Reviews Completed Change Requests Opened Change Requests Resolved Units Designed Units Coded Units Integrated Test Cases Attempted Test Cases Passed Action Items Opened Action Items Completed Components Integrated Functionality Integrated
Resources and Cost	Personnel Effort Financial Performance Environmental and Support Resources	Staff Level Development Effort Experience Level Staff Turnover BCWS, BCWP, ACWP Budget Cost Quantity Needed Quantity Available Time Available Time Used
Product Size and Stability	Physical Size and Stability Functional Size and Stability	Database Size Components Interfaces Lines of Code Requirements Functional Changes Function Points
Product Quality	Functional Correctness Maintainability Efficiency Portability Usability Reliability	Defects Age of Defects Technical Performance Level Time to Restore Cyclomatic Complexity Utilization Throughput Response Time Standards Compliance Operator Errors Mean-Time-to-Failure
Process Performance	Process Compliance Process Efficiency Process Effectiveness	Reference Maturity Rating Process Audit Findings Productivity Cycle Time Defects Contained Defects Escaping Rework Effort Rework Components
Technology Effectiveness	Technology Suitability Technology Volatility	Requirements Coverage Baseline Changes
Customer Satisfaction	Customer Feedback Customer Support	Satisfaction Ratings Award Fee Requests for Support Support Time

Figure 3-2   Information category measure mapping

Project Information Needs	Probability of Occurrence	Relative Impact	Project Exposure
Aggressive Schedule	1.0	10	10.0
Budget Constraints	1.0	10	10.0
Unstable Requirements	1.0	8	8.0
Subcontractor Integration	0.7	6	5.6
Staff Turnover	1.0	6	6.0
Staff Experience	1.0	5	5.0
Changing Mission	0.7	6	4.2
Critical Dependencies	0.5	7	3.5
Reliability Requirements	1.0	3	3.0
Concurrent Activities	1.0	2	2.0
COTS Performance	0.2	9	1.8
Questionable Size Estimates	1.0	1	1.0

Figure 3-3   Information need prioritization example

occurrence by the relative impact) relate to aggressive schedule, budget constraints, and requirements changes. The measurement process should address these information needs first.

When risk assessment results are used, the impact of risks, problems, and other concerns should be estimated using the method defined by the risk process. All issues should be prioritized together.

Prioritization approaches always reflect some degree of subjectivity. Some planners may be tempted to diminish measurement requirements by minimizing the estimated impact or by reducing the priority of information needs inappropriately. This must be avoided. No matter how the information needs are prioritized, similar information needs should be grouped. This makes it easier to select measures that address multiple information needs.

The prioritization of the project information needs is dynamic. Additional information needs may be identified once the project is underway, and the probability and impact of risks change as the project matures. Timing is also important. Priorities and mitigation tactics will change as the estimated date of a projected impact nears. Risks must be managed continually. Thus, the measurement process has to change to keep pace with changing priorities.

3.2   **Select and Specify Measures**

This section describes how base measures, derived measures, and indicators are selected and specified to address identified information needs. Since every project is described by a unique set of information needs, processes, and products, the set of measures applied to each project is also unique.

The steps in the measurement selection task include, mapping the appropriate measurable concepts to each identified information need, identifying candidate measures, and specifying measurement constructs that organize these measures to implement each measurable concept most effectively.

Although project information needs drive the selection of appropriate software measures, the overall characteristics of the project and its development approach must also be considered. The types of analysis and models used also affect measurement choices. For example, most parametric estimation models require a defined set of inputs. Thus, selecting a specific estimation model implies selecting the associated measures. Anticipating the types of analyses and reports that will be needed helps to define the required measures.

Mapping project information needs to information categories and measurable concepts helps to select appropriate measures. Figure 3-4 illustrates this relationship. Each information category has one or more associated measurable concepts. Each measurable concept can be implemented in many different ways. However, these constructs typically incorporate elements from a specific set of base and derived measures. While this mapping is presented as a hierarchical decomposition in this figure, in reality some base and derived measures apply to many different measurable concepts and associated measurement constructs.

The predefined information categories, measurable concepts, and measures in Figure 3-2 provide a starting point for measurement selection and specification. They are intended to be modified and adapted to meet individual project needs.

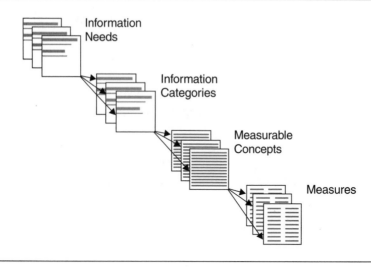

Figure 3-4   PSM measurement selection mechanisms

Characterizing Project Context

The definition of a measure does not depend solely on identified information needs. The technical and management processes of the project must also be considered. Project information needs identify the information that the measurement process must derive from the data. The various project management and technical engineering processes determine specific data that may be collected and how the resulting information will be used. Defining an effective measurement program requires an understanding of the context in which measurement occurs. It makes little sense to define measures that cannot be implemented within an existing process.

Some key project factors to consider are:

- The life-cycle model or activity structure used to define the software supplier's process

- The product structure, including increments and allocation of various tasks to subcontractors and outside vendors

- Current measurement activities

- System and software technology, including design techniques, software programming languages, environment, and tools

- Planned sources of software components, such as nondeveloped, newly developed, or reused components

- Management, coordination, review, test, and inspection practices

- Engineering and management standards to be applied

- Process maturity of each software organization involved in the project

The supplier's process has a major impact on the cost and effectiveness of the measurement program. Whenever possible, current practices and existing data collection mechanisms should be used, and new measurement requirements should be minimized. The project's Work Breakdown Structure (WBS) can provide the basis for collecting and aggregating data. To the extent that the activities of the development process are well defined, they can be reviewed for useful information. An ad hoc or ill-defined process makes it difficult to tell exactly what is being measured. Consequently, the maturity of a development process (i.e., the Capability Maturity Model level) affects the efficiency and accuracy of measurement. Experience has shown that organizations with ad hoc or ill-defined processes are likely to misuse measurement data.

For many information needs, the available data changes across life-cycle activities. For example, during implementation, progress may be measured in terms of software units specified, designed, and built. During integration and test, progress may be measured in terms of test cases executed and passed.

The results of project characterization are used to identify opportunities for measurement.

Defining the Measurable Concepts

Once the project information needs are identified, prioritized, and mapped to measurement categories, and the project context has been characterized, the measurement analyst can develop a concept of how to satisfy the information needs. As discussed in Chapter 2, a **measurable concept** is an idea about how certain activities and products may be related to the information need. A given measurable concept may be implemented in multiple ways. A specific way of implementing a measurable concept is called a **measurement construct.** Measurement constructs are combinations of base measures, derived measures, and indicators. Measurement constructs for a given measurable concept tend to be developed from a small set of base and derived measures.

In general, at least one measurable concept should be selected for each information need or information category. Figure 3-5 provides a list of commonly used measurable concepts for each of the information categories. The figure also includes an example question that may be addressed by each measurable concept.

Figure 3-5 helps in finding the measurable concept or concepts that most closely align with a project information need. For example, if the project information need is "the progress of software integration," then Work Unit Progress is an appropriate measurable concept because the information need is related to the progress of a specific activity, namely, integration. If the project information need is "the amount of additional budget required to fix unanticipated problems," then Financial Performance is pertinent because it addresses the extra cost that will be incurred to correct latent defects.

The measurable concept that provides the best fit for the information need should be selected. For critical or high-priority information needs, more than one measurable concept may be selected. In addition, measurable concepts should be selected to provide leading indicators of issues, before they become more difficult to correct. Chapter 4 discusses an analysis model that organizes common software issues in terms of their basic "cause-and-effect" relationships.

Selecting the Applicable Measures

The next step in selecting and specifying project measures associated with a measurable concept is to choose the best fit from among the base and derived measures associated with each measurement category. Base measures are the lowest level at which data will be collected. Consider the alignment of potential measures with the information need, as well as the efficiency and effectiveness of the measures themselves and the ability of the project to produce them. For example, if the degree of product volatility is an information need, then requirements and product-oriented size measures may be selected. The appropriate measure depends on the nature of the project. Programming language and application domain influence the choice of a software size measure, such as number of function points or

Information Category	Measurable Concept	Questions Addressed
Schedule and Progress	Milestone Completion	Is the project meeting scheduled milestones?
	Critical Path Performance	Are critical tasks or delivery dates slipping?
	Work Unit Progress	How are specific activities and products progressing?
	Incremental Capability	Is capability being delivered as scheduled in incremental builds and releases?
Resource and Cost	Personnel Effort	Is effort being expended according to plan? Is there enough staff with the required skills?
	Financial Performance	Is project spending meeting budget and schedule objectives?
	Environment and Support Resources	Are needed facilities, equipment, and materials available?
Product Size and Stability	Physical Size and Stability	How much are the product's size, content, physical characteristics, or interfaces changing?
	Functional Size and Stability	How much are the requirements and associated functionality changing?
Product Quality	Functional Correctness	Is the product good enough for delivery to the user? Are identified problems being resolved?
	Maintainability	How much maintenance does the system require? How difficult is it to maintain?
	Efficiency	Does the target system make efficient use of system resources?
	Portability	To what extent can the functionality be re-hosted on different platforms?
	Usability	Is the user interface adequate and appropriate for operations? Are operator errors within acceptable bounds?
	Reliability	How often is service to users interrupted? Are failure rates within acceptable bounds?
Process Performance	Process Compliance	How consistently does the project implement the defined processes?
	Process Efficiency	Are the processes efficient enough to meet current commitments and planned objectives?
	Process Effectiveness	How much additional effort is being expended because of rework?
Technology Effectiveness	Technology Suitability	Can technology meet all allocated requirements, or will additional technology be needed?
	Technology Volatility	Does new technology pose a risk because of too many changes?
Customer Satisfaction	Customer Feedback	How do our customers perceive the performance on this project? Is the project meeting user expectations?
	Customer Support	How quickly are customer support requests being addressed?

Figure 3-5   Measurable concepts and related questions

lines of code. Many different measures may apply to an information need. In most cases, it is not practical to collect all or even most of the potential measures. Generally, more measures should be collected to track high-priority information needs.

The following measurement selection criteria can help identify the best measures for the project:

- *Measurement effectiveness:* How effective is the measure in providing the desired insight? Is it a direct measure of the process or product characteristic in question? Does the measure provide insight that relates to more than one information need?

- *Domain characteristics:* Are certain measures better in a given domain? For example, response time is widely used to measure computer resource utilization in information systems, while memory utilization is more widely used in embedded systems (e.g., flight control for aircraft).

- *Project management practices:* Can existing management practices be leveraged to support the measurement requirements? For example, is there a scheduling system in use that provides one or more of the desired measures? Is there an estimation model in use that requires specific measurement inputs?

- *Cost and availability:* What data should be readily available in the context of the project? How much effort will be required to extract and package the data for analysis? Electronic data collection usually costs less than manual collection.

- *Life-cycle coverage:* Does the measure apply to the development phase under consideration? Does it apply to multiple development phases?

- *External requirements:* Has the overall organization or enterprise imposed any related measurement requirements?

- *Size and origin of system components:* Does the size of the project justify a greater investment in measurement? Does this measure make sense if much of the system involves externally supplied components, software reuse, or commercial, off-the-shelf components?

In most cases, the selection process requires trade-offs among the measurement selection criteria. For example, a given measure may directly address a high-priority project information need, but may be too costly to implement in terms of time and resources. The initial selection of measures are refined further as the measures are incorporated into measurement constructs.

Specifying Measurement Constructs

Once a measurable concept and candidate measures have been selected, base measures, derived measures, and indicators must be defined, as appropriate, to complete the specification of the corresponding measurement construct. This specification provides an operational definition of the relevant measures. Each measurement construct should include all of the elements described in Chapter 2. Figure 3-6 provides a template for specifying measurement constructs. The fields in the template correspond to the

Measurement Construct	
Information Need	
Measurable Concept	
Relevant Entities	
Attributes	
Base Measures	
Measurement Method	
Type of Method	
Scale	
Type of Scale	
Unit of Measurement	
Derived Measure	
Measurement Function	
Indicator	
Analysis Model	
Decision Criteria	

Figure 3-6 Measurement construct template

elements of the Measurement Information Model presented in Chapter 2. Appendix A contains examples of completed templates.

The measurement specifications should be documented for easy reference, usually in the measurement plan. The specifications sometimes vary over the course of the project as processes are modified and updated. Clear and complete specifications and associated definitions help ensure accurate measurement data and meaningful interpretations. Maintaining an experience base of previously developed measurement constructs (stored in the form of completed templates) also facilitates planning. These may be associated with standard organizational processes. Taking advantage of existing measurement specifications and proven data-collection mechanisms improves the overall cost-effectiveness of the measurement program within the organization.

The task of specifying a measurement construct usually is performed iteratively. That is, candidate base measures, derived measures, and indicators are sketched out and then adjusted at each level to arrive at a measurement construct that fits the information need.

Many base measures support multiple derived measures and indicators. For example, the Actual Lines of Code Implemented base measure is used to calculate and analyze software development performance in terms of productivity (code/effort—a derived measure) and quality in terms of defect density (defects/code—another derived measure).

The initial selection of measures should be reviewed to ensure that all of the high-priority information needs are addressed.

As discussed in Chapter 2, an **indicator** is a measure that provides an estimate or evaluation of specified attributes derived from an analysis model with respect to defined information needs. Combining base and/or derived measures using a predefined algorithm or model generates an indicator. Typically the value of an indicator is a number or series of numbers. An indicator is often represented as a graph or a table. Base and derived measures can be combined for analysis purposes in many different ways, meaning that various indicators can be constructed from the same set of base and derived measures. This allows tremendous flexibility in analyzing issues and in adapting to new information needs as they arise. A measurement process that is based only on the periodic delivery of predefined graphs does not have this flexibility.

Nevertheless, measurement procedures usually define a basic set of regularly produced indicators. As will be discussed in Chapter 4, the analysis activity must be responsive to management questions stimulated by a regular reporting cycle. This means measurement constructs may be redefined or new constructs introduced during analysis. The measurement procedures must allow for that flexibility.

A good indicator will:

- Support analysis of the intended information need

- Support the type of analysis needed (estimation, feasibility, or performance analysis)

- Provide the appropriate level of detail

- Indicate a possible management action

- Provide timely information for making decisions and taking action

Indicators typically compare actual measured values with an *expectation* of what they should be. The expectation may be based on historical averages, planning numbers, specific limit values, or threshold ranges. Models and decision criteria help to decide whether or not the difference between actual data and expected data is significant.

Figure 3-7 provides an example of a coding progress indicator. Note the following:

- The expected values are represented by a base measure containing cumulative data (the "planned" series), which shows the amount of coding that should be accomplished over the period of time for which the code phase is planned.

- The actual values are represented by a separate base measure, also containing cumulative data (the "actuals" series), which is updated each period and shows the total number of units that have completed coding to date.

- The variance is the gap between the actual and the planned values. The decision criteria for this indicator specifies that a variance of more than 20 percent requires further analysis. For example, for 29 October, the cumulative variance is a negative 25 percent, requiring further investigation. (The model specifies that the cumulative num-

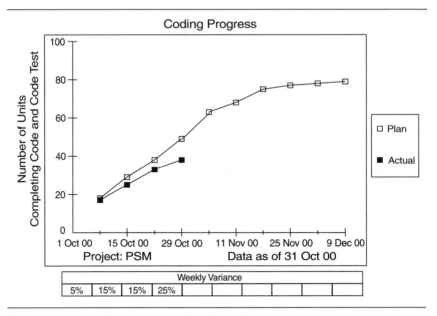

Figure 3-7 Graphical representation of a coding progress indicator

ber of units completed is divided by the cumulative number of units planned, and the product is multiplied by 100.)

Developing and disseminating clear specifications for all measurement constructs facilitate the collection of accurate and consistent data. Even obvious terms, such as lines of code or staff-months of effort, often are defined differently by different organizations. For example, lines of code may be interpreted to mean physical lines, noncomment lines, executable statements, or other variations. Similarly, different organizations may specify a different number of hours of effort per staff-month. Carefully completing the template provided in Figure 3-6 ensures that all the necessary information has been specified.

3.3 Integrate the Measurement Approach into Project Processes

Up to this point, measurement planning has focused on what the project manager needs to know. The next task is to examine how the data will be collected and analyzed to satisfy the project's information needs. The measurement approach should be integrated into the project's technical and management processes. This includes both integrating data collection procedures into processes providing data, and integrating analysis and reporting procedures into decision-making processes. In the final planning task, opportunities for measurement are investigated, procedures for collecting and analyzing the data are developed, and the measurement specifications and procedures are documented to complete the measurement plan.

Identifying Measurement Opportunities

During measurement planning, identifying and exploiting any measurement mechanisms already in place should be a high priority. *This is especially important when implementing measurement on an existing project.* The use of existing data sources offers the advantage of familiarity and potentially lowers the cost of implementing the measurement program. A measurement plan can be implemented more quickly when the data providers and decision makers already know some elements of the measurement process.

Measurement data potentially comes from many sources. Special attention should be given to existing databases and tools that support project management, quality assurance, and configuration management. Extracting and delivering data from electronic sources is usually more cost-effective than manual collection methods.

Measurement data can typically be described as originating from one of three primary sources:

- *Historical data:* This includes data collected from past projects. This data helps in generating estimates and in determining the feasibility of plans.

- *Planning data:* This data typically represents project estimates and expected values. It generally contains the budgets and schedules against which progress and expenditures will be measured. Data must be collected from both initial plans and revised plans, including incremental changes to plans.

- *Actual performance data:* As a project evolves, actual data will become available. Many sources of data exist within the technical and management processes. Problem reports may be obtained from problem-tracking systems. Defect counts may be obtained from configuration management systems. Counts of hours expended by activity may be collected from financial management records. Progress data usually comes from the detailed work plans maintained by technical managers and team leaders. Consistent use of project management tools facilitates data collection.

Measures of components, software units or lines of code, and changes to other deliverables or documentation are usually obtained from configuration management records and reports. A source code analyzer may be used to count lines of code. Product information, such as requirements, components, or number of pages, can also be captured from requirements and design tools and during reviews and inspections. Note that in all these cases, the most efficient method of collecting the desired data depends on the nature of the technical and management processes. To the maximum extent possible, data collection should be automated so that it is a byproduct of normal project activities. Figure 3-8 shows some examples of common data sources.

For high-priority information needs, sources of data available early in the project life cycle should be considered. For example, if quality is a major concern, inspection data during design provides earlier sources of data than problem report data from testing.

When implementing measurement on existing projects, recognize that information needs may have already been identified and some measurement activities may already be implemented. Existing data should be used, if it supports the identified information needs. However, the existing measures often are not defined to the level of detail described in this section. Establishing good specifications is just as important for utilizing existing data as it is when implementing a new set of measures. Without clear definitions, objective communication and meaningful interpretation of the data are impossible.

Developing Measurement Procedures

A well-thought-out set of measurement constructs, by itself, does not adequately define a measurement program. The physical implementation of a given measurement construct may take many different forms. For example, a base measure that quantifies lines of Ada code by counting semi-

Measurable Concepts	Electronic Source	Hard Copy Source
Milestone Completion	Project Management System/ Project Scheduling Tools	Schedule
Work Unit Progress	Project Scheduling Tools Configuration Management System	Status Reports
Incremental Capability	Configuration Management System	Build Reports Status Accounting Records
Personnel Effort	Cost Accounting System Time Reporting System Estimation Tools	Time Sheets
Financial Performance	Performance Management System Financial System	Earned Value Reports Financial Records
Physical Size and Stability	Static Analysis Systems Configuration Management System Computer Models	Product Listing Product Spec Sheets Laboratory Test Records
Functional Size and Stability	Function Point Counting Systems Change Request Tracking System Configuration Management System Computer-Aided Software Engineering (CASE) Tools	Requirements and Design Specifications Change Requests
Functional Correctness	Defect/Problem Tracking System Configuration Management System CASE Tools Test Automation Tools	Test Incident Reports Review/Inspection Reports Design Review Notes and Actions
Maintainability	Static Analysis Tools Problem or Failure Tracking System	Review/Inspection Reports Problem Reports Maintenance Reports
Efficiency	Dynamic Analysis Tools System Monitoring Tools	Performance Analysis Reports
Usability	Problem or Failure Tracking System Help Desk System	Operator Problem Reports
Process Compliance	Process Enactment Tools	Assessment Findings Audit Reports
Process Efficiency	Project Management System Time Reporting System	Time Sheets Process Reviews Findings
Process Effectiveness	Defect/Problem Tracking System Time Reporting System	Test Incident Reports Review/Inspection Reports Time Sheets
Customer Feedback	On-line Feedback Systems	Survey Results Comment Forms

Figure 3-8 Example data sources

colons could be implemented with one of several commercially available source analyzers or even manually. Moreover, unless someone is assigned responsibility for code counting at some regular interval, whether by manual or automated means, it is not likely to get done. Typically, measurement procedures address these assignments and decisions. Procedures should be developed for both the collection and storage of data, as well as for its analysis and reporting.

The following sections examine considerations that must be addressed when developing project measurement procedures.

Aggregation Structures

Base measures may be generated from many different entities in the project environment. Many of these entities are related to each other. A software product, for example, may be made up of several different components. Measuring a component also can provide information about the software product to which it belongs, if the relationship is understood. Aggregation structures capture the relationships among the measured entities so that data can be combined and decomposed as appropriate to the question being considered.

Three common aggregation structures are as follows:

- *Component structure:* The organization of the software product into subsystems, components, units, and so forth, provides a basis for aggregating information about product size and quality. Thus, the high-level software design is one commonly used aggregation structure.

- *Functional structure:* The decomposition of requirements into functions provides a useful basis for aggregating information about functional size and quality.

- *Activity structure:* The organization of the work processes into elements and tasks provides a basis for aggregating effort and other resource data. Typical activities include requirements analysis, design, implementation, integration, and testing.

Simplified examples of each type of aggregation structure are depicted in Figure 3-9. (In the figure, individual design components are designated as

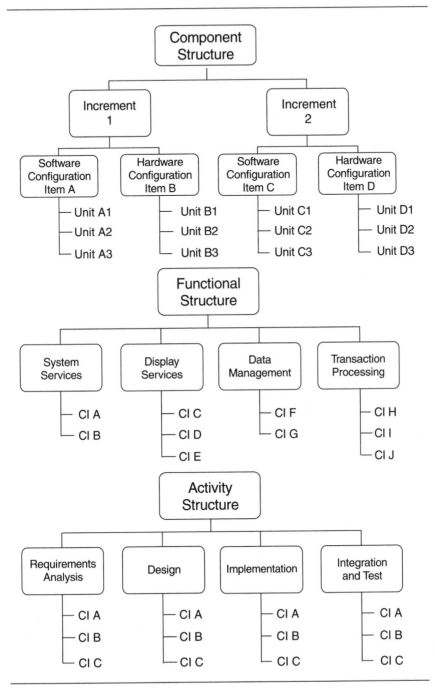

Figure 3-9   Measurement aggregation structures

CIs—configuration items.) One common project-planning construct, the Work Breakdown Structure, combines both the component and activity structures.

Each entity may be mapped to one or more aggregation structures so that data can be combined appropriately during analysis. Alternatively, the position of each measured entity in the structure may be recorded along with the value of the measure, for each aggregation structure used.

Periodicity
Collection, analysis, and reporting of data need to occur on a frequent enough basis to support the decision-making process that generated the information need. These three activities often are scheduled to occur with the same frequency (e.g., monthly or weekly). It does not make sense for reporting to occur more often than analysis (since there are no new results to report) or for analysis to occur more often than collection (since there is no new data to analyze). However, it may be necessary to collect data more frequently than it is analyzed to ensure data quality. Human memory and records may deteriorate or get lost, even over the course of a month. Most project management measures are collected and analyzed monthly. However, problem report data may be analyzed weekly during the final stages of integration and testing. Some data may be collected only occasionally such as at the completion of a major project.

Responsible Individuals
Many people participate in the measurement process, including those who provide data and perform analysis, as well as the decision makers who use measurement results. Responsibility for each step of the measurement process should be assigned to the appropriate individuals.

Source
Specify the phase and activity during which each base measure is collected and analyzed. This may be captured in the aggregation structure. Some measures apply to multiple phase or activities, but may be collected from only some of them.

Analysis and Reporting Mechanisms

The tools and procedures for analyzing base and derived measures to produce indicators should be identified. Analysis can be as difficult and costly as data collection. Even for data that is readily available, the lack of an appropriate analysis tool may make use of the data uneconomical. Data from different organizations and processes may need to be normalized.

Plans and Actuals

Many analyses involve comparisons of actual performance against plans. Thus, data collection usually begins during the project-planning phase. Many measures will include an estimate or plan, and then the actual result. Updates of plans and estimates should result in updates to the data.

Configuration Management

Ideally, collection, analysis, and reporting follow the measurement plan and stay synchronized. However, data has the potential to get lost, and mistakes are inevitably made. Consequently, it may be necessary to go back to previous versions of data and reports. The configuration of the final and intermediate products of the measurement process should be managed, just as the software is. At the minimum, the dates of collection and analysis need to be associated with the data and reports.

Documenting the Project Measurement Plan

The final task of the planning process is documenting the project measurement plan. The plan should contain all planning results including information needs, measurable concepts, measurement constructs, and measurement procedures. The plan should explain how the measurement process will be integrated into the project management process so that decision makers can use the measurement results.

The project measurement plan may be formal or informal. A viewgraph presentation can be an effective vehicle for documenting and communicating the measurement plan. Modify the plan as required to accommodate changes in information needs, in measure availability, and in project

---

Part 1—Introduction
• Purpose and Scope

Part 2—Project Description
• Technical and Project Management Characteristics

Part 3—Measurement Roles, Responsibilities, and Communications
• How Measurement Is Integrated into the Project Processes
• Measurement Points of Contact (acquirer, supplier, subcontractors)
• Measurement Responsibilities
• Organizational Communications and Interfaces
• Tools and Databases
• Phased Implementation (if applicable)
• Evaluation Criteria

Part 4—Description of Project Information Needs
• Organizational Goals/Issues
• Prioritized List of Project Information Needs

Part 5—Measurement Specifications (include for each
        identified information need)
• Measurable Concept
• Relevant Entities
• Attributes
• Base Measures
• Measurement Method
• Type of Method
• Scale
• Type of Scale
• Unit of Measurement
• Derived Measure
• Measurement Function
• Indicator
• Analysis Model
• Decision Criteria

Part 6—Project Aggregation Structures
• Component Aggregation Structure (CIs, units, etc.)
• Activity Aggregation Structure (such as requirements
  analysis, design, implementation, and integration and test)
• Functional Aggregation Structure

Part 7—Reporting Mechanisms and Periodicity
• Reporting Mechanism and Periodicity
• Content of Reports

Figure 3-10   Project measurement plan outline

processes as the project context changes. The plan may be produced as a separate document, although it is commonly included in the software development plan, project plan, or similar planning document. Figure 3-10 shows a typical outline for a measurement plan.

The project measurement plan should be coordinated with the project risk management plan. All significant quantifiable risks should be reflected in the measurement plan. For small projects, all of this information may be included in a single plan.

A careful and complete measurement plan and well-defined measurement constructs are essential to good data. Clear definitions ensure that the following are true:

- The measurement process is repeatable.

- Data providers, those doing analysis, and the decision makers understand the measures and the associated analysis and recommendations.

- Comparisons can be made across the project or at an organizational level.

- The measurement process can be maintained, even with personnel changes.

4

Perform Measurement

Chapter 3 explains how project information needs are identified and how a measurement plan is developed to address those needs. This chapter describes how the plan is implemented to produce the information products required by the project manager to make informed software decisions. Figure 4-1 shows the three tasks associated with performing measurement on a software project.

The measurement plan provides the road map for implementing measurement on the project. The first task in performance measurement involves

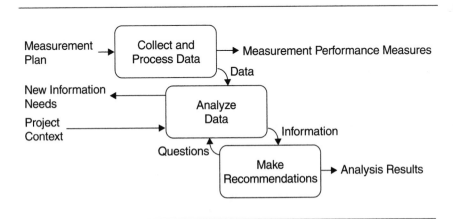

Figure 4-1   Perform Measurement tasks

implementing the data collection procedures to collect the base measures defined in the plan. Next, the data analysis procedures are executed to produce the designated indicators necessary to performing the planned analysis. Finally, the information gained through analysis is used to formulate recommendations that are reported to the project decision makers. These recommendations are conveyed along with the associated measurement analysis results. Questions raised by the project manager usually require that some of the analysis activities be repeated. These three perform measurement tasks are repeated throughout the project life cycle on a periodic basis, reflecting changing project information needs and the changing characteristics of the project.

The following is an example of performing measurement on a project. In this case, one of the information needs identified by the project manager is knowing whether the project is on schedule. Knowledge about progress during the software-coding phase of the project, therefore, is important. The project manager has a number of new programmers on board and wants to monitor their progress closely in an attempt to reduce schedule slippage during the latter stages of the project. As a result, the project manager develops detailed plans for individual software component development that include assignments, effort estimates, and planned start and stop dates. The project manager establishes procedures where programmers are required to check their code into the configuration library when they complete their assignments.

Each week during the coding phase of the project, the project manager produces an indicator using two base measures: planned components complete and actual components complete. (This indicator is similar to Figure 3-7 in Chapter 3.) The indicator displays the complete profile for the number of components that were supposed to be completed by the end of each week, and plots the actual number of components checked into the configuration library for that time period. The graph is designed to show cumulative progress over time, so the picture of coding progress "grows" with each passing week. The project team reviews its progress each week during the weekly staff meeting against the defined decision criterion established—not more than 10 percent behind schedule. Early in the coding stage, progress begins to slip behind plan. Additional analysis shows that some of the new programmers are having trouble completing their assignments on time. The team decides to modify its process to use programming pairs for certain components, and a number of coding assignments are modified based on earlier lessons learned. Through continuous monitoring and corrective actions, the project is able to stay on track.

This simple example illustrates one way that measurement can be used on a project. More details on the three basic Perform Measurement tasks— collect and process data, analyze data, and make recommendations— along with additional fundamental measurement analysis concepts, are presented in this chapter. Chapter 5 provides additional details regarding three specific applications of measurement analysis.

4.1   Collect and Process Data

This task involves collecting data from the various sources identified in the measurement plan, preparing it for analysis, and then storing it where it will be accessible for analysis. The three basic areas that must be addressed in this task are (1) how to make the data visible and to capture it properly, (2) how to ensure the quality of the data, and (3) how to store and manage the data for analysis. The answers to these questions should be developed and documented during the Plan Measurement activity. This section discusses some of the practical issues related to data collection that may not be obvious during the planning process.

How data is captured during project activities affects the cost and accuracy of this task. In many cases, data can be captured *automatically*. For example, code analysis tools are used to analyze source code and automatically generate measures of the code's size in lines of code, code complexity, and other code characteristics. In other cases data may be captured through *manual* processes. For example, testers may generate individual defect reports during the testing process as they identify each problem. How data is stored once it is generated and captured is also important. An accessible electronic format for data storage is most desirable. For example, some code analysis tools may store their results in a database or spreadsheet-compatible file. Other tools may be limited and report results only through a printed report or through an on-screen display. In the case of defect data, testers may have the ability to enter defect reports directly into a defect tracking system or may be required to complete a paper form.

Plan or "baseline" measures are usually generated at different points in time from actual performance data. Since these two types of data are often combined to analyze project performance, how and where plan data is stored also influences this task. Plan data is often generated at the beginning of a project and may be revised periodically. Plan data may be stored in project plans created using a word-processing tool, project-planning tool, or spreadsheet. Other plan data (e.g., thresholds, norms, or control limits generated from past projects' actual performance data) may have been generated outside the project process and stored in an organizational database. In contrast, actual performance data is generated and accumulates gradually over time and may be stored in different systems (e.g., time-reporting systems, spreadsheets, or defect-tracking systems) to accommodate continual data generation, collection, and storage.

Continuing with the coding progress example, Figure 4-2 shows how plan and actual data was stored in different locations on a project. Also shown is how the measurement constructs specified in the measurement plan provide a road map for pulling the data together for analysis. As discussed in Chapter 3, the measurement method for each base measure and the measurement procedure provide the "how to" details, including how data will be captured and how and where it will be stored. In this case, the measurement methods for both planned and actual base measures describe how data is aggregated by week and accumulated over time. A derived measure is produced from the plan and actual base measures to provide an indication of the percentage of variance that exists each week between the plan and actual performance. These measures are then combined into an indicator, in this case represented by a line graph and variance table, that the project manager and development team can review and use as the basis of their discussion of coding status and progress.

As this example shows, base measures often require additional "processing" prior to, or as part of, the analysis. This may involve aggregating the data, normalizing the data, or deriving additional measures by applying a mathematical formula or measurement function to the data.

The reliability of a flexible analysis process depends on effective data management. As with any other important project asset, values of base measures and indicators should be managed and controlled. (Values of derived measures can be computed from values of base measures.) Configuration management concepts, such as controlled write access and using version numbers for electronic files and data sets, should be applied to maintain the integrity of the data. Keeping data synchronized is also important when data must be extracted from its original source and stored elsewhere to facilitate analysis. All data should be identified by its collection date and source; this will help the measurement analysts align findings and conclusions with project events and will allow comparison of data over time and from different sources.

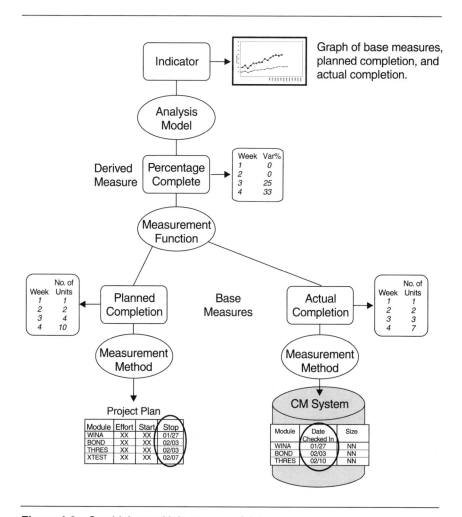

Figure 4-2 Combining multiple sources of data

Well-defined measurement constructs and processes improve data quality and, ultimately, the value of performing measurement on a project. Even seemingly obvious terms must be defined. For example, a "lines of code" base measure may be interpreted to mean all physical lines, only noncomment lines, or executable statements. Even the specification for a unit of measure can be ambiguous; for example, the number of hours in a "staff-month" varies from organization to organization. Even if specifications are precise and well understood by the process owners, many data problems still arise whenever data is being generated, captured, stored, and processed. Typical problems include the following:

- *Data not captured:* When the generation of data depends on a manual activity, what happens when the activity is bypassed? For example, if defect data is generated when testers record defects found during testing in a defect-tracking system, they may fail to enter all defects found because of time constraints. The process may allow alternative ways of getting the defect fixed, such as communicating informally with the coder. Many organizations integrate the measurement process into the development process. For example, one approach is to mandate that code cannot be modified unless it is checked out of a controlled library and that it cannot be checked out unless a defect report is opened against the component.

- *Wrong values captured:* Even when base measures are clearly specified and people are trained in how to record data, deficient information is still entered. One common problem arises when, despite documented definitions for defect severity codes, individuals develop their own rules for what should be considered a "major" versus a "minor" defect. Because of this, the project manager may be misinformed regarding the number of major open problems and their impact on the project.

- *Measurement system errors:* Most measurement "systems" are comprised of off-the-shelf tools, homegrown spreadsheets, or databases that are constantly undergoing changes. These changes can lead to data collection and processing errors. For example, a query developed to extract information from an existing database and to store it in a spreadsheet for analysis may (1) not extract all relevant records, (2) not capture all relevant fields, (3) transform fields or accumulate records incorrectly, or (4) overwrite data. All changes and enhancements to the measurement system and associated tools should be tested.

Data should be verified before it is used for analysis. Data verification should consider both the accuracy of the data as it is recorded and the fidelity with which it is processed. An examination of data stores can often uncover problems. Data verification requires accurate measurement specifications and an understanding of the project's defined process. Checklists can provide a useful tool for data verification. Figure 4-3 contains an example of a data verification checklist.

Any data concerns or inconsistencies should be resolved through communication with the data providers on the project team. Missing data, significant changes in values, or changes in the data structure should always be discussed with the project team. Even accurate and verified engineering data may be "noisy." Software development is a human-intensive activity; things seldom go exactly as planned. Because performance varies from week to week, it is rare that actual results exactly match the plan.

4.2   Analyze Data

The principal task of the Perform Measurement activity is to analyze data. This is where much of the project's measurement effort will be focused. This task transforms values of base measures into values for indicators, the basic building blocks of analysis. Indicators and associated decision criteria are used to make planning decisions or determine the need for corrective action once the project has started. These analyses are performed by executing the data analysis procedures defined in the measurement plan. However, since all information needs and management questions cannot be anticipated during planning, the data analysis procedure must also provide for the use of alternative analysis techniques.

Figure 4-4 shows the three types of analysis typically employed to support project management decisions: estimating, feasability analysis, and performance analysis. Each type of analysis relies on unique measurement techniques, has its own inputs, and produces different types of results. The focus of analysis always changes over the course of a project, and for most projects, all three types usually must be addressed

Early in the software project, and when plans are updated, the focus is on *estimation* to support project planning. Estimation establishes target values for product size, project effort, project schedules, and other key objec-

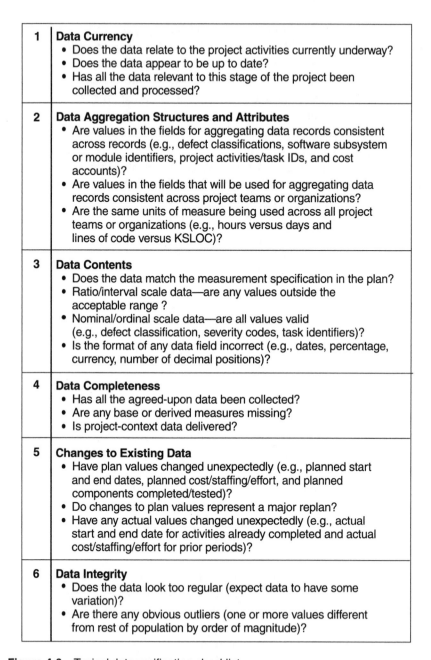

1	**Data Currency** • Does the data relate to the project activities currently underway? • Does the data appear to be up to date? • Has all the data relevant to this stage of the project been collected and processed?
2	**Data Aggregation Structures and Attributes** • Are values in the fields for aggregating data records consistent across records (e.g., defect classifications, software subsystem or module identifiers, project activities/task IDs, and cost accounts)? • Are values in the fields that will be used for aggregating data records consistent across project teams or organizations? • Are the same units of measure being used across all project teams or organizations (e.g., hours versus days and lines of code versus KSLOC)?
3	**Data Contents** • Does the data match the measurement specification in the plan? • Ratio/interval scale data—are any values outside the acceptable range ? • Nominal/ordinal scale data—are all values valid (e.g., defect classification, severity codes, task identifiers)? • Is the format of any data field incorrect (e.g., dates, percentage, currency, number of decimal positions)?
4	**Data Completeness** • Has all the agreed-upon data been collected? • Are any base or derived measures missing? • Is project-context data delivered?
5	**Changes to Existing Data** • Have plan values changed unexpectedly (e.g., planned start and end dates, planned cost/staffing/effort, and planned components completed/tested)? • Do changes to plan values represent a major replan? • Have any actual values changed unexpectedly (e.g., actual start and end date for activities already completed and actual cost/staffing/effort for prior periods)?
6	**Data Integrity** • Does the data look too regular (expect data to have some variation)? • Are there any obvious outliers (one or more values different from rest of population by order of magnitude)?

Figure 4-3 Typical data verification checklist

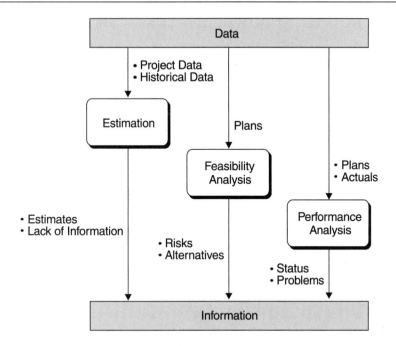

Figure 4-4 Three types of analysis

tives. Estimation usually starts with historical data and assumptions about the project's process and products. Estimation also identifies uncertainties that feed back into the identification of information needs. Estimation should be conducted during the initial project-planning phase and whenever replans are generated.

As project planning nears completion, the focus shifts to *feasibility analysis*. This type of analysis determines whether project plans and targets are realistic and achievable. Feasibility analysis uses historical data, experience, and consistency checks to evaluate the project plans. It also helps to define the interdependencies between the key planning parameters related to product capability, cost, and schedule. Risks identified during this stage should be incorporated into the project's risk management process. Feasibility analysis should be conducted during the initial project-planning phase and during all subsequent replans.

Once the project has begun, *performance analysis* determines whether the project is meeting defined plans, assumptions, and targets. Inputs include plan and actual performance data. Performance analysis is designed to identify risks, problems, and prospective corrective actions. Performance analysis should be conducted on a regular basis throughout the project's life cycle.

Chapter 5 provides more guidance on the specific measurement techniques used in these three types of analysis.

Indicator Generation

As described in Chapter 2, indicators are combinations of base and/or derived measures and predefined decision or evaluation criteria. Chapter 3 explained that an initial set of indicators is designed during the measurement planning activity to support identified information needs. However, new and additional indicators may be needed to address new issues and management questions that arise during analysis. This section examines the details of indicator generation as part of the analysis process.

Few information needs can be addressed by collecting only "current," or actual, performance data. Actual data must be compared with an *expectation* of what it should be. That expectation may be expressed in planned values, historical averages, derived limits, or thresholds (these are discussed in more detail in Chapter 5). These expected values usually become base measures in an indicator. In addition, predefined decision criteria are used to decide whether or not the difference between actual data and expected data is significant.

Figure 4-5 shows how the indicator of coding progress was generated for the example project described earlier. Note the following:

- The *expected values* are represented by a single data series (the planned series) containing cumulative data that shows the amount of coding that should be accomplished over the period of time for which the code phase is planned.

- The *actual values* are represented by a separate data series (the actuals series), also containing cumulative data that is updated each period to show the total number of units that have completed coding to date.

- The *variance* is the gap between the actual and the last-plan values. This is derived from the two base measures.

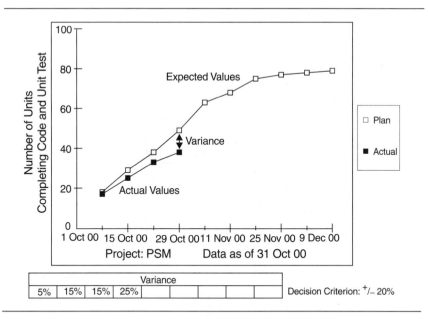

Figure 4-5 Example of a graphical representation of an indicator

- The *decision criterion* specifies that a variance of more than 20 percent requires further analysis. For example, for Week 4, the variance
  is a negative 25 percent, derived by dividing the cumulative difference between the number of units planned and actually complete by
  the cumulative number of units planned, multiplied by 100.

On most projects, information needs evolve rapidly. While the measurement plan may contain a set of predefined indicators designed to provide
insight into known information needs, the project's measurement process
should allow for the dynamic generation of indicators to help investigate
problems as they arise. Because base and derived measures can be combined in many different ways, various indicators can be constructed from
the same set of measures. This allows tremendous flexibility in addressing
information needs and analyzing issues and in adapting to changing information requirements. A measurement process that is based only on the
periodic delivery of a static set of indicators does not have the flexibility to
address changing project information needs.

Figures 4-6, 4-7, and 4-8 are examples of a set of defect indicators generated from a small set of base measures. For this project, defect open date,

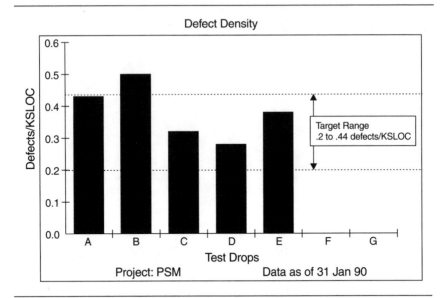

Figure 4-6 Multiple indicators from a few measures—Defect Density

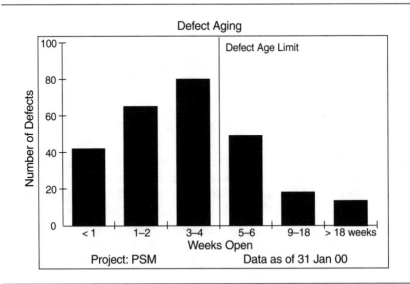

Figure 4-7 Multiple indicators from a few measures—Defect Aging

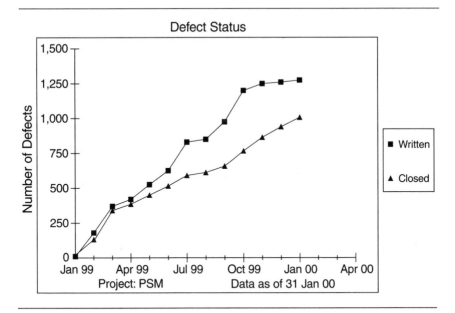

Figure 4-8 Multiple indicators from a few measures—Defect Status

defect close date, and the identification of the unit in which the defect was found are collected for all discovered defects. In addition, the size of the unit is recorded. These base measures are combined in different ways to derive the Defect Density (Figure 4-6), Defect Aging (Figure 4-7), and Defect Status (Figure 4-8) indicators. Figure 4-9 presents a composite view of this approach

When closure rates are not keeping pace with project expectations and/or when defect densities are higher than expected, more detailed indicators can be generated to help uncover the root causes of these problems. The types of defects found, the locations of defects, and the age of open defects are examples of indicators that might be generated to answer certain questions during this problem-solving activity. The new indicators can help determine what types of defects are occurring most often, which subsystems are the most defect-prone, and how long certain defects have been open.

Indicator Representation

Indicators are often best displayed graphically rather than as a table of numbers. Graphs make trends in data, variances, and relationships more obvious and easier to interpret. Many simple charting techniques can be

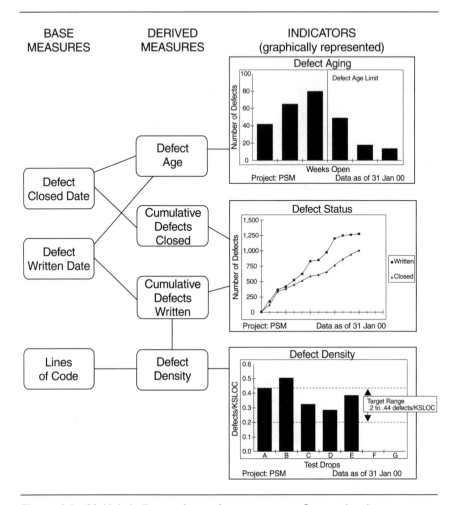

Figure 4-9   Multiple indicators from a few measures—Composite view

used to produce graphical representations of measurement data. The ability to extract the pertinent information contained in the measurement data can be improved with proper selection and use of these charting techniques. The three most commonly used charting techniques are described as follows:

- *Line charts* provide a way to represent a series of measurement data values over time. The x-axis of a line chart is often used to represent the time dimension of a project. The y-axis of the chart may be used to represent the units being counted. Multiple series of data may be shown on a single graph. For example, the expected and actual values in Figure 4-5 represent two series of data; the variance table at the bottom represents a third, derived series. A series either may contain data for a particular period or may be cumulative. Values are plotted as points on the graph and are connected with lines to help show progress or trends.

- *Bar charts* provide a way to represent the count or frequency of a set of components or events. Nominal data, with categorical data groupings, is often shown across the chart's x-axis. Bars are typically drawn vertically; and each bar contains data associated with a category or other nominal grouping of data. The y-axis represents the units or events being counted (see Figure 4-10). Understanding the distribution of the data across the groups is often useful. For example, the bar might represent the number of defects detected (1) for each product component, or (2) within each phase of the software development life cycle. Sets of bars can also be used to compare two series, such as measured and expected values, or, as in Figure 4-9, an average can be used for comparison.

- *Scatter charts* are used to show possible relationships between two factors. They are produced by plotting a series of x and y coordi-

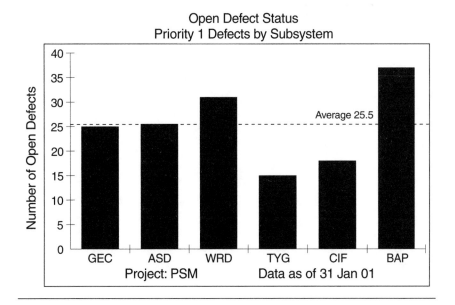

Figure 4-10   Example of a bar chart

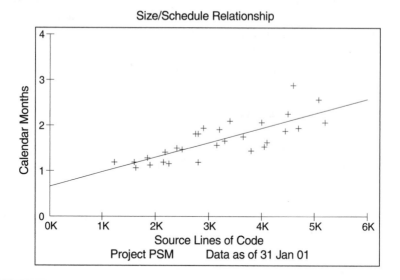

Figure 4-11 Example of a scatter chart

nates. For example, two measures, collected on a number of completed projects, might be plotted. As shown in Figure 4-11, project
size, measured in lines of code, is assigned to the x-axis and schedule
is assigned to the y-axis. When all points are plotted, the strength of
the relationship is illustrated by the tendency of the points to cluster
along a center line and/or within confidence limits.

Well-designed graphs facilitate communication of measurement results.
Graphs should not be complex. They should convey a clear message. It is
better to have multiple graphs rather than to have many measures on
one graph. Some guidelines for developing effective graphs include the
following:

- Provide a descriptive title to identify the information need or measurable concept represented by the graph.

- Include the project name as a header or footer on the graph.

- Ensure axis labels include units of measure and scale markers.

- Provide annotations of major project milestones when showing time
  trends.

- Use the connect-the-dots technique rather than curve-fitting to show trends.

- Show an as-of line or include a date indicating the reporting period represented by the data. Many graphs will show plans or projections beyond the as-of date.

- Use contrasting styles for lines, bars, and data points that represent different base or derived measures.

- Label the line, bar, and data points directly on the figure, if possible. Otherwise, use a key that associates a label with each contrasting style of line, bar, or data point.

- Identify the source of the data. Include the version number of documents.

- Use similar conventions for all reports. For example, on all line graphs, use a solid box style (■) for actual data points and an open box style (□) for plan data points.

- Adjust the horizontal axis to show the expected time frame of the data plotted.

- Label significant events and trends in the data.

- Check that the use of percentages does not hide significant trends in the data.

- Use the same axes on both graphs when comparing two graphs.

The Integrated Analysis Model

So far in this chapter, the focus has been on the generation of a single indicator to provide insight into a project information need. It is important to note that the information categories common to software projects are not independent of one another. For example, most project managers know that unplanned staff turnover or personnel unavailability will most likely impact schedule and progress. "Scope creep" is known to result in a need for more resources and schedule than planned. Problems with product quality can cause cost and schedule overruns when rework effort has not been sufficiently accounted for in schedules and budgets.

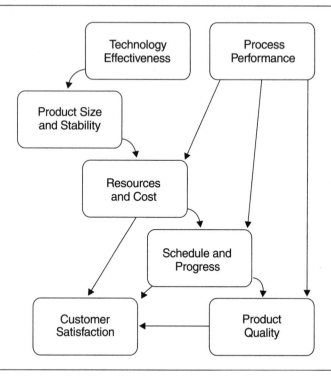

Figure 4-12 Integrated Analysis Model

The Integrated Analysis Model in Figure 4-12 shows the relationships between information categories. This model helps build "early warning" capabilities into the measurement process and helps to relate project information needs and issues in terms of cause and effect.

Each of the arrows in the figure represents a relationship. For example, as Product Size and Stability changes, so do project Resources and Cost. Each of the common information categories is related to its neighbor in the integrated analysis model. This means that "upstream" issues can serve as leading indicators of problems with "downstream" issues. Upstream issues can also be investigated to uncover the *root cause* of a current problem. For example, if schedules are beginning to slip and/or progress is slowing, effort or size might be investigated as the cause of the schedule problem. Moreover, proactively monitoring effort and size measures can serve as an "early warning system" for schedule issues. Early identification of an unplanned size increase can be used to support management decision making, such as adding more people to the project or asking for a schedule extension before the project is in jeopardy of missing key dates.

Figure 4-13 provides a further refinement of the Integrated Analysis Model, showing relationships between measurable concepts that are common to software development projects.

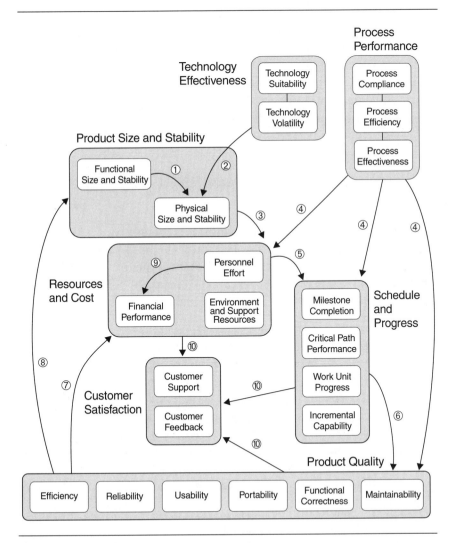

Figure 4-13   Detailed Integrated Analysis Model

The following relationships correspond to the numbered circles in the figure:

1. Functional size represents the amount of functionality the project is expected to provide. This is usually determined by requirements, change requests, or function points. Functional size is a primary determinant of physical size (the amount of product that must be developed or maintained).

2. Most innovative technical approaches attempt to minimize the quantity of new product that must be implemented for a given function. Examples of technical approaches include using purchased software, common architectures, and reusable components. If the effectiveness of the approach does not yield all of the desired benefit, more of the system must be developed than planned. For example, if a purchased system does not satisfy all of the required functionality as originally intended, custom code may have to be developed. The volatility of any new technology also influences product size.

3. Increases in product size, and overall size instability, usually result in the need for additional personnel.

4. Process performance—The maturity or capability of a developer's process—contributes to the need for personnel resources and influences development schedules and product quality. A development team with a more mature and capable process performs better than a team with an ad-hoc or ill-defined one, assuming other factors are constant.

5. Adding more personnel impacts schedule and progress. If personnel are added early in the project and if the appropriate training and communications are in place, the schedule may be shortened. If personnel are added later, the schedule may actually be *lengthened* because of the disruptions caused by adding new personnel not familiar with the project environment, processes, and/or domain. Schedule shortfalls are associated with milestone slips and delays in completing planned life-cycle activities and products, and often necessitate reductions in build and release requirements.

6. Schedule shortfalls can cause product quality problems, including defects in the product, maintainability issues, and performance issues. This happens when test efforts are curtailed in order to meet

tight schedules. Problems left open and not corrected during reviews and testing are also a cause of quality problems.

7. Latent quality problems represent rework that requires additional resources to make current or future releases acceptable to the user. The project manager will usually make a delivery decision based on the number of open problems, fixing some high-priority problems and deferring others to the operations and maintenance phase.

8. Quality problems also worsen product stability and impact cost. Managers may be forced to modify or eliminate some mission requirements to stay within cost and schedule constraints.

9. For software projects, personnel effort, including rework, is the primary determinant of project cost. Cost control can be achieved only by controlling other upstream factors.

10. Problems with resource and schedule overruns, as well as problems with product quality, all impact customer satisfaction.

The following example shows the use of the Integrated Analysis Model. Two areas of concern for this particular project were the uncertainty of software requirements and ability to meet cost and schedule commitments. Figure 4-14 shows how the estimated size of a pertinent software component has grown since the initial estimate.

The Integrated Analysis Model shows that size growth is a leading indicator of a projected increase in development effort (and cost), which, in turn, has the potential to impact project schedules.

Figure 4-15 shows the variance to date between planned and actual effort for this project. Although the applied effort was originally tracking close to plan, indications of the size growth problem are starting to become visible. The planned effort probably has not been revised to reflect the re-estimate of size depicted in Figure 4-14. This is critical, given the downstream impact of size on cost and schedule.

The size growth indicator in Figure 4-14 can also be used to help predict the amount of expected additional effort that will be required. Using the **estimator** depicted in Figure 4-16, the amount of size growth in Figure 4-14 is used to define a new plan for total project effort.

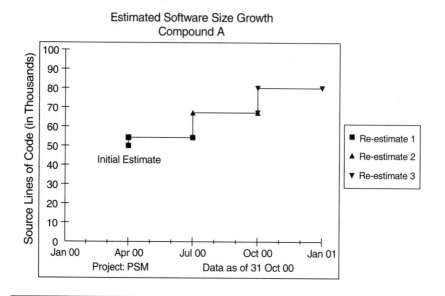

Figure 4-14   Software size growth

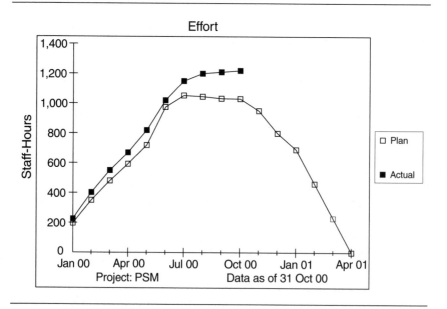

Figure 4-15   Software effort

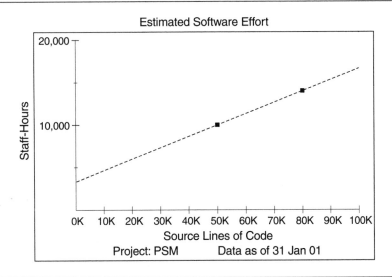

Figure 4-16 Software size used to re-estimate development effort

This example shows how the Integrated Analysis Model can be used as a tool for solving problems, projecting or predicting outcomes, and formulating recommendations. It also illustrates that the analysis process and the generation of indicators are dynamic. Indicators may change and evolve over time to answer different, but related, questions and to provide different views of the measurement results. Each information need may require applying a different set of analysis techniques in order to isolate, understand, and facilitate resolution of a problem or to better understand and mitigate a risk. As project problems, risks, and information change, the types of analyses performed and the indicators generated must be revised.

The Integrated Analysis Model applies equally to estimation, feasibility analysis, and performance analysis, as discussed in the next chapter.

4.3 Make Recommendations

The ultimate purpose of measurement is to help engineers, customers, and managers make more informed decisions. The final task in the Perform Measurement activity involves formulating recommendations and communicating those recommendations along with the analysis results to the appropriate decision makers. As results are discussed and information is communicated to various parties, additional questions may arise. This Make Recommendations task and the Analyze Data task may be executed iteratively until all information needed to make a decision has been presented.

The analysis of project issues should result in the following:

- *Overall evaluation of the project:* Evaluation should include status regarding known project information needs and projections of performance through completion.

- *Identification of specific problems, risks, and lack of information:* The location, cause, and impact of current or potential obstacles to project success should be described, along with any noteworthy outliers or trends.

- *Recommendations*: These should include alternative actions, with advantages and disadvantages of each, to address the underlying risks and problems identified in the analysis.

- *Potential new issues:* The nature of the problem or proposed actions may result in *new information needs,* which may affect the focus of the measurement process.

Measurement results should be incorporated into project status reports given to senior managers and customers. Many project teams are required to present their status at various internal management reviews and, sometimes, to customers at periodic milestone reviews. Using the Integrated Analysis Model helps to explain how different factors (e.g., a growth in size) contribute to certain project results (e.g., schedule slips). This aids in steering the decision makers toward a productive and nonargumentative discussion of alternatives when some corrective action is required.

Action must be taken to realize any benefit from measurement. Well-formulated recommendations facilitate action. These actions typically involve making adjustments to project resources to optimize performance within the project's established constraints. Others actions may require outside decision makers such as senior management or the customer to take action. These may include actions such as:

- Extending the project schedule to maintain quality

- Adding development resources to stay on schedule

- Deleting functional capabilities to control costs

- Changing the development approach or acquisition process to improve performance

- Reallocating project resources and budgets to support key activities

Some of these courses of action affect external project commitments and may not be taken unilaterally. Decision makers need to know how analysis results and recommendations were derived. All assumptions should be well defined. If they are, managers can justify decisions and trace recommendations back to the underlying data.

Measurement is more readily accepted and more effectively utilized when the results are widely available. There are many methods for accomplishing this. Project staff meetings provide a common forum for reviewing indicators, drawing conclusions, and formulating recommendations. This type of team interaction may uncover events and qualitative information that help to explain the data. Web-based systems are another increasingly popular approach to making measurement results available. Formal reports and e-mail also may be used.

5

Analysis Techniques

Fundamental software measurement analysis concepts were introduced in Chapter 4. In this chapter, the three primary types of analysis are presented, along with analysis techniques specific to each type. The types addressed are:

- **Estimation:** Producing estimates of size, effort, schedule, and quality

- **Feasibility analysis**: Assessing the feasibility of project plans during initial planning and replanning activities

- **Performance analysis**: Assessing the project's actual performance against plans throughout the project

These three measurement activities are usually performed iteratively throughout the project's life cycle.

Early in the software project, measurement focuses on estimation to support project planning. The output of estimation is the primary input to the project planning process. As project planning nears completion, feasibility analysis helps to determine whether or not project plans and targets are realistic and achievable. Both estimation and feasibility analysis use historical data extensively. The resulting project plans are then used to direct project execution. Performance analysis determines whether the project is meeting defined plans, assumptions, and targets. When performance deviates from plans or when requirements, constraints, or assumptions change, project teams should re-examine and revise their estimates and re-plan their work accordingly.

5.1 Estimation

Estimation produces quantitative projections of key project attributes. Software project projections typically include product size, amount of required effort, and project duration or schedule. The expected level of product quality also may be estimated. These projections, or forecasts, form the basis for initial project plans. Estimation results in effort and schedule expectations that are used throughout project planning and execution.

Estimation is usually the first type of measurement analysis performed on most projects. The initial round of estimation often occurs early in the project, before the project team is even selected. These initial estimates often establish overall funding and schedule commitments. However, early estimates are often imprecise. They must be updated throughout the project life cycle. Estimation should be performed at various times during a project, and the resulting measures should be used to update plans and track performance.

Poor estimates and misconceptions about the estimating process often contribute to failed projects. In many cases, poor estimates lead to planning targets that are impossible to achieve. Implementing such plans results in missed deadlines, inadequate performance, and poor software quality. Poor estimation can be attributed to a number of factors:

- Lack of estimating experience

- Lack of historical data on which to base estimates

- Lack of a systematic estimation process, sound techniques, or models suited to the project's needs

- Failure to include essential project activities and products within the scope of the estimates

- Unrealistic expectations or assumptions

- Failure to recognize and address the uncertainty inherent in project estimates

The guidance in this chapter cannot substitute for valid historical data or estimation experience. However, it does describe the kinds of data, models, and tools needed to estimate software parameters in a systematic manner. This chapter presents a basic estimation process, supported by the Integrated Analysis Model and widely used software project estimation techniques. This process helps ensure that comprehensive and realistic estimates are produced and incorporated into a project's plans.

Using the Integrated Analysis Model for Estimation

The Integrated Analysis Model described in Chapter 4 is used to support the software estimation process. Upstream elements drive the estimation of downstream elements. For example, software size is the primary input to effort estimation. As product size projections increase, the project effort projections also increase. Similarly, effort serves as the primary input to most schedule estimation approaches. Additionally, most estimation approaches also recognize that the project's use of technology and the expected level of process performance represent *performance factors* that must be accounted for in the estimates.

Actually, any element in the Integrated Analysis Model that is upstream from another given element can be used as a basis for estimation. However, the strongest relationships are found between elements pictured close together in the model, shown in Figures 4-12 and 4-13.

Estimators

Estimation involves using one measure to predict the value of another, using a special type of indicator called an *estimator*. Just like other indicators, estimators are generated from base and derived measures. A unique characteristic of measures used to produce estimators is that they typically are composed of data from past projects. Estimators, like other indicators, are defined using an analysis model. The model specifies the predictive relationship that exists between two measures. Examples of common predictive relationships include

- Functional size to predict product size

- Functional size to predict effort

- Product size to predict effort

- Effort to predict schedule

- Effort to predict cost

- Product size to predict the number of defects (quality)

These estimating relationships are often domain-specific. Analysis models used for estimation typically include performance factors that adjust the predicted value in some way to account for the specific project environment and characteristics. Examples of performance factors include staff skills, staff experience levels, historical productivity rates, the organization's level of process maturity, and the specific kinds of technology and tools used. Other unique project characteristics included as factors are the expected degree of requirements volatility and the complexity of the software being built. Software estimation models vary in their use of estimating relationships and performance factors. For example, some models assume linear relationships between size and effort, while others assume nonlinear relationships.

Figure 5-1 shows a simple estimator for software effort based on software product size. The solid line shows the estimating relationship between size and effort. As product size increases, the amount of effort required to produce the software also increases. The plotted points represent data from past projects. The dashed lines define a region around the estimating relationship into which 95 percent of the data falls. For any given product size, there is a 95 percent chance of the amount of actual effort falling somewhere in that region.

Note that not all of the points lie on the center line. This indicates that the relationship between size and effort is not *deterministic*. This means that, even if the precise value of size is known, only a range of likely values of effort can be determined. Unfortunately, many estimation models produce only single point estimates. A probabilistic statement of the estimate, such as that shown in Figure 5-1, provides a more realistic representation of the actual situation. Figure 5-1 shows that the 95 percent confidence interval for the effort required to develop 10,000 lines of code ranges from about 8 to 100 staff-months. In this example, the confidence interval includes a rather wide range of likely values. Additional filters on the data and additional parameters help to narrow the range. While estimators predict an outcome, they can also be used to assess the associated variability, or level

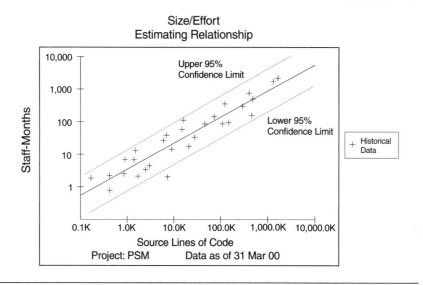

Figure 5-1 Estimator for software effort

of uncertainty, that exists in the estimate. It is always important to understand and communicate the level of confidence in an estimate as well as the estimated value itself.

Estimation Process Overview

Estimation can be viewed as a four-step process, as shown in Figure 5-2. The first step is to select the estimation approach from the many different approaches available. The second step is to map the approach to the project's sequence of life-cycle activities and products and to calibrate associated estimation models with historical data from the organization. The third step involves computing estimates of size, effort, schedule, and/or quality using the approach or model. The fourth step is to evaluate the estimates and to determine if adjustments are needed to bring estimates in line with project constraints.

Estimates provide the foundation for more detailed planning and should be documented in the project's software development plan. Re-estimates should be performed periodically throughout the project life cycle, at major milestones and when changes or project constraints require a new

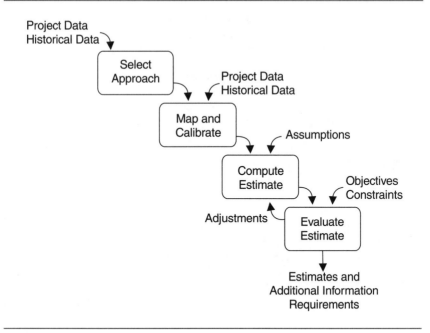

Figure 5-2 Estimation process

plan. As the project progresses and actual performance data becomes available, the accuracy of the estimates increases.

A Survey of Software Estimation Approaches

Software estimation approaches may be composed of a complex mathematical model, a simple arithmetical expression, a set of rules, or a list of descriptive statements. Regardless of the selected approach's sophistication, the quality of the estimates is no better than the assumptions and the actual data put into the model. Four major types of estimating approaches are described in this section: parametric models, activity-based models, analogy, and simple estimating relationships.

Parametric Models
Parametric models assume that a specific mathematical relationship exists between size, effort, schedule, and quality. These models also assume that

the relationships are affected by measurable performance factors (also called *parameters*). The relationships are based on theoretical reasoning or analysis of historical data.

Parametric models for estimating effort generally take the form

$$\text{Effort} = A \times (\text{Size})^B \times C$$

The model's output is estimated effort expressed in hours or person-months. The most important input into the model is software size, which represents the amount of software functionality or product. Parameter A is a constant. Parameter B is an aggregation of performance factors that affect the model output (effort) in a nonlinear manner. These nonlinear performance factors adjust a large input value for size more dramatically than a small size value. This causes the factors to have more influence on projects with larger software products than those with smaller products. Parameter C is an aggregation of performance factors that affect effort in a linear manner. These linear factors have a directly proportional influence on effort regardless of software size.

Performance factors generally fall into two categories: process factors and product factors. Process factors are based on the characteristics of the project's life-cycle processes, including the tools used and the skill level of project personnel. Product factors include attributes such as the operational environment, required reliability, and application complexity. The values of these parameters are selected to raise or lower productivity to more accurately reflect expected project conditions. While estimation models may provide 15 to 100 adjustment factors, most organizations find that only a few factors substantially affect their performance.

For the best results, parametric models must be calibrated to data from the local development environment. Most estimation tools recommend calibration. Calibration usually adjusts only the constants in the model (such as the constant A described in the general model just discussed). While calibrating all of the parameters takes a tremendous amount of data, only a few data points may be required to calibrate a model's constants to local development conditions, with a resulting improvement in model accuracy.

The COnstructive COst MOdel II (COCOMOII) (Abts, Boehm, et al., 2000) is an example of a parametric model for estimating effort and schedule from software size, either in source lines of code or function points. After size is entered, 22 performance factors are applied to yield an effort estimate in person-months. For example, one of these factors is applications experience, which is a linear performance factor. A high level of experience reduces the estimated effort by 23 percent, while a low level of experience increases it by 22 percent.

Most parametric models assume that schedule is a function of effort. Schedule is determined by spreading effort estimates across a predefined set of major activities or phases. An optimum staffing profile for these phases is assumed. Sometimes, these assumptions do not match the project plans, necessitating adjustments.

Few parametric models support both effort/schedule estimation and quality estimation. There are numerous tools for parametric effort and schedule estimation, and few for quality estimation. Some are free, while others are quite expensive. The level of vendor support also varies.

Activity-Based Models
Activity-based estimation is sometimes referred to as *activity-based costing* or *bottom-up estimating*. The activity-based approach is based on the collection of engineering estimates of size, effort, and/or schedule for all products and activities in a project. The low-level estimates for each individual activity or work product are derived from (1) engineering judgment, (2) historical data, or (3) a combination of the two. The estimates are then aggregated to produce a project-level estimate. For example, effort to design each lower-level component may be estimated and then added together for an estimate of system design effort.

Some bottom-up approaches use project-level characteristics to inflate or deflate the estimate for product, project, and technical risks. The activity-based estimation approach requires detailed knowledge of the product and process. When developing an activity-based estimate, the effort to produce all products and documentation should be included, regardless of whether they are used internally or delivered to the customer.

Analogy
The analogy approach is based on a comparison of the characteristics of the proposed project with other previously completed projects. Data from

similar, or analogous, projects is the basis for the proposed project's estimates. Differences between the projects are identified, and appropriate
changes are made to adjust the size, effort, schedule, and quality to fit the
new situation. Estimates based on analogy can be generated from just one
similar project. However, a good estimate requires a detailed understanding of both the analogous and estimated project contexts and characteristics. Direct quantitative comparisons between individual projects must be
done with extreme care.

Simple Estimating Relationships

Another estimation approach is a simplification of the parametric modeling approach. Simple estimating relationships based on local historical data are used instead of a comprehensive mathematical model. Examples of simple estimating relationships include estimates of effort as a
function of product size and productivity, and the prediction of error rate
as a function of size. As shown in this example, productivity can be used to
estimate the effort required to develop a new product within the same
organization:

$$\text{Effort} = \text{Product Size} \times \text{Productivity}$$

The productivity number is determined from past projects. The size
input is an estimate of the new product's size. The result is the estimated
person-months of effort. This estimate is then used with data on the
percentage of effort spent in each phase of the development (collected
from past projects) to estimate the amount of effort for each phase of
the new project. For example, assume that the effort estimate for the
new project was 50 person-months and the percentage of effort spent
in the design phase from previous projects was 33 percent. In this
case, the estimated design effort required for the new project would be
16.5 person-months.

Estimating relationships generally do not apply outside of the organization
and domain that provided the data. This is because a simple relationship
(such as productivity) assumes that all of the factors that affect effort are
similar among past and future projects. If these factors are significantly
different, then a parametric model should be used.

Selecting an Estimation Approach

All of these estimating approaches can yield good results under the right circumstances. When selecting an estimation approach, consider how closely its assumptions match the project and whether the data required by the approach is available from a reliable source. Some questions to ask when selecting an estimation approach include the following:

- Do the activities covered by the model or approach match the planned activities for this project?

- What degree of granularity is needed? What is the right level at which to apply this approach? (Some approaches are better applied at the system level than at the component level.)

- Is the right quantity, quality, and type of historical data needed for this approach available?

- Is local historical data available to calibrate the model?

- Does the build/buy strategy for the product (e.g., use of purchased or reused software) match the assumptions built into the approach?

- Is there enough understanding of the project to use this approach?

- Are reasonably estimated values for the parameters that must be provided as input to the model or approach available?

- Can the organization afford to buy an estimation tool? Is there adequate documentation and tool support available?

Three of the most important factors to consider in selecting an estimation approach are the level of understanding of the software problem, the nature and amount of historical data required, and the mathematical difficulty of implementing the approach and understanding its results. Figure 5-3 summarizes these factors for the four basic estimation approaches.

Differences and Similarities in the Four Approaches

The four estimation approaches differ significantly in the assumed level of understanding of the intended project's environment. Most parametric models require only an estimate of size and a general understanding of performance factors—enough to provide a relative-importance weighting,

Estimation Approach	Assumed Understanding	Historical Data Required	Mathematical Complexity
Parametric Models	General descriptive information	Data to calibrate the model	Complex statistical techniques
Activity-Based Models	Detailed process and product information	Very detailed data f a few projects	Arithmetic
Analogy	Detailed product information	At least one similar project	Arithmetic
Simple Estimating Relationships	General descriptive information	Multiple projects	Simple statistical techniques

Figure 5-3 Key considerations in selecting an estimation approach

or ranking. Activity-based estimation requires a detailed understanding of both the product to be implemented and the process to be followed. Analogy requires detailed project knowledge to recognize specific differences between the proposed project and the projects used in the estimate. Simple estimating relationships require minimal knowledge of the application.

All four estimation approaches require some historical data to produce meaningful results. Most parametric models are based on an analysis of extensive historical data from many organizations. However, the best results are obtained when the model has been calibrated with local data. A parametric model should be used without calibration only as a last resort. Activity-based estimation requires a detailed work breakdown structure for the project and corresponding detailed actual performance data from past projects. Typically, data should be available for several projects so that a probable range of performance can be estimated. Analogy requires data from at least one similar project. Simple estimating relationships require data from multiple projects within the organization developing the project.

The conceptual and mathematical difficulty of the four approaches varies considerably. This is an important consideration when trying to understand the meaning of the estimate. Parametric models generally involve complex mathematical formulas. Calibrating a parametric model may require knowledge of statistical techniques such as multiple and nonlinear regression. Activity-based estimation and analogy require only basic arithmetic. However, product and process structures can be complex, and estimating each component arduous. Simple estimating relationships require only a limited knowledge of statistical concepts.

Using Different Approaches throughout the Project Life Cycle

Parametric models are often used early in the life cycle because they produce an estimate based on a minimal amount of input data. Of course, estimates based on models that have not been calibrated with local data or that use performance factors that have not been adjusted to the realities of the project frequently turn out to be wrong by an order of magnitude. Unfortunately, many project managers act on these early estimates as if they were certainties. Two things can reduce uncertainty: using multiple approaches and performing periodic re-estimating. Confidence in an estimate increases when more than one approach is used. For example, the results of a parametric model can be checked against results from a simple estimating relationship.

It is also important to re-estimate at various points throughout the project. Information increases over the life of the project, yielding better estimates. These later estimates should be based on actual project data collected to date. There are several ways in which new estimates can be performed. For example, a parametric model could be re-run with new size inputs that may include the actual results for some product components. The budget and schedule expended to date can be used to predict the estimate to complete. Alternatively, the profile generated by the estimate can be compared with actual project performance. For example, if the project has consistently overrun its original budget and schedule by 30 percent, the estimate for the remaining activities could be increased by 30 percent.

Few of the popular parametric models work well when applied to software maintenance projects. The problem begins with size. In many cases, neither function points nor lines of code accurately reflect the workload of a maintenance project. Maintenance projects often emphasize change requests and problem reports, and the technical activities tend to be organized differently from those in development projects. Simple estimating relationships based on local data can provide good results. For example, many organizations base their maintenance estimates on the average effort per change request. Data from both earlier releases and from similar maintenance projects is used. Major enhancement projects are often handled like new development projects.

Mapping and Calibrating

Each estimation approach must be tailored to the unique characteristics of the project. Tailoring involves two major activities: mapping the model's assumptions to the project's characteristics, and calibrating the model with local historical data.

Most estimation approaches make some assumptions about the activities and products included in the estimate. For example, many parametric models do not cover requirements analysis. Another example is that some models assume that a minimal level of documentation will be produced. It is a useful exercise to inventory all the model's assumptions and map them to the project's characteristics. This will identify the differences that need to be accounted for after the model has produced its results.

Calibration is another important ongoing estimation activity. Analogy, activity-based estimating, and simple estimating relationships must use some historical data from the local organization. Parametric models generally are developed based on historical data from many organizations, none of which may be similar to the local organization. Some estimation tools provide a facility for entering local data and "running the model in reverse" to calibrate it. The historical data used to calibrate a model should be as similar as possible to the proposed project, including the application domain, process, and personnel. Once the project is underway, data from early activities can be used to calibrate the estimation approach.

There are several points to consider when using historical data to estimate or to calibrate a model:

- *Source of the data:* It is important to know the characteristics of the project that supplied the data, such as the duration of the project, the application domain, project problems (e.g., high staff turnover, change in funding level, excessive overtime), and when the project was completed.

- *Scope of the data:* Product and activity data can cover different contiguous phases of the life cycle (e.g., software requirements and design, high-level and detailed design, software coding and testing). Having separate data for each phase is most useful because it can be organized to match the phases being estimated. If data is not available for each individual phase, adjustments must be made for the percentage differences between what the data covers and what is needed.

- *Level of detail:* Measures are not always available at lower levels of product and activity detail. It is important to understand the aggregation structure of the data. Parts of past projects may be a close match to the project under estimation, but the data may also include dissimilar pieces.

- *Data context:* Other factors to consider with historical data include product factors such as required reliability, amount of reuse achieved, product complexity, and documentation requirements. The experience and turnover of people affect schedule and effort. The use of modern development technologies can also influence what data is available.

Figure 5-4 summarizes some additional questions that often arise when historical data is used to estimate and calibrate models.

Many of the problems associated with using historical data can be avoided by identifying projects within the same organization that are similar in size, application domain, anticipated staffing level, and anticipated schedule. The opportunity to improve estimation accuracy motivates many organizations to collect and store data on multiple projects within an organizational repository.

Computing the Estimate

The estimation process can produce numerical predictions for the size, effort, schedule, and quality of the project. These estimates are dependent on each other and are usually performed in the order listed. However, it is frequently necessary to iterate these tasks to achieve an estimate that satisfies all project constraints.

Types of Data	Typical Questions about Historical Data
General	• Did this data come from a successful project?
Effort Data	• What staff-hours (or days or months) are included? Are administrative, managerial, and technical staff-hours included? • What is the effort by time period (weekly, monthly)? What is the effort by phase? • If the data is expressed in staff-months, what is the number of hours in a staff-month for data normalization?
Schedule Data	• What are actual phase start and end dates? • What activities were included in this project and within each phase?
Size Data	• Does size include added, modified, or reused units? • Does size data include both the deliverable product and supporting products, such as test products? • For lines of code, what counting rules or what code-counting tool were used? • For lines of code, what programming language was used?
Quality/Defect Data	• What is the quality level associated with the effort/schedule data? (When using historical effort and schedule data, it is important to know the quality of the product, since quality can be sacrificed for effort and schedule.) • What is included in the defect data (e.g., are only bug fixes counted or does data include change requests and enhancements also)? • Are all defect severity levels included?

Figure 5-4   Questions concerning historical data

Size Estimation

Typically, the first component of an estimate is software size. The software size estimate may be prepared in terms of functional size, physical size, or both. Since it is the first activity in the estimation process, obtaining a good size estimate is essential to generating accurate estimates of effort, schedule, and quality. The type of work to be performed (e.g., new development, integration of nondeveloped components, maintenance) must be considered in estimating size. Unfortunately, few of the models and tools available accommodate the full range of common project scenarios.

The first step in estimating size is to select a size measure. Two common size measures used in software estimation are function points and lines of code.

- The *function points*, or *functional size*, measure considers software from an *external systems* perspective. It counts observable system functionality such as inputs, outputs, interfaces, and reports. Function points are especially useful in user-driven systems such as transaction processing and information systems. One advantage of function points over lines of code is that function points can be counted early in the project life cycle directly from requirements or design specifications. Function point estimation requires a good understanding of the system's functionality and an understanding of the function point counting methodology (ISO/IEC 14143, 1998).

- The *lines of code* measure considers software from an *internal structural* perspective. Counts of lines of code require knowledge of the potential software design or the impact of requested changes on an existing design. This makes them difficult to estimate early in the project life cycle. Lines of code often work best with analogy and activity-based estimation methods. Typically, separate size estimates are produced for each software component. The best results are obtained by estimating size to the lowest degree of resolution that is economically possible. The rules for counting lines of code are simpler than those for function points, although the way that the rules are applied varies widely across the software industry (Park, 1992).

Software size estimates should be updated during the course of development. For example, if an incremental-build approach is being used, actual size measures from the first build can be used to validate original size assumptions and to adjust size estimates (and corresponding effort and schedule estimates) for subsequent builds.

Effort Estimation

Effort estimation is widely understood and is supported by most estimation models and tools. During this activity, the software size estimate is converted into an estimate of effort by applying an appropriate estimating relationship.

An important consideration when estimating effort involves nondeveloped components. Most of the effort associated with reused and purchased software comes from the need to integrate that software with developed code. The cost of integration can be significant. If any nondeveloped components must be modified as part of the project, effort will increase dramatically. Purchased software may also have a licensing or purchase cost that must be included in the project estimate, even though this does not contribute to the effort estimate.

Schedule Estimation

Schedule estimation primarily answers the question: "How long will the project take?" Most parametric models provide an estimate of project duration as a function of the estimated effort required for the project. The bottom-up or activity-based method estimates the calendar time required to perform each constituent activity. This method can be used to develop detailed plans for the project. However, a parametric model should also be used to provide a sensibility check on a bottom-up or activity-based estimate.

One of the primary mistakes made when estimating the development schedule is to ignore critical path dependencies between components. There are limits to parallel development and schedule compression. What may seem logical from a mathematical perspective may be infeasible in reality.

Another important question that schedule estimation can help answer is: "What is the best staffing profile (in terms of applied effort per month) over the project duration?" There are several mathematical models for estimating optimum effort distribution, including the Raleigh curve (Putnam and Myers, 1992). The estimation models often produce an effort curve with a single peak, indicating a gradual buildup and a gradual decline of resources throughout the project (see Figure 5-5 for an example). This information is especially valuable during the initial stages of project planning to determine the peak level of personnel resources needed. However, while this is often useful for larger projects, many short-duration projects and maintenance organizations operate with a fixed staff level.

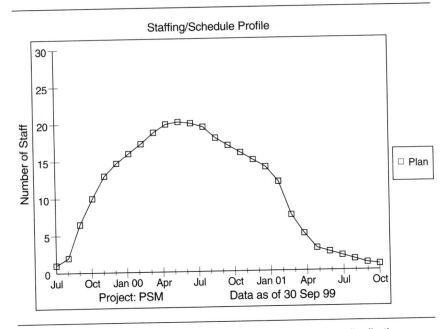

Figure 5-5 Staffing/schedule profile based on a Raleigh curve distribution

Quality Estimation

Software must often meet certain quality objectives. For example, on some projects, an objective might be "all known Priority 1 failures must be corrected prior to delivery." For another project, system reliability may be an issue with specific acceptance criteria stated in terms of a minimum mean-time-to-failure. In order to achieve such quality objectives, the likely error content of the software must be estimated, and actual error trends must be tracked.

Defect rates from past projects can be used to make initial estimates of quality. Estimating defects from ongoing project performance is more difficult. Models that support this type of quality estimation fall into two categories:

- *Reliability models,* which measure mean-time-to-failure, usually during integration and test

- *Transaction models,* which measure defect insertion and detection rates throughout the life cycle

Both models require systematic collection of defect data over multiple projects before good estimates for a specific project can be made (Lyu, 1996).

Evaluating the Estimate

The last step in the four-step estimation process involves evaluating the estimate before it is used in project planning or replanning. The estimates should be evaluated from three perspectives:

- *Quality of the estimate:* Are estimates complete, consistent, and reliable?

- *Satisfaction of constraints*: Are estimates within project constraints of cost and schedule?

- *Documentation of the estimate:* Are estimation approaches, assumptions, and results fully recorded?

Key considerations in determining the quality of an estimate include the following:

- Has a firm foundation been established for the estimate of product size?

- How well does the life cycle assumed by the estimation model map to the project's process?

- Has the estimation model been calibrated with local historical data or recent project performance data?

- Have reasonable assumptions been made about performance factors affecting productivity, schedule, and quality?

- Are aggressive goals or targets supported by realistic strategies for achieving them?

- Are the results of alternative estimation methods consistent?

- Has the level of uncertainty for inputs and outputs of the estimation process been identified?

- Have estimating relationships been adjusted so that the results meet predefined project constraints?

Estimates that do not satisfy these evaluation criteria should be recalculated. Poor estimates reduce the likelihood of project success.

Projects are often constrained by overall cost or required delivery dates. Even a good estimate may return results outside those limits. If estimates resulting from the preceding tasks overrun constraints, appropriate adjustments must be made after trade-offs are considered. For example, reducing functionality may be an effective strategy for reducing costs to meet a project constraint. All adjustments and rationales should be fully documented.

Good documentation provides a foundation for improving the estimation process and facilitates periodic re-estimation. During re-estimation, determine if initial assumptions have changed. Information about the estimation process identifies potential areas for improvement.

5.2 Feasibility Analysis

Feasibility analysis evaluates the accuracy and realism of project plans. For a project plan to be feasible, the individual elements of the plan must be technically realistic and achievable, and the elements must be consistent in relation to each other. For example, Figure 5-6 shows a milestone (Gantt) chart and staffing profile for a project. Note the highly parallel design and implementation schedule between June and November during an interval of decreasing staffing. While the overall schedule may be adequate and the overall staffing may be sufficient, the allocation of staffing over time does not match the schedule. If this plan is followed, the project will experience periods of overstaffing and periods of understaffing.

When there is a feasibility problem, only parts of the overall project plan may be unrealistic. It is important to recognize and correct those situations to ensure project success. Feasibility analyses should be performed throughout the software life cycle as plans are developed and revised. Research has shown that two of the main reasons software projects fail are a lack of planning and unrealistic plans and objectives.

Three types of situations should be examined during feasibility analysis:

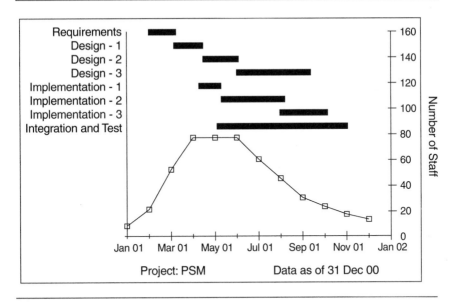

Figure 5-6 Software development schedule and staffing plans

- Feasibility analysis of measures related to the project's high-priority information needs should be performed. The analysis should look at any plans associated with high-priority project information needs (such as schedule) to check the plans for accuracy and consistency. The analyst should review the schedule at a high level (such as milestone schedules) and at a low level (such as work unit progress) of detail.

- Plan elements that are upstream from the high-priority information needs should be assessed individually because their validity will influence the feasibility of downstream plans. For example, if a primary concern is schedule, and the schedule plan looks feasible, effort should also be reviewed. Schedule could still be jeopardized if the amount of planned effort is unrealistic.

- Plan elements should be assessed for consistency with other project information. For example, even if the individual elements of schedule and effort allocation are feasible, they may not be synchronized with staff availability. These situations must be recognized and resolved to maximize project success.

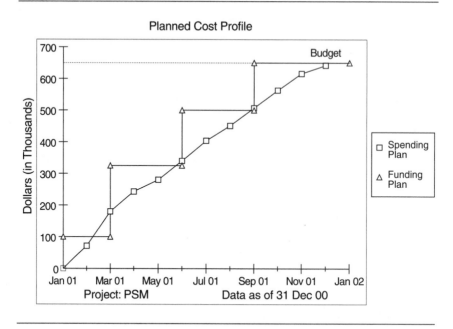

Figure 5-7   Cumulative plan example

Feasibility Indicators

Plan or "baseline" measures (the expected values) are the focus during feasibility analysis. These measures are typically compared with other baseline measures to assess the realism and internal consistency of the project plans. Historical data, preset thresholds, or established norms may be used to evaluate the plan's feasibility. Two types of indicators are used: those based on trends and those incorporating thresholds or targets. The following sections provide examples and evaluation guidelines for both types.

Indicators Based on Trends

Sometimes plans are represented as trends over time. Trends are usually represented in one of two ways: as cumulative plans or as profile plans. A cumulative plan shows the total quantity planned to be achieved to date, such as the total cost to date. Figure 5-7 is an example of a cumulative plan. A line chart is used to represent a spending plan as well as a funding plan for the project. In this case, funding will be provided in increments, and the expenditure rate is relatively consistent across the project life

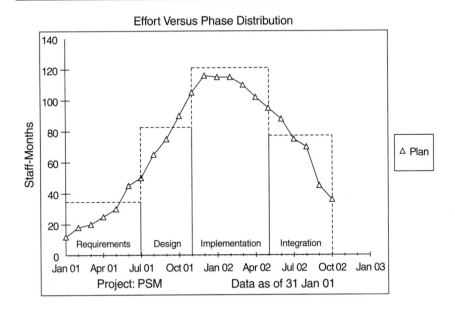

Figure 5-8   Planned effort profile example

cycle. This cost plan should be compared with schedules and staffing plans for consistency.

A profile plan shows the planned quantity apportioned to each reporting period, such as the number of staff assigned to the project each month. Figure 5-8 provides an example of a profile plan with two planning baselines. Total effort for the project was allocated over the project life cycle and presented as a line chart. The allocation in this example is being checked against a phase distribution profile based on historical effort data from past projects for realism. This plan appears to map to the historical performance data.

Indicators Based on Thresholds or Targets
Sometimes, a planning baseline is really a single value—such as a target, goal, limit, or threshold—against which a set of actual values will be compared. Many of these targets originate with product requirements, such as code complexity, response time, or memory utilization.

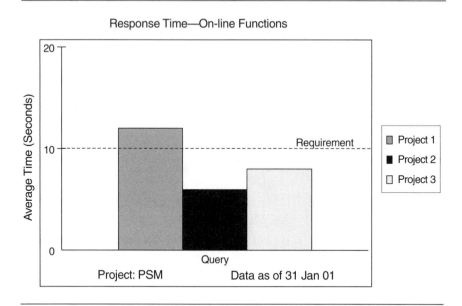

Figure 5-9   Threshold baseline example

They may also be the basis for final software acceptance criteria. These types of baselines are typically represented as straight lines on a graph. For example, Figure 5-9 shows how data from previous projects can be used to assess the realism of a response time limit. Notice that several past projects met or came close to the limit. Therefore, the baseline appears reasonable.

Rules of thumb are sometimes used to derive the measurement baseline for an indicator. For example, in a maintenance environment, a rule of thumb might be that the backlog of change requests should not exceed some pre-defined number. Another example is that no more than a certain percentage of discovered defects should remain open at any point in time. These rules of thumb can be applied against an actual backlog and actual percentage of open problems during performance analysis.

Feasibility Analysis Process Overview

Feasibility analysis can be viewed as a three-step process as depicted in Figure 5-10.

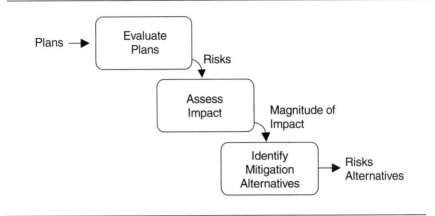

Figure 5-10 Feasibility analysis process

The first step is to evaluate the feasibility of project plans. Inputs to this step are the planning data and estimates, as well as any external constraints. Indicators are generated to support the analysis. If plans are unachievable or unrealistic, this is identified as a risk, and the next two steps should be executed to characterize and assess the risk. The source of the risk should be localized, and the scope of the risk should be evaluated to assess impact. More indicators may be generated to help assess the risk of proceeding with the current set of plans. Once the magnitude of the problem is understood, alternatives, including revisions to plans, development strategies, and approaches, should be discussed.

Evaluating Project Plans

Projects often run into trouble because their plans provide insufficient detail to effectively coordinate project activities. Most projects develop high-level estimates of size, effort, cost, and schedule, but fail to allocate the estimates to lower-level project components and activities. Without these detailed plans, status cannot be evaluated objectively. Moreover, the lack of detail makes it easier for important project components to be omitted from the plan. If not discovered until late in the project, these omissions could seriously impact project success. Thus, the first activity in analyzing the feasibility of plans is to check that they are complete and sufficiently detailed

Some key factors in determining the overall feasibility of plans are as follows:

- *Planning basis:* How completely was the problem analyzed? How reliable is the historical data? Are the measures well defined?

- *Completeness of plan:* Have all significant activities and products been accounted for?

- *Confidence in process:* Has the process for determining plans or targets been used before? Did it yield good results?

- *Historical performance:* Is planned performance in the same range as that achieved on similar projects?

Plan elements often conflict because different people develop them at different times using different strategies. For example, the project manager may use one strategy for allocating cost and effort, while a technical manager may use a different strategy for creating a detailed work unit delivery plan. Feasibility analysis is complicated by the fact that various types and levels of plans often exist.

The planning process can also run into problems when too many participants are involved. Detailed project plans are often developed by individuals who did not create the original project estimates. Assumptions may not be carried over to the detailed planning process, or new assumptions may render the original estimates infeasible. The latter situation often occurs when estimates are elevated through multiple levels of management approval. Feasibility analysis helps ensure that plans are based on sound engineering judgment or historical data, rather than on unrealistic constraints.

Each individual plan element related to a high-priority information need should be evaluated. Related plan elements should then be compared for consistency, using the Integrated Analysis Model. For example, physical size estimates should be compared to the planned effort, and planned effort should be compared to scheduled activities.

Plans should be evaluated for both *depth* and *breadth*. The *depth* of a plan focuses on technical feasibility and the internal consistency of each planned element (such as schedule). For example, aggregated totals and schedules should be compared to more detailed counts and scheduled dates contained in low-level plans for consistency. The *breadth* of a plan focuses on consistency and compatibility across plan elements. For example, effort allocation peaks and valleys should correlate to the number of concurrent activities on project schedules. Breadth is particularly important when considering how one incompatible element can adversely impact related plan elements.

Consider these questions when assessing the feasibility of specific plan elements:

- Are important activities missing (schedule)?

- Are holidays and vacations considered in plans (schedule, effort)?

- Is the overlap between project activities reasonable (schedule)?

- Is the expenditure rate, or rate of progress (slope on the indicator), reasonable?

- Are targets such as complexity and defect density reasonable within the project context (quality)?

Consider these questions when comparing plan elements:

- Do totals, such as total number of software components and total effort, match across plans?

- Do summary figures match more detailed breakdowns?

- Do dates, milestones, and time frames match across plans?

- Does the effort allocated for a specific time frame match workload scheduled for that time frame?

- Does the effort allocated match cost/budget plans?

- Does any other project information contradict plans?

Feasibility analyses should be conducted during initial planning and whenever significant changes are made to plans. One event that should trigger feasibility analysis is a change in the scope of work. Plans should be re-evaluated whenever functionality or requirements increase or decrease. Plans should also be re-evaluated whenever staffing changes occur on the project. Consider also performing a feasibility analysis when performance is significantly below plan.

Assessing the Impact of Planning Risks

A variety of planning risks may be identified when plans are evaluated. In order to assess the impact of those risks, the source of the planning problem must be localized, and its scope must be evaluated. This may require an examination of both the planning assumptions and the basis for the estimates. The estimation techniques discussed in section 5.1 of this chapter can help assess the impact of a planning problem. The outcomes for both the best- and the worst-case situations should be assessed. The impact of each identified problem and risk should always be assessed, especially on critical path items.

Identifying Mitigation Alternatives

Alternative courses of action to deal with infeasible plans include suggesting changes to the plans, development strategies and approaches, project assumptions, and constraints. For example, if a project's scheduled delivery date is infeasible, the following alternatives might be considered:

- Reducing requirements

- Increasing staffing

- Adding more experienced staff

- Extending the delivery date

- Using purchased components or leveraging reuse

Some alternatives may not be viable, given project constraints, and others may add risk. All reasonable alternatives should be documented and discussed so that the project manager can evaluate them and either take action or make a recommendation. In general, the sooner the plan is revised, the more likely the new performance requirements can be achieved.

5.3   Performance Analysis

Performance analysis determines if the project is meeting its plans and targets. Regardless of its feasibility, once a project has committed to a plan, performance can be measured against the plan. The project manager must pay close attention to how well the project adheres to the plan. Even when the project begins with a good plan, if performance begins to deviate from the plan, the reasons for the deviation must be identified and corrective actions must be taken to ensure success. The goal of performance analysis is to provide information for making decisions *in time to affect the project outcome*. Performance analysis should be conducted regularly throughout the project's life cycle.

The guidance in this section is not intended as a prescriptive approach to performance analysis. The process must be flexible in analyzing important project issues. Performance analysis should be viewed as an *investigative activity* in which measurement analysis is used to track down and isolate problems. This may require the use of slightly different data, the generation of different indicators, and the identification of alternative courses of actions each time performance is analyzed. The following sections describe several analysis tools and a straightforward process for gaining insight into project performance.

Using the Integrated Analysis Model for Performance Analysis

The Integrated Analysis Model described in Chapter 4 serves as a useful performance analysis "road map." It leads to several implications for analyzing project performance:

- Projects need direct measures of their high-priority information needs. If the concern is staying within cost, then cost indicators should be monitored regularly. However, if the high-priority information need is downstream in the model, by the time a problem becomes visible, it may represent a significant threat to project success.

- Always monitor elements that are upstream from the primary information needs because they represent *leading indicators* for those information needs. For example, requirements changes usually precede size and effort increases. If the primary concern is staying within a fixed cost, effort should be measured along with product size, process performance, and technology effectiveness.

- When investigating problems, the relationships between multiple information categories should be considered. Sometimes a variety of factors are contributing to a specific problem.

- When evaluating alternatives, always weigh the trade-offs between information categories. Optimizing a primary information need may negatively impact another information need that is equally important to project success. For example, attempting to make up a schedule slippage by increasing the number of personnel increases overall cost.

- Sometimes two related indicators suggest different situations. Neither variance alone may be large enough to suggest a problem, but taken together, they indicate that an element is not working as planned.

- Individual points that are not part of a trend, but that show unusual behavior, should also be investigated. Examples include a large change in productivity, error rate, or complexity.

Performance Indicators

The same two general types of indicators used to monitor feasibility are used to monitor performance: those based on trends and those based on thresholds or targets. The primary distinction between the two is whether the expected plan or target is relatively constant or changes over time. The following sections explain these indicator types in more detail.

Indicators Based on Trends

Trend-based performance indicators are used when the expected or planned value changes regularly over time. Figure 5-11 shows a trend-based indicator where a plan for the number of *work units completed* has been set for each week, and actual units completed have also been captured weekly. Both plan and actual values have been depicted as cumulative trend lines. Performance analysis of a trend-based indicator determines if the actual project performance corresponds to the plan. Notice that the number of actual units completed began deviating from plan almost immediately and that, while the planned number of units are now complete, this phase of the project finished four weeks later than planned.

In another example, a trend-based indicator tracks work backlogs for items such as problem reports. The amount of work to be completed, represented

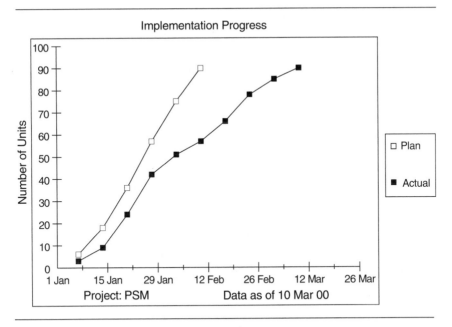

Figure 5-11 Trend-based indicator example

by the number of open problem reports, is not known in advance. The indicator must be developed week by week as new problems are discovered.

Problems in trend-based indicators may be detected with visual clues including the following:

- There may be an unusual individual result. This unique occurrence may not require any immediate action. However, the reason behind the deviation may be important.

- There may be a constant variance of actual performance from the planned baseline. In this case, performance is outside the threshold, but it parallels the planned baseline. This may be due to a one-time perturbation in the project. Managers must either compensate for the deviation or accept the deviation and replan accordingly.

- There may be an increasing variance between actual performance and the planned baseline. This is serious and warrants immediate management action. The deviation may be caused by systemic problems that inhibit projected performance, or estimation errors that make the plans infeasible.

Indicators Based on Thresholds or Targets

Performance indicators based on thresholds or targets are used when the expected value remains relatively constant over time. Performance analysis determines whether the actual project performance meets or exceeds its established bounds. Figure 5-12 is an example of a threshold-based indicator for response time. Performance is acceptable as long as the actual response time remains within the planned threshold (which may be a specified requirement). Whenever actual values exceed the threshold, the cause should be investigated. In this example, response time was exceeded for on-line functions, but test results from the last two builds indicate that the problems have been corrected.

In many cases, thresholds or targets are specified as requirements. In other cases, they represent values established by the project manager. Other common examples of threshold- or target-based indicators are defect density thresholds, complexity thresholds, computer utilization targets, and productivity targets.

Setting Thresholds on Trend-based Indicators

A common technique for monitoring performance is to set thresholds based on planned performance. As long as the project progresses

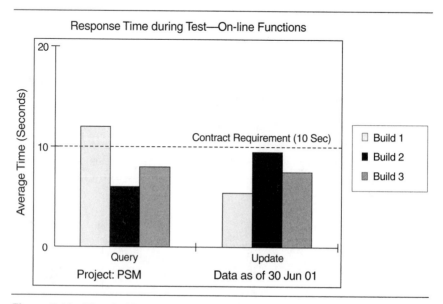

Figure 5-12   Threshold-based indicator example

according to plan and within the threshold, no management action is necessary. Thresholds may be displayed visually as boundaries around trend lines.

There are three approaches for setting thresholds:

- *Arbitrary:* This is usually a percentage based on engineering judgment. It may not reflect a real need to take action when the threshold is crossed. In fact, the threshold may be ignored if it is not useful. This is the least desirable, but easiest threshold to set. This type of threshold is represented by a line parallel to the trend line or constant boundaries around a limit. Arbitrary thresholds usually reflect the decision maker's "trigger point" for taking action.

- *Management reserve:* A reserve is the amount of unallocated resources that can be used for remaining work. A management reserve may be planned, such as a schedule reserve built into the plans. Another type of management reserve may not be explicitly planned, such as overtime effort. The threshold must be recomputed when any of the management reserve is consumed. This type of threshold typically narrows down over time as the management reserve is consumed.

- *Statistical limits:* With this approach, actual data is used to calculate statistical thresholds. These may be limits or confidence intervals based on statistical data that represent the probability of getting results some distance from the average. These are the hardest thresholds to set because they require good data over an extended period of time. However, the use of data removes the subjectivity associated with arbitrary thresholds.

Thresholds are cues to alert management to investigate and possibly take action. Falling outside a threshold indicates that work will not finish on schedule unless requirements or processes change.

Performance Analysis Process

Performance analysis consists of four steps, as shown in Figure 5-13. The first step evaluates actual performance against the plan. During this step, indicators are generated and analyzed. If problems or risks are identified, the next three steps must be performed. The second step is to assess problem

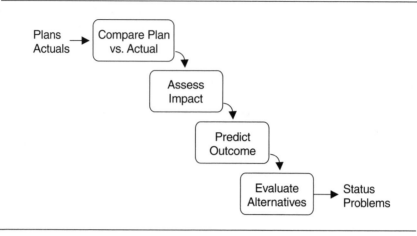

Figure 5-13   Performance analysis process

impact by localizing the problem source(s) and evaluating the scope of the problem. Additional indicators may need to be generated during this step. Next, the project outcome is predicted, usually by extrapolating from current trends in the data. Finally, if the predicted outcome does not meet project objectives, then alternative actions must be identified and evaluated. The resulting information is provided to the project manager as an input to decision making.

Several of these performance analysis tasks require non-measurement information. Decisions cannot be based solely on quantitative data. Project context information may be collected from customers, developers, technical and management reviews, document reviews, and risk analyses. Gathering and integrating non-quantitative information is essential to successful measurement.

Comparing Plans with Actuals

In order to evaluate performance, the basic indicators that correspond to each information need are examined. Problems are identified by quantifying the difference between plans and actuals. If the difference exceeds the threshold acceptable to management, then the situation should be investigated further. Both the trend and the absolute magnitude of the difference should be analyzed. If a variance has been growing steadily over time, it should be investigated, even if it hasn't exceeded a predefined threshold.

Because project issues are not independent, an *integrated analysis* using multiple indicators also must be performed. For example, a problem in one issue area, such as unplanned increases in effort, may be disguised by an accommodation in another issue area, such as schedule. Figures 5-14 and 5-15 show a problem visible through the analysis of multiple indicators. Figure 5-14 is a design progress indicator. While actual design progress appears to be only slightly behind the plan, the number of open problem reports generated during design inspections, as shown in Figure 5-15, continues to increase. These open problem reports represent rework that must be completed before the design activity can be completed.

Context information is usually needed to make valid interpretations about the cause of a problem. For example, simply noting a discrepancy between the original size estimates and the current (or actual) size estimates does not provide enough information for management action. The size difference may result from (1) poor initial size estimates, (2) significant requirement changes, or (3) changes in the way size is counted. Depending on the cause of the variance, different actions may be required.

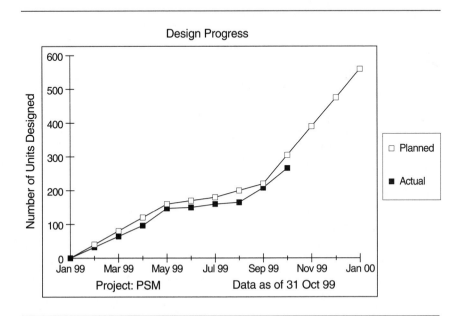

Figure 5-14   Design progress indicator

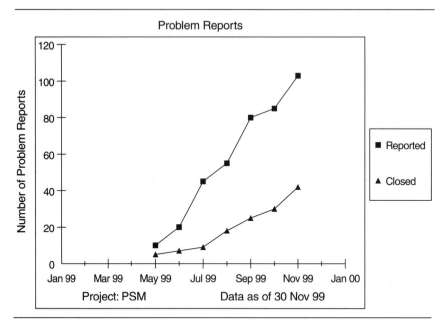

Figure 5-15   Problem report status indicator

Software Quality

Component	Size (KSLOC)	Total Valid Defects	Defect Density	Number of Units	Average Complexity	Units with Complexity >10
Navigation	124.8	42	0.34	156	9.2	26
Sensors	45.6	12	0.26	68	6.7	15
Communications	56.6	14	0.25	75	5.2	8
System Services	75.3	20	0.27	102	7.5	16
Display Services	168.0	32	0.19	125	8.6	12
Training	25.5	3	0.12	42	4.2	3
Total / Average	495.8	123	0.25	568	6.9	80

Project: PSM   Data as of 31 March 01

Figure 5-16   Comparative component measurement results

In many cases, measurement results can be compared and evaluated within the boundaries of the project to identify problems. This is especially true for large projects with many activities and components. For example, if a project has a large number of subsystems, defect densities of the subsystems can be compared to identify "outliers," or those areas with an unusually high number of defects. Figure 5-16 shows an example of this type of analysis. In this example, the Navigation subsystem experienced the highest defect density, but also demonstrated the highest complexity. This analysis suggests that extra attention should be placed here, perhaps in the form of increased levels of inspection or testing.

Sometimes inconsistent, incorrect, or inaccurate data may cause an indicator to suggest a problem where none exists. All data anomalies and other potential inconsistencies should be reviewed with the process/data owner. However, when multiple indicators point to a problem, it is usually not just a data issue.

Assessing Impact

The first task in assessing the impact of a performance problem is to localize the source of the detected variance and to evaluate its scope. This may require additional focused data collection, but usually can be satisfied by producing more detailed indicators using existing measures. For example, to assess the impact of the large number of open design defects shown in Figure 5-15, an analysis of open problem reports could be conducted. Figure 5-17 shows open problems by problem type. Note that a large percentage of the open design problems are related to performance deficiencies. This certainly points to an area to investigate further. A breakdown of the

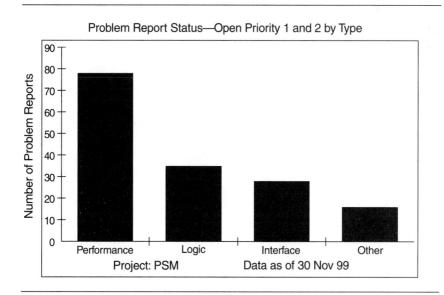

Figure 5-17   Open problem reports by type

problem data by software component, depicted in Figure 5-18, provides additional information about which components have the most open problems. It indicates that component F has the most open problems, followed closely by component C and component B.

Sometimes a substantial difference between planned and actual values may be caused by *outliers,* which are values that do not appear to be consistent with other data. For example, the average cyclomatic complexity (McCabe, Watson, 1996) of a component may be significantly higher than others in the system because of one or two unusually complex units. These outliers should not bias judgments about the whole system.

Once the source and scope of the problem have been identified, its potential impact on project success can be assessed. The magnitude of the impact is not always proportional to the difference between planned and actual values. Sometimes, a small problem that arises in one issue area may have a ripple effect on another issue, multiplying its effect.

Predicting Outcome

Assessing the current impact of a problem helps in understanding the probable impact on the project. However, to fully appreciate the significance of a problem, its impact must be projected into the future. Project outcome can be predicted by projecting current trends as straight lines (for measures such as work unit progress, size growth, and requirements changes) or by employing more sophisticated parametric estimation models (for measures related to effort, size, schedule, and problem reports).

Alternatively, the variance to date can predict future performance, and future plans can be adjusted accordingly. For example, if progress to date has been 20 percent below plan, it may be assumed that future progress will also lag by 20 percent, *unless some specific action is taken to change the project's performance.*

These projection techniques can be used to evaluate the effects of changes on project outcomes. Exploring "what-if" scenarios helps in understanding those factors that most strongly influence project outcomes. It also helps to determine whether a project can make up the gap between planned and actual performance. Throughout these studies, keep in mind the

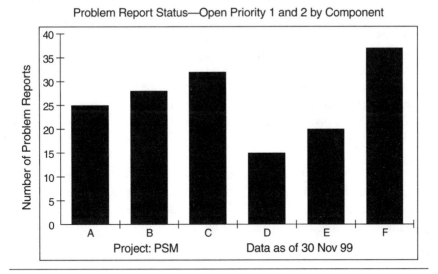

Problem Report Status—Open Priority 1 and 2 by Component

Figure 5-18 Open problem reports by component

imprecise nature of such projections. Small differences in predicted out-comes are probably meaningless.

Evaluating Alternatives

If the predicted outcome does not satisfy project objectives, alternative courses of action must be investigated. Measurement assists in predicting project outcomes given different scenarios and actions. Current trends can be projected into the future. Historical data and qualitative experience from similar projects also help in evaluating alternatives.

The integrated analysis model can be used to identify where trade-offs can be made to bring the project plan into line with project objectives. For example, if the projected cost from a task exceeds the project constraint, upstream issues may be identified to reduce the cost of that task. Eliminat-ing requirements might reduce the amount of work to be done. If the cur-rent schedule is aggressive, some late benefits of reduced rework may be obtained by extending the schedule. Increasing the level of automation might enhance productivity if provided early.

The effect of each alternative on the risk and financial status of the project should be considered, as well as on the current problem. An action that addresses a current problem could increase the risk exposure of the project in other ways. For example, purchasing and implementing a productivity aid such as a design tool might lower costs in the future. The risk of delays in acquiring, installing, and learning the tool might make this course of action undesirable in the near term. Focusing on current problems can force a project into a situation where it cannot recover from a significant risk.

The viability of each proposed course of action should also be weighed against financial performance. The budget and schedule may affect the implementation of a proposed action. All these sources of information help the project manager arrive at an optimum decision within the bounds of project constraints.

The purpose of this task is to identify specific actions that can be taken to change the outcome of the project. Just changing the assumptions behind the project plan does not make the plan any more viable. For example, assuming increased productivity without taking any real action will not prevent cost overruns.

Underlying problems and potential actions should be reviewed with the project team and modified as appropriate. The data, performance indicators, and context information about the project and recent events should all be considered. Conclusions should not be based on a single item, whether quantitative or qualitative. In deciding on a specific recommendation, the nature and effectiveness (or impact) of previous corrective actions must also be considered.

Once a likely alternative has been identified, it needs to be fed back to the Predict Outcome task. In order to make a decision, the project manager needs to know what alternatives are available, as well as the likely consequences of each. One result of the analysis process may be to identify a new information need and to recommend the collection of additional data to track it. This may require revisiting the Plan Measurement activity described in Chapter 3.

6

Evaluate Measurement

The objective of a measurement program is to generate information that provides insight into project information needs so that the project manager can make informed decisions. It is unlikely that the first implementation of a measurement program will accomplish this perfectly. Experience will uncover better measures and methods of processing and analyzing data. As the project and organizational capability matures, information needs will expand, and there will be more users of the measurement results. The measurement program should be evaluated regularly and actions taken to continually improve it.

The Evaluate Measurement activity includes four tasks, as shown in Figure 6-1. The first task, Evaluate Measures, considers whether the measurement constructs, the base measures, derived measures, and indicators, satisfy the project manager's information needs. The second task, Evaluate the Measurement Process, examines the operation of the project's measurement process. The evaluation of a measurement process should consider three dimensions:

- Quantitative performance of the process

- Conformance of the measurement process to the measurement plan

- Capability (maturity) of the measurement process relative to expected standards

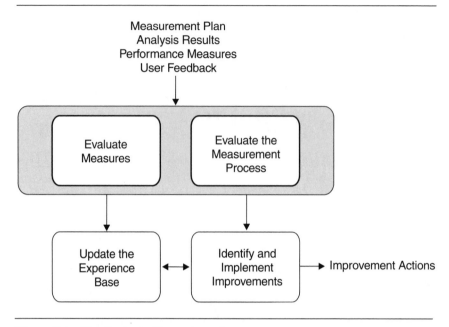

Figure 6-1   The Evaluate Measurement process

The third task, Update the Experience Base, identifies and captures lessons learned from evaluating the measures and process. Some of these lessons may be implemented on the current project, while others may benefit only future projects. The final task, Identify and Implement Improvements, identifies the specific actions taken to improve the measures or the measurement process in an ongoing project. These improvements may be accomplished by updating the measurement plan in the next cycle through the Plan Measurement activity, or as a parallel improvement initiative.

Evaluate both the measures and measurement process regularly. Planning these evaluations in advance helps to ensure that they occur. Evaluation plans may be part of the measurement plan or the organizational process improvement plan. Defining the evaluation criteria up front contributes to the objectivity of the evaluation activity as well as ensuring full coverage of data, information products, measurement activities, resources, and infrastructure. A good evaluation process may even enhance an already adequate measurement program.

The evaluation tasks described in this section rely on predefined criteria. Figure 6-2 shows how these criteria relate to the measurable concepts that

Evaluation Task	Evaluation Criteria (and Indicators)	Measurable Concept	Information Category
Measures	Accuracy Usability Reliability	Functional Correctness Usability Reliability	Product Quality
Process Performance	Timeliness Efficiency Defect Containment Customer Satisfaction	Process Efficiency Process Efficiency Process Effectiveness Customer Feedback	Process Performance
Process Conformance	Audit Checklists	Process Compliance	Process Performance
Process Capability	Reference Model	Process Compliance	Process Performance

Figure 6-2   Criteria for evaluation of a measurement process mapped to measurable concepts

were discussed in Chapter 3. Some of these criteria may be assessed using quantitative indicators. Others require subjective assessment methods.

The following sections describe the measurement evaluation tasks and criteria in more detail.

6.1   Evaluate the Measures

The first task in the Evaluate Measurement activity assesses the products of the measurement process: base measures, derived measures, indicators, and analysis results. The effectiveness of each of these measurement products should be evaluated against predefined criteria. The following criteria are adapted from ISO/IEC Standard 15939, "Software Measurement Process." Note that many of these criteria are subjective. Some criteria are specific to measures or analysis results. These criteria are not necessarily independent of each other.

Measurement Products Use

This criterion measures the extent to which the project manager or other measurement user actually uses the analysis results and interpretations produced by the measurement process. For example, how often does an inspection moderator use defined decision criteria to determine whether a re-inspection should be performed? Most of the following criteria have an influence on the use of measurement results.

Confidence in Measurement Results

This criterion considers the extent to which the users of the information products have confidence in the measures, and interpretations incorporated in the measurement results. Greater confidence is achieved when the measurement users consider the analysts to be competent and unbiased. Confidence also is increased if the data providers are involved in the process, such as through regular feedback sessions.

Measurement Fitness for Purpose

This criterion assesses the extent to which the measurement results can be demonstrated to effectively satisfy the identified information need. The interpretation of indicators must consider the context in which measurement is being performed. Not all indicators work well in all situations. A given measure may be easier or harder to collect under different circumstances, thus affecting the desirability of using a specific measure in an information product. Confidence in the fitness for purpose of an information product will increase as evidence accumulates for its effectiveness in certain environments.

Fitness for purpose includes

- The extent to which the measures actually measure what they are intended to measure

- The extent to which the measures have demonstrated the ability to predict what they are intended to predict

To the extent that measurement results provide comprehensive and appropriate feedback relative to an information need, the results may be judged fit for the measurement's purpose.

Understandability of Measurement Results

This criterion gauges the ease with which the measurement user understands the indicators and interpretations produced by the measurement process. Measurement results are less likely to be used if they are difficult to understand. Use of language or "technical jargon" unfamiliar to the user when interpreting or presenting indicators may lead to misunderstanding. Volume alone may be an obstacle to understanding measurement results because lengthy reports are less likely to be read carefully.

Satisfaction of the Assumptions of an Indicator Model

This criterion measures the extent to which assumptions inherent in the model on which an indicator is based have been satisfied (e.g., data distributions, measurement scales, units of measure, sample size). Statistical techniques often rely on assumptions about the input data. Even simple numerical techniques usually depend on some assumptions about what is being measured. For example, many common estimation models rely on statistical regression techniques to derive estimating parameters. Those techniques assume that the data is normally distributed. If that is not true, then the technique should be avoided, or the results should be interpreted with care. More sophisticated techniques generally make more complex assumptions and are more sensitive to violations.

Measurement Accuracy

This criterion examines whether the implementation of a measure conforms to its definition as specified in a measurement procedure. Results may differ from what was intended because of problems such as systematic error in the procedure, random error that is inherent in the underlying measurement method, or poor implementation of the procedure.

The human or automated implementation of a measure may depart from the measure's definition. For example, a static analysis tool may implement a counting algorithm differently from the way it was originally described in the literature. Discrepancies also may be due to ambiguous definitions of measurement methods, scales, units, and so forth. Even good measurement procedures may be inconsistently applied, resulting in the loss of data or the introduction of erroneous data.

Subjective measurement methods depend on human interpretation. For example, the formulation of survey questionnaire items may leave respondents uncertain about the question and even bias the responses. Clear, concise instructions help to increase the accuracy of surveys.

Measurement accuracy can be enhanced by ensuring that the following are true:

- The amount of missing data is within specified thresholds.

- The number of flagged inconsistencies in data entry is within specified thresholds.

- The number of missed measurement opportunities is within specified thresholds such as the number of inspections for which no data was collected.

- No inappropriate selection exists in the sampling process. Examples of inappropriate selection include surveying only continuing users to evaluate user satisfaction, or evaluating only successful projects to determine overall productivity.

- All base measures are well defined, and those definitions are communicated to both data providers and users.

Poorly defined measures tend to yield inaccurate data. The reliability of the underlying measurement method may also limit the potential accuracy of a measurement procedure.

Measurement Reliability

This criterion measures the extent to which the repeated application of the measurement method yields consistent results. Random measurement error reduces reliability.

The reliability of a measurement should be considered from two perspectives:

- *Repeatability*: the degree to which the repeated use of the measure in the same organization following the same measurement method under the *same* conditions (such as tools or individuals performing the measurement) produces results that can be accepted as being identical.

- *Reproducibility:* the degree to which the repeated use of the measure in the same organization following the same measurement method under *different* conditions (such as whether tools or individuals are performing the measurement) produces results that can be accepted as identical.

Subjective measurement methods tend to exhibit lower reliability than objective methods.

6.2 Evaluate the Measurement Process

Defining good measures is not enough to ensure success. Even a measurement process based on appropriate and proven measures may be rendered ineffective by a clumsy and unresponsive measurement process. The operation of the measurement process may be evaluated from three perspectives:

- *Performance:* evaluation of the inputs, outputs, and effects of the measurement process

- *Conformance:* comparison of the actual measurement process with a description of its intended implementation

- *Maturity:* comparison of the measurement process with an external benchmark of process maturity

All three views of process operation should be assessed regularly. Evaluating performance quantitatively requires a significant amount of data. One year's worth of data is generally recommended. Conformance should be audited on a semiannual basis, while assessments of maturity typically are conducted every two to three years. The measurement analyst usually evaluates measurement process performance, while independent groups typically conduct conformance audits and capability assessments of process maturity.

The following sections describe these views of the operation of a measurement process in more detail.

Performance

The measurement process is in itself an entity subject to measurement. When evaluating the performance of the measurement process, consider objective measures of output, schedule, and resource utilization as well as subjective feedback from the project manager and other users. The measures selected should address the information needs of measurement users, analysts, and data providers. The data collected may also help to plan future measurement processes.

Four criteria have proven especially useful for evaluating the performance of a measurement process:

- Timeliness
- Efficiency
- Defect containment
- Customer satisfaction

The following sections describe the application of these example criteria to the evaluation of a measurement process.

Timeliness

The measurement process should provide information to the project manager so that decisions can be made in time to affect the outcome of the measured activity. Depending on the phase of the project and the decision being supported, "timely" may mean daily, weekly, or monthly. A typical base measure would be the cycle time from collecting data to delivering analysis results. However, short cycle times are not as important as synchronizing delivery of information with the project manager's needs, so an alternative might be to measure the number of days late (or days early) for each scheduled report. Late measurement information is seldom used to make decisions.

Measurement Process Efficiency

The benefits of the measurement process should outweigh the cost to perform it. A larger cost/benefit ratio indicates a more efficient process. As an alternative to the cost/benefit ratio, a return on investment figure may be calculated to consider inflation and the cost of money. Both approaches require information about benefits and costs. Determining the cost of a measurement process is generally less difficult than estimating the benefits, since many benefits, such as improved communication, are difficult to quantify.

Measurement process expenses include both investment and operational costs. Examples of investment costs include training, tool acquisition, and other setup costs. Operational costs consist primarily of the labor to plan, collect data, analyze, and report results to project management. Increased automation is an investment cost that usually results in reduced operational costs for long-term projects or for measurement programs that can be reused from project to project.

No benefits can be realized from a measurement process unless action is taken based on the measurement results. The only way to separate the benefits of the action from the benefits of measurement is to clarify that the action could not have been taken without the insight from measurement. The benefits of a measurement process often result in cost avoidances, specifically through identifying and avoiding risks and problems so that their effects can be minimized. Benefits may be represented by the costs that would have been incurred if the problems had actually occurred. Some other benefits may be intangible, such as improved employee morale resulting from the improved communication of project objectives and status.

Another approach to determining benefit is to measure the cost of an operation at two points in time. First, the cost of the operation is measured before the measurement process is implemented, and the same operation is again measured some time after the measurement process has matured. Credit should be allocated for the change in operating costs between the measurement process and any other improvement initiatives undertaken.

Defect Containment

The measurement process should minimize the introduction of erroneous data and results, while removing any defects as soon as possible. Chapter 4 discusses some general strategies for verifying data and analyses, and each organization is likely to discover some unique problematic areas. Gathering feedback on defects discovered after delivery of analysis results helps to develop additional strategies for containing defects within the measurement process. Typical base measures are the total number of problems found and the number discovered prior to the presentation of the analysis results.

Customer Satisfaction

The project manager and other users of the measurement information should be satisfied with the information provided by the measurement process. Satisfaction results not only from the production of standard reports, but also from the support provided in response to special information requests. Customer satisfaction indicates the measurement user's judgment of the quality of the information products relative to the performance of the measurement process, measured in terms of timeliness, efficiency, and defect containment. Satisfaction may be affected by the user's expectations of the level of quality and performance to be provided.

Customer satisfaction data often is obtained through a periodic survey of the project manager and other measurement users. The survey should ask measurement users to assess the value of the reports they receive based on their content, timeliness, and usability.

Measurement Process Compliance

A measurement process may be evaluated in terms of its compliance with a description of its intended function. This description usually is defined in the measurement plan and supplementary documentation. The plan may be derived from the organization's documented process, such as standards and procedures, or adapted from an external reference such as the PSM guidance or ISO/IEC Standard 15939. Compliance with the plan usually is determined by an independent audit. For example, audits may be conducted by the quality assurance group or as part of an ISO 9000 review of the organization's quality management system.

This section provides some guidelines and example criteria for auditing a measurement process. These criteria are based on the activities described in Chapters 3 and 4. The checklist of criteria provided here should be tailored to correspond to the intended local measurement implementation before conducting an audit.

These criteria verify measurement process adherence to the measurement procedures and work products defined in the original measurement plan. Definitions of the measures, data collection procedures, and measurement-database management procedures are examples of work products that may be defined in the measurement plan and should be reviewed. Significant deviations from the planned process should be justified.

Auditing the Plan Measurement Activity

Figure 6-3 defines key audit considerations for each task within the Plan Measurement activity. The items in the figure probe whether or not the principal outcomes of each task have been accomplished. The first task in the Plan Measurement activity is to identify and prioritize project-specific information needs. This means that a well-articulated set of project information needs should have been produced and prioritized. During the next tailoring task, appropriate measures are selected and specified for each of the high-priority information needs. The final task produces a measurement plan that takes the project's technology and the developer's process into consideration.

The auditor should carefully examine the measurement plan. While this plan need not be a formal deliverable, certain key items should be addressed (see Chapter 3). Moreover, the information needs of a project usually change as it progresses through its life cycle. The measurement plan for a healthy measurement process should carry a change history that corresponds to major milestones and project replans.

Auditing the Perform Measurement Activity

Figure 6-4 defines key audit considerations for each task of the Perform Measurement activity. These items explore whether or not the principal outcomes of each task have been accomplished. The first task in the Perform Measurement activity is to collect and process data. Inconsistent or inaccurate data may degrade the analysis. Common causes of data problems include poor definitions, inconsistent formats, and data entry

A compliance audit may review these sample tasks in the PSM Plan Measurement activity:
A. Identify and Prioritize information Needs.
• Does a prioritized list of project information needs exist? • Were the project information needs arrived at in a systematic manner? • Have the information needs changed since initially identified?
B. Select and Specify Measures.
• Do the selected measures clearly relate to the high-priority information needs? • Are the base measures difficult to obtain? • Are the indicators appropriate to the information needs?
C. Integrate into the Project's Processes.
• Has an adequate measurement plan been produced? • Were the project's processes and technology considered when specifying the measures? • Are the base measure definitions and collection procedures clear?

Figure 6-3 Sample audit criteria for the Plan Measurement activity

errors. The next task involves using the data to generate indicators that provide insight into the project's information needs. Common analysis problems include failure to satisfy assumptions of the analysis or to consider all relevant factors in the analysis. The final task uses those indicators and their interpretations to support a manager in making decisions. Problems commonly result from poorly designed and communicated reports. A successful measurement process becomes a tool that the project manager relies on.

The level of the analyst's interaction with data providers and decision makers gives a good indication of the effectiveness of a measurement process. Data and analysis results should be reviewed with the data providers to ensure their accuracy and consistency. Indicators and interpretations should be discussed with decision makers so that any supplemental questions that arise can be answered. Broad involvement in the measurement process across the organization will ensure success.

A compliance audit may review these sample tasks in the PSM Perform Measurement activity:
A. Collect and Process Data.
• Is measurement data being generated as scheduled? • Are there adequate resources provided to collect and manage data? • Are the base measures being consistently reported according to the procedures defined in the measurement plan?
B. Analyze Data.
• Are indicators being produced for all high-priority information needs? • Have all identified anomalies been investigated and the underlying causes described? • Are the probable impacts of problems on project success estimated?
C. Make Recommendations.
• Are indicators and interpretations provided to the decision makers as scheduled? • Are appropriate corrective actions identified? • Are corrective actions tracked to closure and their impacts assessed?

Figure 6-4   Sample audit criteria for the Perform Measurement activity

Evaluating the Establish and Sustain Commitment Activity

Successful execution of the Plan Measurement and Perform Measurement activities depends on implementing an effective support structure for the measurement process. Figure 6-5 defines key audit considerations for each task of the Establish and Sustain Commitment activity. The items in the figure probe whether or not the principal outcomes of each task have been accomplished. The first task in the Establish and Sustain Commitment activity is to obtain commitment. Commitment must be demonstrated in a tangible form. Once commitment is obtained, roles and responsibilities can be assigned. Next, appropriate resources are deployed. After these tasks have been completed, the measurement process can be initiated. All involved parties must agree to the initiation schedule.

> **A compliance audit may review these sample tasks in the PSM Establish and Sustain Commitment activity:**
>
> **A. Obtain Organizational Support.**
>
> - Have the benefits of measurement been explained to all levels of the organization?
> - Has senior management demonstrated support for measurement?
> - Have privacy concerns been addressed explicitly?
>
> **B. Define Measurement Responsibilities.**
>
> - Do all members of the organization understand their roles in the measurement process?
> - Are roles assigned to all participants appropriate to their backgrounds?
>
> **C. Provide Measurement Resources.**
>
> - Have appropriate tools and staff been put in place to support measurement?
> - Have all personnel been trained in their roles in the measurement process?
> - Has a schedule for rollout been developed and distributed?

Figure 6-5 PSM sample audit criteria for the Establish Measurement activity

The ISO/IEC Standard 15939 provides task descriptions that may be used instead of those in PSM as a basis for evaluating conformance of the measurement process. This standard addresses only the outcomes, or the effects, of the measurement activities and associated component tasks. An evaluation of the measurement process using this standard does not address the maturity of the measurement process, which is discussed here in the next section.

Measurement Process Maturity

Earlier chapters described the basic tasks that must be performed in any measurement process. However, as a measurement process matures, additional tasks and more detailed guidance for existing tasks may be added to improve process repeatability and performance. The organization may discover these enhancements through its own experience or may adopt them as the result of a comparison with an external benchmark or reference standard of good practices. The Capability Maturity Model Integration (CMMI) products and the ISO/IEC 15504, "Information Technology— Software Process Assessment," both provide methods for evaluating the maturity of a software measurement process.

One or more reference standards are used to evaluate measurement process maturity and the project or organizational measurement process. The results of this evaluation may be used to identify potential improvements to the measurement process, to monitor improvement progress, or to select among alternative measurement processes. This section describes the typical application of the CMMI or ISO/IEC 15504 methods to accomplish this task.

Conducting an effective process maturity assessment requires careful staffing and thorough planning. Regardless of how well defined the process assessment method is, the results of the assessment still involve subjective judgments by the assessment team. The team members must collectively possess the right blend of domain knowledge, engineering experience, and assessment skills for each specific evaluation.

A plan should be developed for each measurement process maturity assessment. Adopting a well-defined and established public method such as the CMMI or ISO/IEC 15504 facilitates planning. The contents of a typical assessment plan should include the following:

- Assessment purpose, defining the alignment of the measurement process with business goals

- Highest measurement process maturity level that will be investigated

- Required inputs needed to perform the assessment

- Activities to be performed during the assessment

- Resources and schedule allocated to the assessment activities

- Information or data that will be collected during the assessment to determine the process maturity or process improvement status

- Selection criteria and responsibilities of all participants in the assessment, including qualifications of the assessors

- Criteria for verification of assessment findings

- Description of the planned assessment outputs, including the owner-ship of the assessment outputs and any restrictions on their use

In most cases, the software measurement process will be assessed as part of an overall assessment of organizational software life-cycle processes. The CMMI defines a Measurement and Analysis Process Area that pro-vides a framework for the assessment of measurement practices. Similarly, ISO/IEC 15504 defines a Measurement Process. The following discussion focuses on evaluating a measurement process as part of a larger software process assessment.

Most assessment methods involve both reviewing documentation and interviewing practitioners. The measurement plan and related policies and procedures provide information essential to the process assessment. Other important artifacts include measurement reports and training materials. The practitioners usually are interviewed in the appropriate functional groups, such as decision makers, measurement analysts, and data providers.

The results of a capability assessment include detailed findings of strengths and weaknesses, as well as a summary maturity level for the measurement process. Each assessment method provides a mechanism for arriving at a maturity level based on observations about the documentation and interviews. The detailed assessment data usually is held confidential so that individual sources cannot be identified. However, composite results (on a practice-by-practice basis) should be provided to the assessed organ-ization so that the problems identified can be better understood and correc-tive actions can be more effective.

6.3 Update the Experience Base

The next task of the Evaluate Measurement activity is to update the meas-urement experience base with lessons learned from the evaluations that are described earlier in this chapter, as well as anecdotal information about successes and failures. The scope of lessons learned should encompass both the measurement process and the measures themselves. Consider both strengths and weaknesses. Capturing the things that did not work is just as important as capturing the things that did.

Store lessons learned in an experience base to make them widely available. The experience base may range from a simple paper file to a separate organization that processes and packages lessons learned for future consumption. Electronic bulletin boards commonly are adopted as an initial approach. As the measurement process matures, more sophisticated technology may be useful in organizing and disseminating the experience base.

A wide range of artifacts and observations may be assembled in the experience base, including the following:

- Measurement plans, policies, and procedures

- Definitions of measures (measurement constructs)

- Data verification techniques

- Measurement customer satisfaction surveys

- Measurement performance analysis reports

- Measurement process audit reports

- Measurement process maturity assessment results

- Observations such as patterns symptomatic of specific problems, successful and unsuccessful corrective actions, implementation problems and results, and tool evaluations

Note that the planned and actual project data accumulates in a project database that usually is physically separate from the experience base. However, archived copies of project data may also be captured as components of the experience base.

6.4 Identify and Implement Improvements

Some of the lessons gathered in the previous task can be implemented as improvements to the current project's measurement process. Others may be stored for the benefit of future projects. This task identifies specific improvements that can be implemented in the current project's measurement process. Consider the costs and benefits of potential improvements when selecting among them. The actual implementation of the selected actions may be undertaken as a revision of the measurement plan in the next iteration of Plan Measurement or initiated as a parallel activity. Changes that commonly affect the elements of a measurement plan include

- Definitions of measures (measurement constructs)

- Analysis techniques

- Data collection and processing procedures

- Staffing and tool support

- Reporting and communicating procedures

Changes should be tracked to determine their effectiveness. Proposed process changes that affect the supplier's activities, such as data generation, should be coordinated with the affected individuals.

7

Establish and Sustain Commitment

The previous chapters of this book describe the measurement process, including planning and performing measurement. A well-defined measurement process, however, is of little value if it cannot be implemented effectively within an organization.

Implementing a measurement process is similar to implementing any new initiative. Measurement may represent a significant change in how an organization does business. The issues and concerns related to this change must be addressed directly. Three key tasks that must be performed to effectively introduce measurement into an organization are illustrated in Figure 7-1, along with a fourth task that ensures measurement is sustained. These tasks can be accomplished sequentially or in parallel. Once these tasks are in place, the measurement process is initiated.

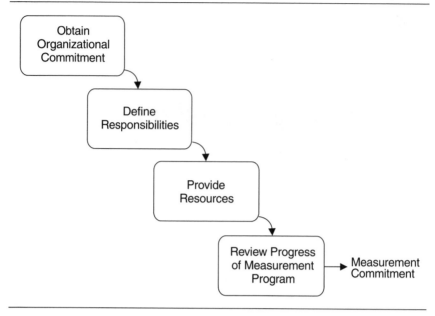

Figure 7-1 Establish and maintain commitment tasks

7.1 Obtain Organizational Commitment

The objective of the first task, Obtain Organizational Commitment, is to develop support for measurement at all levels within the organization. Measurement programs mandated by management will seldom succeed without buy-in and support from project technical and management staff members. Staff members at all levels need to understand how measurement will directly benefit their projects and their own work processes.

Implementing measurement often requires a significant cultural change within an organization. Just as with any other change, uncertainties associated with the introduction of measurement may cause anxiety. Concerns about change can be overcome by communicating to the staff a clear understanding of the measurement process and how the measurement results will be used at all levels within the organization. Some people may fear that measurement results will be used improperly to evaluate individual performance. Measurement is most effective within a culture that encourages people to articulate problems and risks. This can be a major shift for many organizations.

Successful measurement programs must be adopted by both management and the technical staff. Management support, involvement, and leadership are critical to successfully implement a measurement process. Support goes beyond the senior managers' stating that measurement is "a good idea." Support involves establishing measurement policies, providing adequate resources, creating a focus on measurement by communicating objectives, and defining critical success factors. It also includes reviewing the measurement data and analyses through routine feedback loops and then acting on the recommendations from these analyses.

Many managers and staff members first learn about software measurement when some significant software "event" brings into question the way a project or organization is being managed. Others learn about it as a result of a policy directive or initiative. Few individuals are first introduced to software measurement as an effective project management process that can help to achieve personal, project, and organizational objectives. In many cases, management and staff view measurement as "another thing to do" and as something that will require resources that are already overcommitted. To counteract this perspective, the benefits of measurement to the organization, project, and individual need to be clearly identified.

With effective management leadership, the entire organization will usually recognize the importance of measurement and actively support the process. Involvement of the technical staff in defining measures and the measurement process helps to encourage ownership. The staff should be invited to suggest specific data and indicators that are relevant to the objectives and information needs. Their recommendations should also be used to develop better collection methods for their data.

Addressing the issue of "what's in it for me?" also helps to build support at all levels. It helps individuals and organizations to set goals for themselves and provides a mechanism to measure the progress toward those goals. Management benefits by experiencing fewer surprises and being able to make decisions based on more and better information. Measurement often benefits the staff by making management more proactive and by providing a basis for more realistic planning.

7.2 Define Measurement Responsibilities

The size and structure of each organization determine how measurement responsibilities are assigned. The number of people involved and the allocation of measurement tasks vary considerably from organization to organization, depending on the size and scope of the project. The measurement team may consist of a part-time measurement analyst or a team of people. A group of people may be organized as the measurement steering committee. The primary responsibility for the measurement process is at the management level, represented by either the executive manager or the project manager.

The executive manager could be the CEO, CIO, business sector manager, risk manager, or other upper-level manager who generally has responsibility for an organization that controls more than one project. The executive manager's decisions materially affect all of the projects within the organization. Measurement helps the executive manager determine the status of individual projects and make decisions that apply across the organization.

The project manager has direct responsibility for the success of a software-intensive system. In most cases, the project manager is the primary user of the measurement results. This person is responsible for identifying and managing the software information needs and communicating with the senior levels of executive management. The project manager uses measurement to make project decisions.

It is the project manager's responsibility to ensure that measurement is integrated into the project. Integration includes all of the supporting activities that make the measurement process a part of the overall project management and technical processes.

While management is responsible for integrating and using measurement within the organization, the project technical staff is usually assigned the day-to-day tasks related to planning and performing measurement. Generally an individual or team has the primary responsibility for planning measurement, collecting and processing the measurement data, analyzing the measurement results, and reporting the results to management.

To coordinate measurement activities, organizations often establish a measurement steering committee with representation from many projects and from support staff functions. These people could include project managers, programmers, testers, or accounting department personnel. The steering committee usually takes responsibility for the policies, procedures, and common measurement definitions. It often operates like a configuration control board, by applying internal procedures to ensure that changes to the measurement plan are evaluated and properly implemented. Some organizations may be too small to support a measurement steering committee, and in those cases, the project managers usually have to maintain their own plans and data sets.

Depending on the size and scope of the project, the measurement team can consist of a part-time measurement analyst or a multi-person team. In either case, the primary measurement responsibility for the project must be assigned to a specific individual, and that individual must interface directly with the project development organization. Above all, the personnel responsible for measurement must be able to independently arrive at objective answers and alternatives and be able to provide results directly to the project decision makers.

Other members of the project technical staff also have responsibility within the measurement process. Each should understand how the process works and what information it can provide to them. They should also support measurement analysis efforts by helping to identify project events that may have an impact on interpreting the measurement data.

The measurement results are most effective when used by the software development team on a day-to-day basis. In addition to helping to communicate issues and solutions, the development team uses the measurement results to identify and correct problems quickly as a part of its regular work.

7.3   Provide Resources

Experience indicates that a measurement program requires 1 to 5 percent of the project budget. The actual cost of a specific measurement program is determined by the scope of data collected and the ability of planners to integrate data collection and analysis into existing management and technical processes.

As with any initiative, there are some start-up costs associated with implementing a measurement program. The cost of measurement for individual projects will diminish as measurement becomes an established activity within the organization. It is important to view the measurement process as a long-term investment. Within a relatively short period of time after it is established, measurement should become self-supporting, saving at least as much as it costs.

In some organizations, measurement costs for individual projects may be reduced by establishing a measurement team as an organizational resource. As long as there is a primary analyst assigned to work independently on each project, the measurement team can share resources, tools, and expertise.

Measurement costs include labor, training, and tools to generate, process, analyze, and report data. Project teams with mature engineering processes use measurement data internally to manage their projects. Subsequently, there should be little additional cost to collect and report this data at the organizational level. If a project team is not using measurement, their life-cycle process may not be very mature.

Measurement Training

Personnel at all levels of the organization require measurement training that directly addresses the skills required for their roles. Figure 7-2 gives an example of general training requirements for different roles in an organization.

Role				Measurement Training Requirement
Executive Manager	Project Manager	Measurement Analyst	Project Team	
●	●	●	●	Using Measurement Results for Decision Making
●	●	●	●	Measurement Overview
	●	●	●	Data Collection and Management
		●		Measurement Analysis

Figure 7-2 Measurement training requirements

Executive and project managers may require training in the relationship of the measurement program to the organization's engineering processes and products. These managers must understand the capabilities and limitations of the measurement process to provide information that can be used for decision making.

Project managers must understand the measurement results presented to them. They must understand how to interpret the results and take effective actions. They also need confidence in the data collection process.

Analysts need training or experience in basic measurement skills. Additional training may be required for more advanced analysis, such as estimation, modeling, and statistical analysis.

Project team members must be trained as data providers. They cannot perform their roles in the measurement process if they do not understand the data collection requirements and reporting formats.

Measurement Tools

Once the specific measurement requirements and procedures have been defined, the tools to collect, process, and analyze the data must be identified. On small projects, the measurement process can be supported on a personal computer with off-the-shelf office software. On larger projects, or those that require more advanced analysis techniques, additional measurement tools are usually required. Specific tools should not be purchased before determining if they actually support the information needs of a project. The project information needs and the measurement process drive the tool requirements, not the other way around. An existing set of measurement tools should not be used to define a measurement process.

Several classes of tools are commonly applied to the measurement process, as described in Figure 7-3.

Some general guidelines for selecting measurement support tools are as follows:

- Select tools that can be customized to meet specific project needs.

- Evaluate tools that are already available within the organization.

Type of Tool	Support Function
Database, Graphing, and Reporting	Store and manage measurement data to produce graphical and text-based reports
Estimation Models	Provide predictive capabilities, such as cost-estimation models and reliability models
Statistical Analysis	Provide enhanced analytical capabilities, such as regression
Schedule and Project Management	Assist in project scheduling and tracking resource allocations and expenditures
Financial Management	Support collection and storage of funding data
Product Analysis	Generate automated analyses of specific product characteristics (e.g., complexity)
Data Collection	Automatically extract measurement data from elements of the engineering process

Figure 7-3 Measurement tools

- When selecting engineering tools, consider their ability to provide technical and management process data about the tasks and products they support.

- Do not tailor a measurement program based solely on data from existing tools.

- Select tools that automate the mechanics of data-handling efforts such as collecting, processing, analyzing, exporting/importing, and reporting.

- Select tools that run on a common platform.

7.4   Review the Measurement Program

The point at which a project initiates the measurement process depends on the specific situation. The first three tasks in the Establish and Sustain

Measurement Commitment activity may be conducted in parallel on a project. Once key personnel and resources have been allocated on a project, the Plan Measurement activity may be initiated, even if some personnel have not been trained or some resources are not yet available. Once the activity is initiated, the results need to be reviewed to ensure that information provided to the decision makers is what they need to make the best decision possible, in accordance with the fourth task.

A project may also adopt an incremental approach to implementation by working with a small set of information needs and measures initially, then extending the scope of the measurement program as the organization becomes fully capable. Data collection and analysis should be started on a small scale early to demonstrate the value of the measurement process. Implementing even a few key measures to address the highest-priority information needs provides important new information. Reviews in this environment should be held just prior to the implementation of the new measures. This is to ensure that the existing measures are still applicable and that the new measures and processes do not conflict with the existing measures and processes.

During the initial implementation, it is especially important to focus on getting good data and to ensure that the measurement results are not used to evaluate individuals or compare projects. Results should be discussed with the data providers before reporting them to management. Discussions should focus on obtaining insight and should relate results to project activities. Measurement results and reviews should be shared with all stakeholders, including organizational managers, project managers, and the engineering staff.

7.5 Lessons Learned

The following are some tips for implementing a successful measurement program.

Start Small

A common mistake in measurement implementation is to try to do too much too quickly. Successful measurement programs begin with only a few measures that address key information needs. A comprehensive measurement program is built over time and continues to evolve.

The measurement capability of an organization should grow at a pace that can be learned and implemented effectively by the participants. Each measure should be designed to provide an adequate level of understanding of each information need with the fewest and least costly data elements that can be collected.

Provide Adequate Training

All users at all levels must understand what the measurement data represents. This understanding is vital to the proper interpretation of the measurement analysis results. Everyone in the organization needs to understand both the capabilities and the limitations of the measurement process.

All participants need the tools and training that will help them tailor the measurement results and obtain useful information. Participants at different levels within the same organization have different information needs. Project managers need data and tools to make decisions on a realistic delivery schedule. Executive managers need information to make investment decisions. Each level of management should understand how to use measurement information to derive the information required.

The data to be collected should be rigorously defined, and consensus should be reached with all stakeholders. The measurement program is a resource to help managers make informed decisions, not to automate decisions.

Accurate data collection and recording are key to producing reliable measurements. Accountability for timeliness, accuracy, and completeness should be assigned so that data is collected effectively, consistently, and reliably.

Demonstrate Commitment

Acceptance begins with a demonstration of management commitment. Orientation or training helps to ensure that all participants understand their responsibilities in the measurement process and the benefits they can obtain. However, commitment and acceptance must be sustained over time. Measurement results should be made visible; how the results support both project- and higher-level management objectives should be shown.

Minimize Costs

The measurement process must be cost-effective to succeed. Measures and reports should address key project information needs. Data should not be collected or reports distributed that are not needed or are not used.

Data collection and reporting should be automated whenever possible. Data collection should be an automatic by-product of normal activity. An example of this would be the automatic transfers from other systems such as finance and payroll into a project status report. The measurement process may start with basic, commercially available applications: database, spreadsheet, word processing, and presentation graphics. More advanced tools can be added later.

It is often possible to integrate the data collection and analysis tools with other tools of the software environment. Data collection can also be integrated with other activities, minimizing the amount of "new data" needed to support measurement.

It should not be significantly expensive to provide basic measurement data. The unavailability of data may indicate a low level of maturity in the project engineering processes.

Adopt an Action Orientation

Measures that help address management information needs early in a project should be selected. Information must be obtained early enough to allow managers to take the actions necessary to reduce risks or correct problems.

Management decisions should not wait until the measurement process provides a complete set of perfect data. Management information should be derived from a minimal amount of data, complemented by real-time events and qualitative insight, so that managers can make informed decisions quickly.

Measurement data and information should be available to everyone in the organization. Participants need training, tools, and access to the basic data to help them derive the information they need to support their work.

Standard indicators and report formats can be developed that are tied directly to critical objectives and information needs and easy to read and understand. Standard indicators and reports will foster a common language for communicating status and pointing out anomalies. Managers must be willing to listen to "bad news" reported by the measurement process and to react in a constructive manner.

Use of measurement data should be proactive in order to assess the feasibility of a management action. In many cases, historical data and current project data will indicate that an action is not feasible.

Measurement data and indicators can be used to report project status. Measurement results should not be influenced or skewed. The decision maker should understand how results were derived, what they mean for project issues, and what actions are feasible.

Measurement should be an integral part of the project and the organization; it should support the existing technical and management processes. Measurement should not be treated as an "add-on" but as a part of the organization's normal business and decision-making process.

Communicate

A key to success in a development is to establish an effective interface among the various projects, work groups, and individuals. Different managers and companies offer different perspectives on project performance. Good communication improves understanding on all sides and leads to a win-win situation.

Communication within the company is essential, and timeliness is critical. If a negative trend is noted and not communicated for one or two months, it could lead to a problem not only for the project but also potentially for the entire company. Measurement provides a basis for effective communication within a company, as well as between different organizations.

8

Measure for Success

Top-performing software organizations use measurement to demonstrate and manage their performance. However, they don't all measure the same things. Their business environments and engineering processes vary, as do their information needs and measurement opportunities.

Models of excellence such as the CMMI and Malcolm Baldrige Award recognize the importance of measurement. High scores on these scales depend on effective use of measurement, especially as tied to organizational goals and business objectives. Nevertheless, many attempts at software measurement fail. Why are some organizations successful and others not?

Any implementation of a measurement program must consider the specific organizational context. Two key characteristics of measurement in top-performing software organizations are that it is (1) highly integrated into management and technical processes and (2) supported by the corporate culture. Creating these conditions contributes to the success of a software measurement program.

Integrated Discipline

Software project measurement does not stand alone. The value of measurement information is maximized when considered in the context of other sources of information. Moreover, integrating measurement into other organizational systems helps to sustain the measurement program over a long period of time.

Opportunities for integration exist both within a project and at higher organizational levels. The project manager must consider risk and financial information along with estimates and progress reports in making decisions about project direction. Moreover, measurement provides information that helps to track and assess risk and financial status.

On system development projects, systems and hardware engineering activities must be integrated into project planning and tracking. Overall project success depends on the success of all disciplines in achieving their respective objectives. Many management and engineering tools have the potential to supply measurement data. Taking advantage of those capabilities helps to minimize the cost of data collection as well as to ensure data availability.

Project-level measurement provides the foundation for process management and organizational-level measurement. Most data about software engineering originates within the project context. Establishing an effective project-level measurement program makes available the data necessary to evaluate the performance of processes and organizations, which typically span multiple projects. Using project-level data to support process and organizational management decisions encourages its collection and analysis at the project level.

Regardless of how pervasive measurement becomes within an organization, it may fail to promote the desired results if the organizational culture does not support appropriate use of measurement.

Supportive Culture

Software development and maintenance depend on people. Human performance depends on motivation. Because of its close link to motivation, measurement probably has a greater potential for altering the performance of software organizations than many of the more commonly proposed investments, such as tools.

A successful measurement program is more valuable than efficient data processing and number crunching. Management by fact describes organizational behavior, not just the manipulation of data. A focus on numbers, alone, may lead to counterproductive activity. Measurement is a tool for achieving goals. Meeting the numbers should not be confused with achieving the goals.

Software measurement only approximates the desired objectives. Seldom can an objective be measured directly. Even an objective as simple as "keeping costs within budget" can be deceptive. For example, the cost of a project (relative to its budget) might be reduced by deferring functionality or transferring some activities to other organizational elements, thus increasing opportunity costs (through lost sales) and overhead costs. Even though the project might meet its cost target, the business could still fail because the real objective of capturing a particular market segment was not achieved. Moreover, the true situation might not be recognized by the enterprise if the transfer of cost and reduction of functionality are not visible decisions. The management-by-fact culture uses measurement to understand the true situation so that effective decisions can be made consciously—not to create objectives that encourage surreptitious compromises leading to sub-optimization of performance.

Linking performance measures to compensation and promotions, especially when the relationship of the performance measures to the real business goals of the organization is not understood, tends to produce dysfunctional behavior. Individuals opt to do what's best for them rather than what's best for the organization. See Austin (1996) for further discussion of this problem.

The culture that adopts management by fact must accept occasional failure in meeting well-planned objectives as an opportunity to learn and modify performance or direction. On the other hand, objectives that have no basis in reality often lead to wasted effort or despair.

The culture of management by fact implies some new roles for the software project manager. Rather than just monitoring and reacting to anomalies, the manager must use measurement to investigate and understand project performance so that effective corrective actions can be developed. The project manager must coordinate those actions with enterprise managers by proactively reporting status and issues.

Indications of Success

Establishing the culture necessary to support effective use of measurement isn't easy. There are no simple strategies. However, you can tell that you have been successful when the following are true:

- Data collection is automatic and natural.

- Data is widely available.

- People seek data as a basis for decision making.

- Failure leads to understanding rather than blame.

- Numeric objectives are accompanied by rational plans.

- Improvements are made regularly to the measurement process.

Measurement is an experimental process. No amount of analysis and discussion can identify the perfect measure a priori. Moreover, the "best available" measure may change as a project progresses through its life cycle and more knowledge is gained. Measurement must evolve as information needs evolve. So perhaps "progressive flexibility" best describes the successful measurement program—actual usage drives changes in measures and analysis techniques. A static measurement program usually fades into disuse or misuse.

This also suggests that it may be not be possible to define the perfect measurement program in the beginning of the project's life cycle. It is better to select a few useful measures and get started than to agonize over the ideal choice of measures. Once initiated, the measurement program will evolve with experience to better meet the user's needs.

APPENDIX A

Measurement Construct Examples

Chapter 2 describes the Measurement Information Model and how it can be used to specify measurement constructs to address defined information needs. The Measurement Information Model provides a formal mechanism for linking information needs to measurable attributes of software processes and products. This Appendix offers examples of how the measurement information model is actually applied to define and combine indicators, derived measures, and base measures into a useful information product. Each example includes one or more sample indicators, analysis guidance, and implementation considerations, as well as a table containing each element of the related measurement construct. A general description of each of these elements is presented in Figure A-1.

This material contains examples of how some of the more commonly used measures might be selected, specified, and implemented. While these examples can serve as a guide to the reader, measurement constructs need to be developed to meet each project's individual requirements.

MEASUREMENT INFORMATION MODEL

Information Need Section	Information Need	What the measurement user (e.g., manager or project team member) needs to know in order to make informed decisions.
	Information Category	A logical grouping of information needs that are defined in PSM to provide structure for the Information Model. PSM categories are defined in Chapter 2.
	Measurable Concept	An idea for satisfying the information need by defining the entities and their attributes to be measured.
Indicator Section	Indicator	A display of one or more measures (base and derived) to support the user in deriving information for analysis and decision making. An indicator is often displayed as a graph or chart.
	Analysis Model	A function that applies decision criteria to define the behavior responses to the quantitative results of indicators.
	Decision Criteria	Thresholds, limits, and targets used to trigger action or further investigation.
Derived Measure Specification Section	Derived Measure	A measure that is derived as a function of two or more values of base measures.
	Measurement Function	The formula that is used to calculate the derived measure.
Base Measure Specification Section	Base Measures	A base measure is a measure of a single attribute defined by a specified measurement method (e.g., planned number of lines of code, cumulative cost to date). As data is collected, a value is assigned to a base measure.
	Measurement Method	The logical sequence of operations that define the counting rule to calculate each base measure.
	Type of Method	The type of method used to quantify an attribute, either (1) subjective, involving human judgment, or (2) objective, using only established rules to determine numerical values.
	Scale	The ordered set of values or categories that are used in the base measure.
	Type of Scale	The type of the relationship between values on the scale, either: • *Ratio*—the measurement values have equal increments, beginning at zero, for equal quantities of the attribute, such as size measurement in terms of LOC. • *Interval*—the measurement values have equal increments for equal quantities of the attribute without the use of Ø, such as an additional cyclomatic complexity value for each additional logic path in a software unit. • *Ordinal*—the measurement values are rankings, as in assignment of defects to a severity level. • *Nominal*—the measurement values are categorical, as in defects by their type.
	Unit of Measurement	The standardized quantitative amount that will be counted to derive the value of the base measure, such as an hour or a line of code.
Attribute Section	Relevant Entities	The object that is to be measured. Entities include process or product elements of a project such as project tasks, plans/estimates, resources, and deliverables.
	Attributes	The property or characteristic of an entity that is quantified to obtain a base measure.

Figure A-1 Elements of a measurement construct

Milestone Completion

This measure is used to evaluate the schedule, progress, and interdependencies of key development activities and events. In this example, the project manager needs to objectively assess the progress of the development against the project plan. This information need is addressed by measuring the total days late for all milestones.

The table in Figure A-2 contains an indicator with the base measures of days late for each milestone and overall schedule length. Additionally, the derived measure, milestone schedule variance, is shown in the table. The indicator tells the project manager that schedule is more than 12 percent late (25 days cumulatively). The complete measurement construct for this measure is provided in Figure A-3.

Since the schedule variance exceeds the limit established by the decision criteria (greater than 10% variance), the reason for the delays should be investigated. In particular, the problem in completing the design for Build 1 should be investigated. If necessary, a replan with a more realistic schedule should be generated.

Milestone	Planned Date	Actual Date	Variance	Qtr 1, 2001				Qtr 2, 2001			Qtr 3, 2001		
				Dec	Jan	Feb	Mar	Apr	May	Jun	Jul	Aug	Sep
Project Start	1/1/01	1/1/01	0	◆ Jan 1									
HL Reqs Complete	2/20/01	2/28/01	-8			◆ Feb 28							
Build 1													
Reqs Approved	3/10/01	3/12/01	-2				◆ Mar 12						
Design Complete	4/28/01	Late	-17					◆ Apr 30					
Coding Complete	6/1/01	Started								◆ Jun 1			
Test Drop	6/7/01									◆ Jun 7			
Release	7/2/01										◆ Jul 2		
Build 2													
Reqs Approved	4/2/01	4/2/01	0					◆ Apr 2					
Design Complete	5/4/01	5/2/01	2						◆ May 2				
Coding Complete	6/28/01	Started									◆ Jun 28		
Test Drop	7/9/01											◆ Jul 9	
Release	8/1/01												◆ Aug 1
Total Days Late			-25										
Overall Schedule Length			212										
Milestone Schedule Variance			-12%										

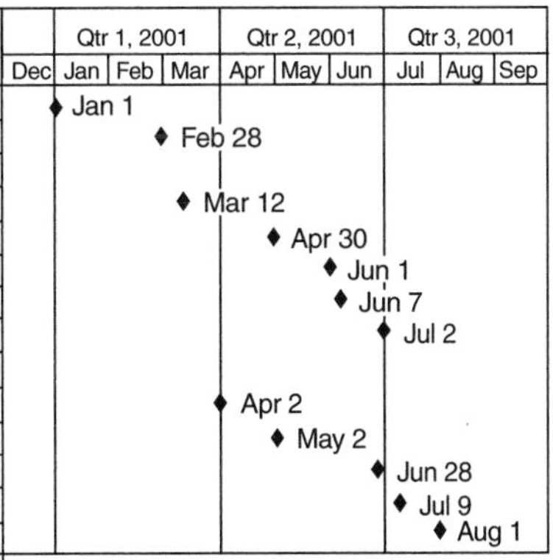

Project: PSM   Data as of 15 May 01

Figure A-2   Milestone completion example

Information Need	Evaluate the schedule, progress, and dependencies of key development activities and events.
Information Category	Schedule and progress
Measurable Concept	Milestone performance (monitoring the status of a project's milestone completion throughout the project)
Indicator	Milestone schedule variance
Analysis Model	Compare the schedule variance to the overall schedule length.
Decision Criteria	Investigation is required if the schedule variance exceeds 10%. Replan the schedule as necessary.
Derived Measure	1. Total days late 2. Schedule variance
Measurement Function	1. Add days late for all milestones. 2. Divide total days late by overall schedule length.
Base Measures	1. Days late for a milestone 2. Overall schedule length
Measurement Method	1. For each milestone, subtract the planned start date from the actual start date 2. Subtract the earliest planned start date from the latest planned end date.
Type of Method	1. Objective 2. Objective
Scale	1. Integers from zero to infinity 2. Integers from zero to infinity
Type of Scale	1. Ratio 2. Ratio
Unit of Measurement	1. Days 2. Days
Relevant Entities	1. Milestone schedule plan 2. Milestone schedule reports
Attributes	1. Milestone dates in project schedule plan 2. Dates that milestones were actually achieved

Figure A-3   Measurement construct—milestone completion

Additional Analysis Guidance

During feasibility analysis, each activity's start and end dates should be evaluated to ensure they are reasonable, given the amount of code that must be produced and the amount of effort to be applied. The evaluation should include an assessment of whether all activities are included, what activities affect the critical path, and the amount of overlap between various activities. Analysis of planning changes should include an assessment of the impact of the changes on future activities. If multiple releases or builds are planned, separate activities and milestones should be defined for each release or build.

During performance analysis, analysis of staffing levels, work unit progress within a particular activity or task, and defect rates can help identify reasons for schedule slips. Slips in activities and milestones on the critical task are of the highest concern, since these have a direct impact on the final delivery schedule.

Implementation Considerations

This schedule measure is typically collected and reported during the entire project. Responsibility for data collection and reporting typically is assigned to a support person working for the project manager. Reporting should be at least monthly and possibly weekly for smaller, shorter projects and where data is available weekly. The aggregation structure used is typically Component, for each deliverable software product, and Activity, for each project activity and task.

Work Unit Progress—Software Design Progress

In this example, the project manager needs to objectively assess the progress of the software design activities against the preestablished project plan. This information need is addressed by measuring the completion of the design of the individual software components or units with respect to defined exit criteria.

In the indicator in Figure A-4, the base measures of design units planned and design units completed for each period were graphed using a cumulative line chart. Additionally, the derived measure, Percent of Design Units Completed, is computed and shown in the graph's data table. The indicator tells the project manager that design progress has been behind the original plan during each of the preceding four months. The complete measurement construct for this measure is provided in Figure A-5.

While corrective actions were taken during each of the four prior months, based on the established decision criteria for the indicator, they did not solve the problem. So in May, a replan of the overall design activity was conducted (Plan 2), and this information was added to the chart. The replan resulted in extending the schedule for design by two months.

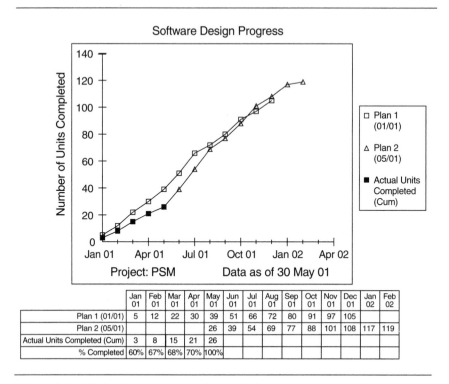

Software Design Progress

	Jan 01	Feb 01	Mar 01	Apr 01	May 01	Jun 01	Jul 01	Aug 01	Sep 01	Oct 01	Nov 01	Dec 01	Jan 02	Feb 02
Plan 1 (01/01)	5	12	22	30	39	51	66	72	80	91	97	105		
Plan 2 (05/01)					26	39	54	69	77	88	101	108	117	119
Actual Units Completed (Cum)	3	8	15	21	26									
% Completed	60%	67%	68%	70%	100%									

Figure A-4   Work unit progress—software design progress example

Additional Analysis Guidance

As part of the feasibility analysis process, the rate of planned progress should be reviewed to ensure it is reasonable and not unusually steep. In addition, the plan should be checked to ensure it reflects the total number of units estimated for the system.

During performance analysis, in addition to using the decision criteria, any major changes in the rate of actual progress should be investigated for the root cause. Once an actual trend line is established, it is difficult to modify the rate of completion unless a corrective action is applied or the process was altered. Also, a more detailed analysis is often required when actual progress lags behind planned progress. For example, analyzing progress by subsystem may help identify which components are most behind schedule. Staffing levels, experience levels, changes in scope, and

Information Need	Evaluate the status of software design activity.
Information Category	Schedule and progress
Measurable Concept	Work unit progress
Indicator	Design completion
Analysis Model	Plot design completion over time. The value of design completion should stay close to 100%.
Decision Criteria	A design completion result of 90% or less, or three consecutive declines in design completion should be investigated.
Derived Measure	Percent design package completed
Measurement Function	Divide total number of design units completed by the estimated units.
Base Measures	1. Design units planned for each period 2. Design units that have completed design
Measurement Method	1. Count the cumulative number of design units planned to date. 2. Count number of approved design units under configuration management.
Type of Method	1. Objective 2. Objective
Scale	1. Integers from zero to infinity 2. Integers from zero to infinity
Type of Scale	1. Ratio 2. Ratio
Unit of Measurement	1. Design unit 2. Design unit
Relevant Entities	1. Design package plan or schedule 2. Configuration management records of completed and approved design units
Attributes	1. Planned design units 2. Status of design units

Figure A-5   Measurement construct—work unit progress—software design progress

quality problems may all be contributors to lack of progress and should be investigated.

Implementation Considerations

Work unit progress measures are typically collected and reported only for a specified project time period—that is, during the time that the design is being developed. Reporting should be at least monthly and possibly weekly for smaller, shorter projects and where data is available weekly. The "owners" of the work units being measured (e.g., the designers) are usually responsible for data delivery. The aggregation structure used is typically Component.

Incremental Capability

In this example, the project manager needs to assess if the incremental builds are being completed as scheduled or if functionality is being deferred to later builds.

The indicator in Figure A-6 includes the base measures of number of units planned for each build for each plan, along with the actual units included in each build. The complete measurement construct for this measure is provided in Figure A-7.

This indicator shows that the threshold in the decision criteria was breached for both Builds 1 and 2, increasing the size of Build 3 by over 30 percent. Build 3 is now significantly larger than either of the previous builds. These deferments will probably result in implementation and test delays for that build, possibly impacting customer delivery milestones. A more realistic replan needs to be developed.

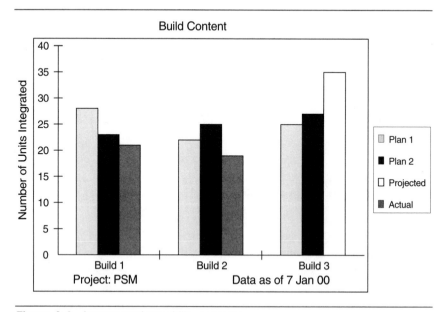

Figure A-6 Incremental capability example

Information Need	Evaluate the status of software coding activity.
Information Category	Schedule and progress
Measurable Concept	Incremental capability
Indicator	Delivery content
Analysis Model	The amount of content in a build reflects how much content was deferred to future builds.
Decision Criteria	A build content derived measure of less than 85% should be investigated.
Derived Measure	1. Build content 2. Build 3 projected content
Measurement Function	1. Divide total number of units completed for each build by the planned units for each build. 2. Calculate the cumulative variance between planned minus actual units per build for Build 1 and Build 2
Base Measures	1. Planned Units Per Build—Plan 1 2. Planned Units Per Build—Plan 2 3. Actual Units Per Build
Measurement Method	1. Count the number of units planned for each build, from Build 1. 2. Count the number of units planned for each build, from Build 2. 3. Count the number of units checked in for each build.
Type of Method	1. Objective 2. Objective 3. Objective
Scale	1. Integers from zero to infinity 2. Integers from zero to infinity 3. Integers from zero to infinity
Type of Scale	1. Ratio 2. Ratio 3. Ratio
Unit of Measurement	1. Code unit 2. Code unit 3. Code unit
Relevant Entities	1. Build plans 2. Configuration management records of completed units
Attributes	1. Units to be completed per build (build content) 2. Units checked in as completed

Figure A-7   Measurement construct—incremental capability

Additional Analysis Guidance

During planning and replanning activities, evaluate the feasibility of the incremental plan. Consider the allocation of components to increments in terms of overlapping work effort and the likelihood of slippage. The sum of components allocated to all increments should equal the total number of components scheduled for the final release.

Schedule and progress data should be evaluated when functionality is deferred to later builds. Effort plans should be compared to schedule plans to determine whether sufficient resources and time have been allocated for overlaps and different build sizes.

Implementation Considerations

Incremental code capability should be tracked during the coding phase, and reporting should occur at least monthly. The software or configuration manager is typically given responsibility for collection and reporting. Data typically come from configuration management reports or electronic spreadsheets. The aggregation structure used is typically Component.

Personnel Effort

In this example, the project manager needs to assess the adequacy of personnel resources to see if sufficient personnel are available to complete the project as scheduled. This information need is addressed by measuring the number of personnel applied to the project compared to the plan. For this measure, it is assumed that the original staffing plan is adequate.

In the indicator in Figure A-8, the base measures of planned number of persons and actual number of persons assigned are plotted. Additionally, the derived measure, Staffing Variance, is shown in the graph's data table. The indicator tells the project manager that staffing for the last period is currently 34 percent below plan. The complete measurement construct for this measure is provided in Figure A-9.

This example shows a staffing plan that builds to a maximum of 46 people over the project schedule of 12 months. While this staffing profile has been incorporated into project plans, actual effort expended on the project to date shows that this level of effort is not being achieved. In April, several staff members on the project were diverted from project work to support a product demonstration, resulting in a 43 percent staffing variance in April. In May, staffing remains below the 15 percent threshold defined in the decision criteria, so additional investigation is needed.

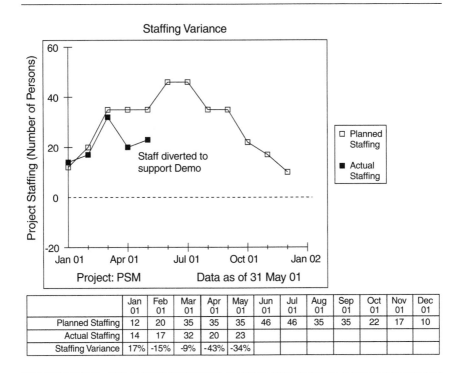

Figure A-8   Personnel effort example

Additional Analysis Guidance

Regular monitoring of staffing can provide an early indication of possible schedule slips and resource availability issues. The scope of work to be performed, staff experience, task assignments, schedules, quality problems, and rework must be considered when analyzing staffing issues and when looking for reasons why staffing may not be following the plan. It is also useful to track where effort is being spent as builds, iterations, or phases are completed. This analysis may indicate that insufficient time is being spent in the early phases of a project. The impact of this type of problem should be thoroughly investigated, as additional time is often needed in later phases to address missing requirements and fix defects, which may result in quality problems and schedule slips.

During feasibility analysis, the distribution of effort between development activities should be evaluated for adequacy. In many projects, requirements and design activities are underestimated. The distribution of effort must

Information Need	Determine if the personnel resources are adequate to meet project commitments.
Information Category	Resources and cost
Measurable Concept	Personnel
Indicator	Staffing variance
Analysis Model	Ratio of actual to planned personnel should stay near 100%.
Decision Criteria	Investigate if the staffing variance exceeds +/–15%.
Derived Measure	Staffing variance
Measurement Function	Divide the actual number of persons by the planned number of persons for each report period.
Base Measures	1. Planned number of persons 2. Actual number of persons assigned
Measurement Method	1. Count the number of positions planned for each personnel category in a project. 2. Count the number of persons that fill each personnel allocation.
Type of Method	1. Objective 2. Objective
Scale	1. Integers from zero to infinity 2. Integers from zero to infinity
Type of Scale	1. Nominal 2. Ratio
Unit of Measurement	1. Person 2. Person
Relevant Entities	1. Staffing plan 2. Personnel directory
Attributes	1. Allocated to the project (or not) 2. Assigned to the project (or not)

Figure A-9 Measurement construct—personnel effort

also be compared to scheduled activities to ensure that sufficient resources are available during periods when multiple activities are occurring.

It is also important to evaluate cumulative variances. If actual data has been below the plan for a long period of time, it is often difficult to recover. The rate of change of effort data must be monitored, since large numbers of people cannot normally be effectively added within a short period. Large overruns during integration and test may indicate quality problems with the code and significant defects that may delay completion.

Implementation Considerations

Staffing should be monitored throughout a project, and reporting should occur at least monthly. The project or personnel manager is usually given responsibility for collection and reporting. Data typically comes from monthly personnel reports. The aggregation structure used is Activity.

Financial Performance—Earned Value

In this example, the project manager needs to assess the earned value performance information. This information need is addressed by comparing the budgeted and actual cost of work performed to the budgeted cost of work scheduled.

In the indicator in Figure A-10, the derived measures of Schedule Performance Index (SPI) and Cost Performance Index (CPI) were graphed. The indicator alerts the project manager that the project has been behind schedule and over cost from early in the project. The complete measurement construct for this measure is provided in Figure A-11.

The large spike in schedule variance in August should have been investigated. It may be related to either actual performance improvement or to problems in the accounting process. Performance for the last three months

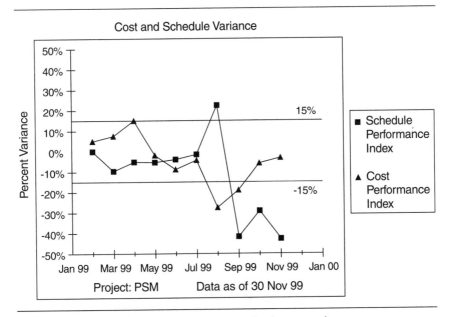

Figure A-10   Financial performance—earned value example

Information Need	Determine if the project will complete scheduled activities on time and within cost.
Information Category	Resources and cost
Measurable Concept	Financial performance
Indicator	Cost and schedule performance
Analysis Model	Both SPI and CPI should stay close to 0. Negative results are an indication that the project is behind schedule or over budgeted cost. Positive results indicate the project is ahead of schedule or under budgeted cost.
Decision Criteria	Investigate if either SPI or CPI exceed +/–15%.
Derived Measure	1. Schedule Performance Index (SPI) 2. Cost Performance Index (CPI)
Measurement Function	1. SPI = (BCWP – BCWS)/BCWS 2. CPI = (BCWP – ACWP)/ACWP
Base Measures	1. Cumulative budgeted costs for work scheduled this month (BCWS) 2. Cumulative actual costs for work scheduled this month (ACWP) 3. Cumulative budgeted cost for work completed this month (BCWP)
Measurement Method	1. Add all budgets for work in each month.
	2. Add all actual expenditures for the month. 3. Add all budgets for work packages scheduled for completion and actually completed in the month (0–100% value method)
Type of Method	1. Objective 2. Objective 3. Objective
Scale	1. Integers from zero to the budget limit 2. Integers from zero to infinity 3. Integers from zero to the budget limit
Type of Scale	1. Ratio 2. Ratio 3. Ratio
Unit of Measurement	1. Dollar 2. Dollar 3. Dollar
Relevant Entities	1. Original cost estimate report 2. Periodic cost accounting reports 3. Periodic cost accounting reports
Attributes	For each work package/WBS element: 1. Budgeted cost/cost estimate per month 2. Actual expenditures per month 3. Budget cost associated with actual expenses

Figure A-11   Measurement construct—financial performance—earned value

is outside of established decision thresholds, indicating that the project is seriously behind schedule and should be investigated. A replan appears necessary.

Additional Analysis Guidance

Large cost or schedule variances should be investigated as soon as possible to quickly determine the problem that must be addressed. When reviewing

SPI and CPI measures, the underlying cause of schedule and cost problems needs to be identified. Further analysis may uncover problems such as infeasible plans, changes in scope, or lack of availability of staff, tools, or test facilities.

If the financial performance baseline is replanned, record the previous data so that the rationale for the change and insight into the cause of previous variances is documented.

Implementation Considerations

There are various ways to measure BCWP (Budgeted Cost of Work Performed), including binary (a package is either counted as 0 percent or 100 percent of its budget), milestone apportionment, and percent complete (0 percent to 50 percent to 100 percent). The approach should be selected and agreed to prior to project execution. Objective exit criteria should be used.

Earned value should be monitored throughout the project, and reporting should occur at least monthly. The project or cost account manager is typically given responsibility for reporting. Data is typically provided via monthly accounting reports. The aggregation structure used is typically either Component or Activity.

Physical Size and Stability

In this example, the software manager needs to assess the adequacy of the original size estimates in order to evaluate schedule and cost implications. This information need is addressed by planned versus actual code production.

In the indicator in Figure A-12, the base measures of planned and actual lines of code produced were graphed. In addition, the derived measure of software size growth ratio was calculated. The complete measurement construct for this measure is provided in Figure A-13.

The indicator seems to indicate that the project production rate is ahead of schedule. However, after further investigation, it turns out that the actual code count for one component was higher than planned due to missing

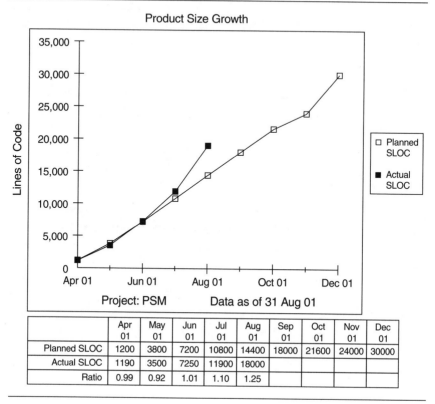

	Apr 01	May 01	Jun 01	Jul 01	Aug 01	Sep 01	Oct 01	Nov 01	Dec 01
Planned SLOC	1200	3800	7200	10800	14400	18000	21600	24000	30000
Actual SLOC	1190	3500	7250	11900	18000				
Ratio	0.99	0.92	1.01	1.10	1.25				

Figure A-12   Physical size and stability example

requirements that were not identified until initial component testing. Resource allocations, schedules, budgets, and test schedules and plans are impacted by this unexpected size growth.

Additional Analysis Guidance

Both code growth and lagging progress in code production are leading indicators of effort and schedule slips, so code growth should be monitored closely throughout development.

Analysis of excessive growth may uncover scope changes, unsatisfied technical assumptions regarding reuse or use of commercial products, or underestimation of code counts.

Information Need	Evaluate the size of a software component to appraise the original budget estimate.
Information Category	Product size and stability
Measurable Concept	Physical size and stability
Indicator	Trend of software size growth
Analysis Model	Increasing software size growth ratio indicates increasing risk to achieving cost and schedule budgets.
Decision Criteria	Investigate if the software size growth ratio exceeds 1.2.
Derived Measure	Software size growth ratio
Measurement Function	Divide the actual lines of code by the planned number of lines of code to date.
Base Measures	1. Planned number of lines of software source code 2. Actual number of lines of software source code
Measurement Method	1. Count the cumulative number of lines of code that were planned to be completed by the current period. 2. Count the number of lines of source code in the currently approved software source code library.
Type of Method	1. Objective 2. Objective
Scale	1. Integers from zero to infinity 2. Integers from zero to infinity
Type of Scale	1. Ratio 2. Ratio
Unit of Measurement	1. Lines of source code 2. Lines of source code
Relevant Entities	1. Software development plan or schedule 2. Baselined software source code library
Attributes	1. Number of lines of code planned for completion in each period 2. Lines of software source code

Figure A-13   Measurement construct—physical size and stability example

Analysis of lagging progress may reveal changing requirements, staffing shortfalls, or lower productivity than planned. The analysis of staffing shortfalls should consider rework, concurrent assignments, nonproject time, and programmer productivity.

Implementation Considerations

Many projects are developing software using several languages. This should be taken into consideration when analyzing code growth and stability. Also, because many projects are working with supplied code libraries, other forms of reusable code, generated code, and modified code as well as new code, these code sources or groupings should also be considered.

Size data is usually collected during the coding and test phases of a project. Data should be collected at least monthly. Configuration tools provide a good means to capture actual lines of code. A configuration manager or software lead is usually given responsibility for collecting and reporting this information. Data are usually collected via configuration management records or a spreadsheet. The aggregation structure used is typically Component.

Functional Size and Stability

In this example, the software manager needs to assess changes to requirements in order to evaluate potential schedule and cost implications. This information need is addressed by evaluating the ratio of requirements that were added, modified, and deleted to the baseline number of requirements.

In the indicator in Figure A-14, the derived measure of total planned requirements is plotted against the derived measure of requirements

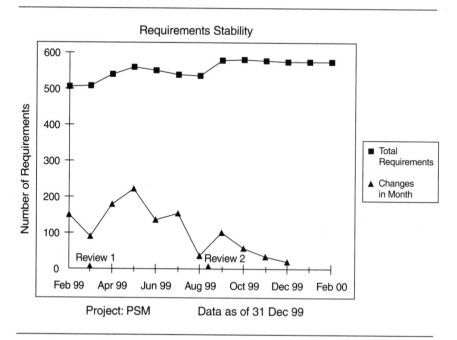

Figure A-14 Functional size and stability example

changes for each month. In this case, total planned requirements is a derived measure calculated by adding the baseline requirements plus new requirements minus deleted requirements. (In other projects, total planned requirements might be a base measure if it can be directly measured from a requirements tool.) The derived measure of requirements stability is calculated and compared to the decision criteria of 10 percent growth to identify issues. In the second sample indicator in Figure A-15, the base measures of number of requirements added, modified, and deleted per month were graphed. Approximately 20 percent of the total requirements were affected after the September review, and total requirements have increased by almost 10 percent. Investigation revealed that the new requirements needed further development and did not stabilize for several months following Review 2. The timing of the requirements changes is a problem because the project is already well into its design phase. The complete measurement construct for all of these measures is provided in Figure A-16.

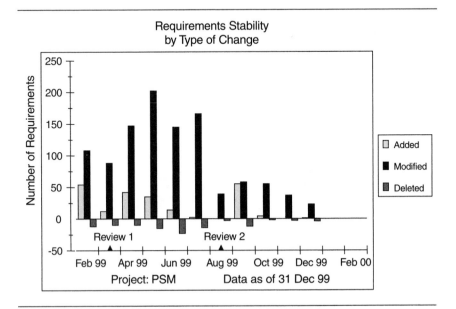

Figure A-15   Functional size and stability example

Information Need	Determine whether the amount of requirements volatility can be handled by the project without additional schedule or budget increases.
Information Category	Product size and stability
Measurable Concept	Functional size and stability
Indicator	1. Requirements stability 2. Requirements stability by type of change
Analysis Model	Some growth after requirements reviews is expected. A small number of requirements changes are expected and can be accommodated.
Decision Criteria	Investigate if the total number of requirements grows by more than 10% or when changes in a particular month exceeds 10% of the current baseline.
Derived Measure	1. Total planned requirements 2. Requirements changes 3. Requirements stability
Measurement Function	1. Calculate total planned requirements by summing baseline requirements and number of requirements added, and deleting requirements deleted. 2. Calculate requirements changes by summing the number of requirements added, modified, deleted. 3. Divide requirements changes by the baselined requirements.
Base Measures	1. Number of baseline requirements 2. Number of requirements added 3. Number of requirements modified 4. Number of requirements deleted
Measurement Method	1. Count the number of requirements in the initial baseline. 2. Add the number of requirements added by all approved change requests. 3. Add the number of requirements modified by all approved change requests. 4. Add the number of requirements deleted by all approved change requests.
Type of Method	1. Objective 2. Objective 3. Objective 4. Objective
Scale	1. Integers from zero to infinity 2. Integers from zero to infinity 3. Integers from zero to infinity 4. Integers from zero to infinity
Type of Scale	1. Ratio 2. Ratio 3. Ratio 4. Ratio
Unit of Measurement	1. Requirement 2. Requirement 3. Requirement 4. Requirement
Relevant Entities	1. Requirements baseline 2. Approved change requests—added requirements 3. Approved change requests—modified requirements 4. Approved change requests—deleted requirements
Attributes	1. Total requirements 2. Requirements added from change requests 3. Requirements modified from change requests 4. Requirements deleted from change requests

Figure A-16 Measurement construct—functional size and stability

Additional Analysis Guidance

Requirements growth and/or requirements volatility are usually leading indicators of cost and schedule increases. Additional analysis into the types of and reasons for the additions and changes to requirements should be conducted. Requirements changes can be classified by area affected (such as system interface, user interface, performance, or key function) or by cause (such as missing, unclear, incomplete, or incorrect). Knowing more about the changes will help the project manager assess the impact of these changes on cost and schedule.

Implementation Considerations

Requirements growth and/or stability should be tracked throughout a project starting as soon as requirements are baselined, since estimates are made and plans are established based on the baselined requirements. Collection and reporting should be monthly. Automation including a requirements management tool/database and a change request system are very helpful in capturing these measures. A configuration manager, systems engineering, or requirements lead are typically given responsibility for reporting on requirements. The aggregation structure used is typically Component.

Functional Correctness—Defects

In this example, the project manager needs to assess whether the system will be ready for the User Acceptance Test in six weeks. In the entrance criteria for User Acceptance Test, all severity 1 defects must be closed prior to the start of this test. Small numbers of lower severity defects are allowed. Therefore, only Severity 1 defects are considered in this measure.

This indicator in Figure A-17 shows two base measures relating information pertaining to severity 1 (high-priority) defects for this project: (1) **new** defects opened within the reporting period (weekly) and (2) defects **closed** within the reporting period, along with one derived measure: (3) the number of **open** defects per reporting period. The measurement construct in Figure A-18 has details of how these derived measures are calculated.

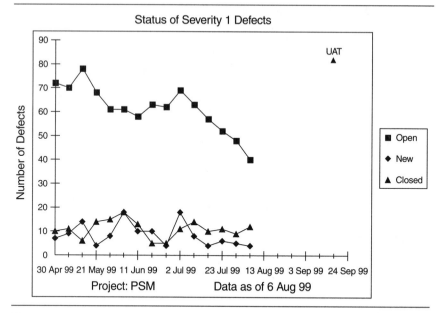

Figure A-17   Functional correctness—defects example

The graph indicates that the closure rate of defects has remained relatively constant, that the number of new defects appears to be slowing, with an associated recent downward trend in open defects. Given that the milestone for User Acceptance Test is in six weeks, these indications are positive signs that the product is nearing readiness for this event.

Additional Analysis Guidance

Open defects represent remaining work (rework), and defect trends provide insight into product maturity. When the number of open defects is large, in addition to indicating quality problems, this may be a leading indicator of later budget and effort overruns and schedule slips from the rework associated with these open defects. Additionally, when analyzing these measures, progress and compliance measures should also be reviewed, since progress shortfalls such as lack of test progress or skipping test steps could result in an apparent downward trend in open defects.

To better understand the defects uncovered on a project, Pareto analyses of defects by location and by type (e.g., logic, interface, data) could be

Information Need	Evaluate product quality and readiness to release by the number of severity 1 defects in the product.
Information Category	Product quality
Measurable Concept	Functional correctness
Indicator	Status of severity 1 defects—track the number of severity 1 defects over time.
Analysis Model	Severity 1 defects make the product unusable.
Decision Criteria	Postpone delivery until the number of open severity 1 defects is zero.
Derived Measure	Number of severity 1 defects open per period
Measurement Function	For all severity 1 defects, subtract the cumulative number of closed defects from the cumulative number of new defects per period.
Base Measures	1. Number of new severity 1 defects reported this period 2. Number of severity 1 defects closed/fixed this period
Measurement Method	1. Count severity 1 defects opened. 2. Count severity 1 defects closed this period.
Type of Method	1. Objective 2. Objective
Scale	1. Integers from zero to infinity 2. Integers from zero to infinity
Type of Scale	1. Ratio 2. Ratio
Unit of Measurement	1. Defect 2. Defect
Relevant Entities	Software defect reports
Attributes	Classification and status of defects

Figure A-18   Measurement construct—functional correctness—defects

performed. This could help isolate the most common causes of defects and could potentially improve product quality by reducing or eliminating the occurrence of future similar defects.

Average weekly closure and discovery rates could be used to quantitatively predict whether the project is likely to be ready for release.

Implementation Considerations

Defects should be tracked throughout the project life cycle, using a single, common defect tracking system. The test manager, QA manager, or software lead is typically given responsibility for defect measurement. Defect status should be reported at least monthly or possibly weekly, especially during the testing phase. A configuration management report typically contains defect rates. The aggregation structure used is typically Component.

Functional Correctness—Defect Density

In this example, the software manager evaluates code quality by monitoring the code inspection process and resulting defect rates from inspections. Each inspection package contains about 1,000 lines of code.

The indicator in Figure A-19 shows defect density rates derived from a project's code inspection process. Upper and lower statistical control limits were established based on historical process performance data. The complete measurement construct for this measure is provided in Figure A-20.

The data reveals that the first inspection had a high defect rate that should have been investigated. However, in more recent inspections, the detection rates have been within expected limits. This means that the variation in detection rates across inspections is due to common causes that exist within the currently defined inspection process and should be expected.

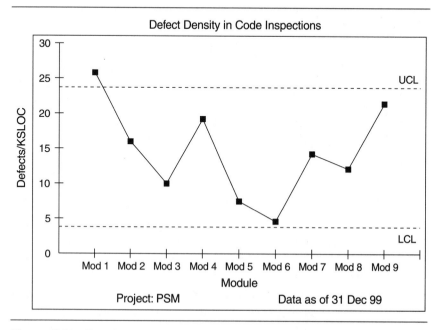

Figure A-19 Functional correctness—defect density example

Information Need	Evaluate code quality by monitoring the code inspection process and resulting defect rates from inspections.
Information Category	Product quality
Measurable Concept	Functional correctness
Indicator	Code inspection defect density control chart
Analysis Model	Use a control chart to monitor defect density and calculate control limits from historical data. Lower or higher than usual defect densities may indicate product quality or process problems.
Decision Criteria	Investigate any out of control situations where values are above or below the control limits and take corrective action.
Derived Measure	Defect density
Measurement Function	Divide the defects found by the lines of code.
Base Measures	1. Actual number of defects found 2. Actual number of lines of code
Measurement Method	1. Count defects found during code inspection. 2. Count lines of code reviewed.
Type of Method	1. Objective 2. Objective
Scale	1. Integers from zero to infinity 2. Integers from zero to infinity
Type of Scale	1. Ratio 2. Ratio
Unit of Measurement	1. Defect 2. Line of code
Relevant Entities	1. Code inspection defect reports 2. Software size
Attributes	1. Classification of defects 2. Product size for the work product reviewed

Figure A-20   Measurement construct—functional correctness—defect density

Additional Analysis Guidance

By tracking defects from design and code inspections, early indicators of product quality can be obtained. Using control charts to monitor product quality helps the project manager monitor the "stability" of the defect removal process. When "out of control" or unstable conditions are present, they should be investigated and the assignable cause of the variation should be determined. Without addressing these conditions, the project may continue to operate in an unstable and unpredictable way and may end up producing more defects or using more resources than planned.

Low defect rates could be due to processes not being performed correctly, lack of preparation for reviews or inspections, or simply higher than usual software quality due to extra time spent in inspections, use of more highly experienced staff, or extra training. Code inspections with high defect rates may indicate a superior inspection process or serious quality problems, in which case the code should be subjected to additional inspections and testing.

Implementation Considerations

Defect density should be tracked throughout the project life cycle, using measures from peer reviews, inspections, and testing. The test manager, QA manager, or software lead should be given responsibility for defect measurement. Control charts should be reviewed after every inspection or test event. The aggregation structure used is typically Component.

Efficiency—Response Time

In this example, the test manager evaluates response time in order to evaluate whether the system will meet the contract-specified response time requirements.

The indicator in Figure A-21 shows the base measures of (1) the contract requirements of 10 seconds and (2) the response time for each type of

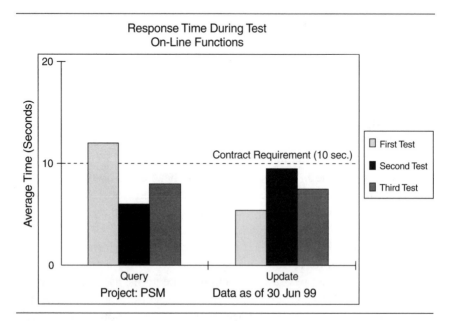

Figure A-21   Efficiency—response time example

function (query, update). This indicator shows that query-type functions initially exceeded response time requirements. These functions were subsequently modified to improve performance and are now within the acceptable range. Initially, update functions performed well, but performance problems were noted in the second test. These were resolved prior to the third test. The complete measurement construct for this measure is provided in Figure A-22.

Additional Analysis Guidance

When comparing different systems, hardware, communications, and database technology should be similar to ensure that historical data is comparable. When results are outside the acceptable range, a more detailed analysis by component or transaction can help identify the problem.

Large decreases in response time between systems should not be expected unless technology or functionality has changed significantly. Performance for the new system can be projected with modeling and simulation techniques.

Information Need	Evaluate the quality of software by measuring the ability to meet the system timing requirements.
Information Category	Product quality
Measurable Concept	Efficiency
Indicator	Response time
Analysis Model	Response time must be less than contract requirement to deliver.
Decision Criteria	Any response time over the contract requirements must be evaluated for improvement opportunities.
Derived Measure	None
Measurement Function	None
Base Measures	1. Contract requirement—10 sec. 2. Actual time for response for each type of function (query, update)
Measurement Method	1. Identify contract requirement. 2. Count time from submittal to response for each type of function (query, update).
Type of Method	1. Objective 2. Objective
Scale	1. Integers from 0 to infinity 2. Integers from 0 to infinity
Type of Scale	1. Ratio 2. Ratio
Unit of Measurement	1. Seconds 2. Seconds
Relevant Entities	System test reports
Attributes	Response time

Figure A-22 Measurement construct—efficiency—response time

Select functions for response-time measurement based on specific criteria, such as functional similarity, criticality, or frequency of use. Also, compare the form of response-time data (an average, sample, or worst case) to the planned or target figure. Factors that may influence the validity of actual response time measures include (1) not simulating sufficient load on the target machine during the tests, (2) not sampling representative functions, (3) not simulating a load representative of an anticipated operational profile, and (4) using a test database that is smaller than the operational version.

Implementation Considerations

Beginning with the design phase, response time should be tracked. It should be tracked using modeling and simulation data during design and implementation phases and actual data from integration and test phases, as well as during operations and maintenance phases.

The test manager or software lead is normally given responsibility for response time analysis and reporting. Data is often available from test logs or problem trouble reporting systems. The aggregation structure used is typically Component.

Process Compliance

In this measure, the project manager evaluates the organization's software development capability relative to the Capability Maturity Model Integrated Systems/Software Engineering model (CMMI). This measure can help to evaluate an organization's process improvement effectiveness or to determine an organization's current process performance. The indicator can be used to answer these questions.

- Is the organization meeting its process performance goals?
- Is this project performing at the same level of performance as the rest of the organization?
- Is the process improvement program working?

The indicator in Figure A-23 graphs the base measure of organizational rating level for each of the three times when an assessment has been con-

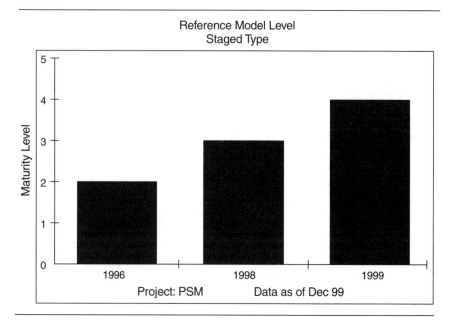

Figure A-23   Process compliance example

ducted. The complete measurement construct for this measure is provided in Figure A-24.

Additional Analysis Guidance

Overall reference model ratings provide limited insight into managing process improvement. Maintaining a detailed list of model practices addressed provides a better indicator of progress.

The reliability of the process maturity score depends on the rigor of the assessment process. A high-maturity score does not guarantee successful development. Project constraints can significantly influence an organization's ability to implement the defined process.

Implementation Considerations

Process compliance should be tracked for all software development activities, using data from reference models evaluation reports. The assessment

Information Need	Evaluate the software development process conformity to a standard model, policies, or procedures.
Information Category	Process performance
Measurable Concept	Process compliance
Indicator	Organization maturity rating
Analysis Model	Compare the number of positive responses to the criteria for the reference model and assign a rating.
Decision Criteria	Investigate if the rating has declined since the last report.
Derived Measure	None
Measurement Function	None
Base Measures	Number of positive responses
Measurement Method	Count the number of positive responses to each item in the standardized reference model.
Type of Method	Objective (individual responses are subjective)
Scale	Integers from zero to total of questionnaire items
Type of Scale	Ratio
Unit of Measurement	Questionnaire item
Relevant Entities	1. Documentation of the key practices of an organization's software development process 2. Reference model questionnaire
Attributes	Satisfaction of questionnaire items

Figure A-24   Measurement construct—process compliance

team lead or Process Improvement (PI) lead is usually given responsibility for data collection and reporting. Data is typically collected whenever an assessment is conducted (typically every six months to one year). The aggregation structure used is typically Organization.

Process Efficiency

In this example, the software manager needs to evaluate the effectiveness of the software development process by comparing achieved productivity to bid rates. For this project, only the code production rate during the coding phase is evaluated.

The indicator in Figure A-25 shows the base measure of the productivity bid rate, along with the derived measure of productivity per period from the project. This example shows that the productivity rate used to bid this software development contract was 500 source lines of code per staff

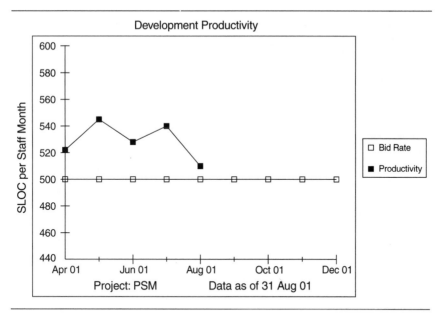

Figure A-25   Process efficiency example

month. For the last five months, the project has been performing above the bid rate. The complete measurement construct for this measure is provided in Figure A-26.

Additional Analysis Guidance

Productivity provides an indication of the amount of work produced relative to the effort expended. Lower than expected productivity may lead to effort and cost overruns. Learning curve, requirements volatility, staffing changes/turnover, and unforeseen product complexities are all factors that affect productivity. It is always useful to base a bid rate on historical past project performance (for similar projects).

Implementation Considerations

Productivity should be monitored throughout the coding process. It can be analyzed monthly at the end of each incremental build or for an interim

Information Need	Evaluate the effectiveness of a software development process.
Information Category	Process performance
Measurable Concept	Process efficiency
Indicator	Average productivity trend for the project
Analysis Model	Decreasing productivity trend for a work center requires management assessment.
Decision Criteria	Decline of productivity for three consecutive months will require evaluation of the project to ensure compliance to the organization's defined process.
Derived Measure	Productivity of the project
Measurement Function	Divide the lines of code produced in the project by the labor hours expended in the project per period.
Base Measures	1. Productivity bid rate (from contract) 2. Total labor hours reported in a period 3. Source lines of code produced in a period
Measurement Method	1. Count productivity bid rate from contract (based on historical data from completed projects). 2. Add timecard entries for cumulative labor hours for each software product. 3. Count the number of source lines of code placed under configuration control for each software product.
Type of Method	1. Objective 2. Objective 3. Objective
Scale	1. Real numbers from zero to infinity 2. Real numbers from zero to infinity 3. Real numbers from zero to infinity
Type of Scale	1. Ratio 2. Ratio 3. Ratio
Unit of Measurement	1. SLOC per labor hour 2. Labor hours 3. Source lines of code
Relevant Entities	1. Historical productivity 2. Employee timecards 3. Configuration management reports
Attributes	1. Historical SLOC per labor hour 2. Timecard entries of labor effort for specific software products 3. Source lines of code in the approved software product baseline

Figure A-26 Measurement construct—process efficiency

release. The software manager is typically responsible for analyzing and reporting productivity. Effort data is usually collected from payroll records, and size data is usually collected from configuration management reports. The aggregation structure used is typically Activity for effort measures and Component for size measures. Productivity is often analyzed at the total organization level (it is often difficult to analyze productivity at a detailed work package level).

Technology Suitability

In this example, the software manager needs to evaluate the ability of a software package to satisfy customer expectations and requirements, as documented in the test cases. Before the system is delivered, 100 percent of the test cases must pass.

The indicator in Figure A-27 shows the derived measures of (1) percent of test cases passed, (2) failed, (3) blocked, and (4) unverified for a commercial package that is being implemented (the measurement construct has definitions of each of these derived measures). The complete measurement construct for this measure is provided in Figure A-28.

The graph shows that as of August 2000, 83 percent of the cases had passed and the percentage passed had been growing steadily over the last 10 weeks of testing. However, 17 percent of the test cases had either failed or had not yet been tested. Further investigation revealed that the package could not support a few key requirements. Because the deadline for implementation was approaching, custom technology alternatives were investigated and ultimately implemented for the critical requirements not met by the package.

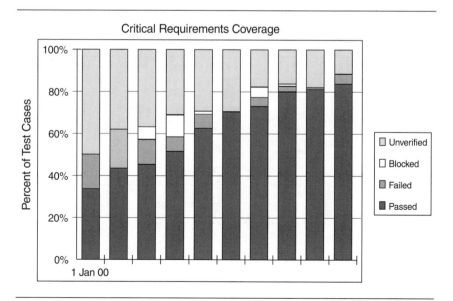

Figure A-27 Technology suitability example

Information Need	Evaluate the ability of a software package to satisfy customer expectations.
Information Category	Technology effectiveness
Measurable Concept	Technology suitability
Indicator	Requirements coverage
Analysis Model	Requirements coverage should be 100% at the end of testing.
Decision Criteria	Software will not be delivered until 100% of requirements that can be executed in test cases are passed.
Derived Measure	1. Percent passed 2. Percent failed 3. Percent blocked 4. Percent unverified
Measurement Function	1. Divide number of test cases passed by total number of test cases. 2. Divide number of test cases failed by total number of test cases. 3. Divide number of test cases blocked by total number of test cases. 4. Subtract (test cases passed + failed + blocked) from total test cases and divide by total test cases.
Base Measures	1. Total test cases 2. Test cases passed 3. Test cases failed 4. Test cases blocked
Measurement Method	1. Count total number of test cases as the number identified in the test plan. 2. Count number of test cases passed. 3. Count number of test cases failed. 4. Count number of test cases blocked (e.g., that cannot be completed because of failures in other test cases).
Type of Method	1. Objective 2. Objective 3. Objective 4. Objective
Scale	1. Integers from zero to infinity 2. Integers from zero to infinity 3. Integers from zero to infinity 4. Integers from zero to infinity
Type of Scale	1. Ratio 2. Ratio 3. Ratio 4. Ratio
Unit of Measurement	1. Test case 2. Test case 3. Test case 4. Test case
Relevant Entities	1. Test plan 2. Test result reports
Attributes	1. Test cases planned 2. Test case status (passed, failed, blocked)

Figure A-28 Measurement construct—technology suitability

Additional Analysis Guidance

Requirements coverage indicators help evaluate the amount of functionality that will be addressed by one or more specific technologies, such as a software package, hardware, or other off-the-shelf component. In some cases reallocations can be made when problems arise. One issue with this measure is that it treats requirements equally in terms of complexity, scope, and effort to implement. Additional analysis of specific requirements is needed to determine effort, cost, and schedule impacts when projecting readiness to implement or when considering reallocation of requirements.

Implementation Considerations

Requirements coverage is typically monitored during key testing activities. It can be analyzed monthly or weekly. The test manager is typically responsible for analyzing and reporting this information. Data is typically available from test records or electronic spreadsheets. The aggregation structure used is typically Component.

Customer Feedback

In this example, the operations and maintenance project manager evaluates customer satisfaction with incremental releases of a delivered product. High levels of dissatisfaction are evaluated for root cause analysis, and a decision is made regarding whether a new product release is warranted.

The indicator in Figure A-29 contains a stacked bar chart of the derived measures of percentage rating for each rating level of Satisfied and Unsatisfied (in actual use there would probably be more categories of responses). The complete measurement construct for this measure is provided in Figure A-30.

This indicator shows that the initial products releases had a relatively high level of unsatisfied responses. A root cause analysis was conducted, and the initial lack of required functionality was identified as the major cause of dissatisfaction. Beginning with release 3, the level of satisfaction has remained above 90 percent. However, the percentage of satisfied customers has dropped significantly with the latest product delivery. A root

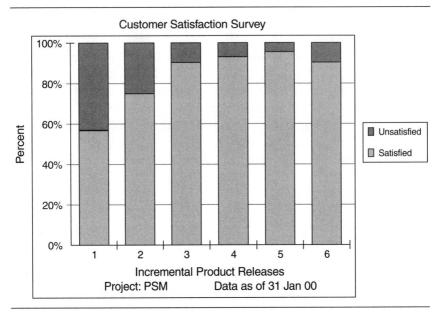

Figure A-29   Implementation considerations—customer feedback

cause analysis will be conducted to identify the problem areas, and a new product release will be generated to address the problems.

Additional Analysis Guidance

Used periodically throughout the project's life, this indicator will gauge changes in customer satisfaction. The customers may have been satisfied with the requirements but may believe the ongoing effort will not adequately address these requirements. A change in survey results will uncover this in time to obtain additional customer feedback for the purpose of understanding and addressing their concerns.

If a survey is used to address satisfaction with a prototype (such as a human-computer interface), then the results can help determine whether a suggested interface is a feasible design.

In cases where the survey indicates dissatisfaction and there is just one customer, the customer and sponsor representatives can meet to discuss the origin of the dissatisfaction. When there is more than one customer, focus groups are sometimes used to provide additional data.

Information Need	Evaluate the level of customers' satisfaction with current products.
Information Category	Customer satisfaction
Measurable Concept	Customer feedback
Indicator	Complaints by survey question
Analysis Model	High levels of dissatisfaction must be evaluated with a root cause analysis.
Decision Criteria	Any survey question with a unsatisfied rating level above 10% must be investigated for root cause and to determine if a new product release is warranted.
Derived Measure	1. Total responses for each survey question 2. Percentage rating for satisfied responses 3. Percentage rating for unsatisfied responses
Measurement Function	1. Add the number of customer responses. 2. Divide the number of satisfied customer responses by the total responses. 3. Divide the number of unsatisfied customer responses by the total responses.
Base Measures	Number of satisfied and unsatisfied customer responses for each product release
Measurement Method	Count the number of satisfied and unsatisfied comments from customer reports.
Type of Method	Subjective
Scale	Rating levels of satisfied, unsatisfied
Type of Scale	Nominal
Unit of Measurement	Number of customer comments
Relevant Entities	Feedback reports received from the customer
Attributes	Count the number of positive and negative customer feedback ratings for each survey question.

Figure A-30   Measurement construct—customer feedback

Implementation Considerations

It is important to design a valid survey instrument and to pretest it prior to implementing a customer satisfaction survey. Surveys can be used throughout a project's life if the instrument is designed correctly.

This measure is typically collected during the operations and maintenance phase of a project once a software product is delivered. This measure is typically collected and reported less frequently than most other project measures (often quarterly or semiannually or in conjunction with product releases), and the data is normally provided via customer comment forms. The marketing manager is typically responsible for reporting this information. The aggregation structure used is typically Delivered Software Components.

APPENDIX B

Information System Case Study

The Information System Case Study describes the development of a military personnel information system for the U.S. Air Force. This example demonstrates the use of measurement on a project that has been under development for some time. The project had recently failed a major acquisition milestone review, and measurement was seen as a way to gain an increased level of control over the software development effort. The system was being developed by an organic Air Force organization working for a program manager within the same command. The development addressed current Department of Defense (DoD) initiatives to promote open systems, interoperability, and the use of commercial, off-the-shelf (COTS) software packages. The technical approach included the use of multiple languages, code generators, and conversion of existing data structures. The critical issues and associated information needs were largely driven by external development dependencies. They included the need to meet aggressive development and deployment schedules, and the requirement that the overall readiness of the software for deployment be determined objectively.

This case study is organized into four sections:

1. *Project Overview:* Describes the technical and management aspects of the software development effort
2. *Getting the Project under Control:* Shows how measurement can be implemented on an existing project to define a realistic project management plan and how to track the development against that plan
3. *Evaluating Readiness for Test:* Illustrates how measurement helps to determine objectively if the software is ready for operational test and subsequent deployment
4. *Installation and Operations and Maintenance:* Shows how measurement is used to identify and correct user problems after the system is fielded

B.1

Project Overview

This chapter introduces the project scenario and illustrates the technical and management aspects of the development effort. The project scenario describes the implementation of a measurement process on an existing project. Special consideration is given to using measurement data that is readily available within the established software and project management processes. The project is representative of a typical information system under development to meet business process reengineering objectives.

B.1.1   Introduction

Over the past several years, Ridgway Air Force Base in Cheyenne, Wyoming, has established itself as a primary source for the development of Air Force business information systems. The software development group at Ridgway began as an organic software maintenance organization and has successfully transitioned its business base function from the support of Air Force logistics and administrative systems to system reengineering and development. Ridgway has benefited from the recent DoD emphasis on upgrading existing information systems into an integrated set of more manageable, cost-effective resources and has become an important resource in the Air Force Materiel Command.

In 1996, the Air Force designated Ridgway Air Force Base as the lead development organization for the Military Automated Personnel System

(MAPS). MAPS represented the Air Force's "next generation" military personnel information system. The project was part of a larger initiative to reengineer the Air Force's administrative business processes. The reengineering plan included service-wide initiatives to modernize information system hardware, software, and communications interfaces at both the base and headquarters levels. Existing mainframes and terminals were to be replaced by client/server architectures, and new capabilities were to be implemented by adapting existing databases and integrating them with newly developed applications software. MAPS was an important link in this business system modernization effort, since it was the first part of the overall system to be developed and delivered. MAPS was scheduled for deployment at a number of Air Force bases during 2000. Needless to say, MAPS was an important and highly visible project.

In 1998, MAPS had been under development for two years. During that time, the Ridgway software development group had tried to keep current with changing DoD acquisition policy and related software initiatives. These included the definition of open systems architectures, the integration of COTS software components, and the use of advanced programming languages and tools.

In November 1998, a new program manager was assigned to the MAPS project. Air Force Lt. Col. Barry Thompson was a 1981 graduate of the Air Force Academy. His background included four years with the Air Force's Operational Test & Evaluation Center and eight years in various Air Force system program offices. His last assignment was as the deputy program manager for a major upgrade to an Air Force system that stored and processed maintenance records for aircraft.

Lt. Col. Thompson's assignment to the MAPS project did not come under the best of circumstances. At the time of his arrival, MAPS had just undergone an unsuccessful review by the DoD's oversight committee for major information systems. MAPS had failed to receive a Milestone C approval for system production and deployment. This was largely a result of problems with the software, especially with respect to the amount of completed functionality and the overall quality of the existing code. The review report indicated that there was little confidence in the cost and schedule estimates presented by the previous program manager in an effort to substantiate his development plan. There was also a lack of available data to show the oversight committee how the program manager was addressing the key MAPS software development issues.

Lt. Col. Thompson arrived at Ridgway with clear direction to get the project under control and to establish an objective, credible plan for the remainder of the development. Lt. Col. Thompson's first task was to review the overall technical and management characteristics of the project. He wanted to identify the events and decisions that had helped to shape the project in order to identify the key software information needs and issues he needed to address.

B.1.2   Air Force Business Process Modernization Initiative

In reviewing the MAPS project history with the Ridgway development team, Lt. Col. Thompson learned exactly how MAPS fit into the Air Force Business Process Modernization Initiative. MAPS was the first application to be developed under the initiative and was intended to reengineer the existing military personnel information system currently in use throughout the Air Force. Subsequent applications to be integrated as part of the initiative included revised supply, finance and accounting, medical, payroll, and base-level maintenance functions. The scope of the initiative was significant. In addition to the upgrade of the base-level business functions, the new applications were required to support a seamless interface at the headquarters level. Thus, almost all key Air Force information systems would be impacted in one way or another.

Lt. Col. Thompson noted several characteristic features of the Air Force Business Process Modernization Initiative:

- *Client/server architecture:* The existing mainframe computers and associated video display terminals were to be replaced by client/server architectures at each base and at each command headquarters.

- *Open systems:* The current dependence on vendor-specific, proprietary operating systems and database management systems was to be replaced by reliance on open system, standards-based architectures. A POSIX-compliant operating system had been selected as part of the software architecture for MAPS and the other Air Force information systems that were to be reengineered.

- *Standard data elements:* The efficient flow of data from one DoD information system to another was an important objective of the initiative. In order to achieve a high level of interoperability, the revised Air Force systems, including MAPS, had to adhere to a standard set of data definitions. The Defense Information Systems Agency (DISA) was responsible for control of the data standardization effort.

- *Process modeling:* All of the business processes that fell under the modernization initiative were to be modeled using the Integrated Computer Aided Manufacturer (ICAM) definition language (IDEF). This modeling effort was important to ensure the efficiency and interoperability of the various information systems that would be reengineered as part of the initiative.

- *Integrated databases:* An important aspect of the modernization initiative was the intent to move away from "stove-piped" business applications, each with its own database and unique application characteristics. Therefore, MAPS had to include an integrated database that could be accessed by the various user applications using a common data interface. The intent was for any given data element to be entered only once, at the point of origination. The data would then be made available to other applications. Development and control of the logical and physical data models rested with DISA, and again the MAPS design had to comply with higher-level requirements.

- *Maximum use of COTS software components:* The use of commercial software packages was strongly encouraged. As part of the modernization initiative, special waivers had to be obtained to develop unique software applications if a commercial counterpart that met the defined requirements was available.

- *Technical Architecture Framework for Information Management (TAFIM):* All of the revised information systems that made up the modernization initiative, including MAPS, were required to be designed and implemented in accordance with the DoD TAFIM. They were required to demonstrate Level-3 compliance with the Defense Information Infrastructure Common Operating Environment (DII COE).

B.1.3   Project Description

Lt. Col. Thompson's staff briefed him on the key project events and the technical and design characteristics of the MAPS project. MAPS began in the summer of 1996. It had been under development since that time by the Air Force's Administrative Systems Development Activity at Ridgway Air Force Base. All of the personnel involved in the MAPS development effort were organic to the activity. That is, they were either civilian or military personnel directly employed by the Air Force. The system and software requirements and high-level design were defined during the first year of the MAPS development. In November 1998, a briefing was given to the DoD oversight committee to support a Milestone C production decision. The members of the group voiced serious concerns during the briefing. The major issues focused on the development of MAPS and included the following:

- The original development schedule had been slipping on an incremental basis. The revised "get well" schedule presented by the previous program manager appeared to be unrealistic and could not be substantiated based on the development performance to date.

- As with the schedule issue, there was no credible basis for the cost projections presented to the oversight committee. It appeared to the oversight committee that the cost of the software was driven by the number of development personnel available, not by the size and capability of the software that had to be developed.

The original MAPS development plan called for two incremental deliveries of the required capability. When Lt. Col. Thompson arrived at Ridgway in November 1998, the software for the first incremental release was under development.

MAPS began under a tailored MIL-STD-498 life-cycle process and was transitioning to IEEE/EIA 12207. The software development languages included both Ada 95 and C. Development tools included a state-of-the-art Ada programming support environment, a graphical user interface (GUI) generator, and a report generator. A COTS relational database was also an integral part of the design.

The MAPS software design included 24 functionally defined Configuration Items (CIs). Thirteen of these were allocated to Increment 1 of the development, and nine were allocated to Increment 2. The remaining two CIs were data conversion software components. For each of these CIs, access to the database was to be implemented using SQL. User access and interface were designed to be implemented using predefined, "user-friendly" screens. Site operators had additional access using SQL. The user interface was to be developed using X-Windows and was designed to be CDE compliant.

B.1.4   System Architecture and Functionality

The primary objective of the MAPS project was to reengineer the existing Air Force military personnel information system to add new functionality and to meet the overall integrated system requirements defined by the Business Process Modernization Initiative. To fully understand the technical implications of migrating the existing system to the new design, Lt. Col. Thompson compared the architecture and functionality of the current military personnel system with the MAPS requirements and specifications.

B.1.4.1   Current Personnel System

Figure B-1 shows the hardware architecture for the current personnel system. The current system actually consists of two separate information systems. One resides at the base level and the other at command headquarters. Both the base level and the headquarters implementations were based on the use of mainframe computers and video display terminals. The applications for both legacy systems were written in COBOL and included hierarchical databases. Both incorporated character-oriented, nongraphical user interfaces.

The operating concept of the current system includes periodic data transactions from the base-level system to the headquarters-level system. Selected data was uploaded to headquarters every 24 hours. As with many legacy information systems, the current military personnel implementation had experienced a significant number of problems with respect to

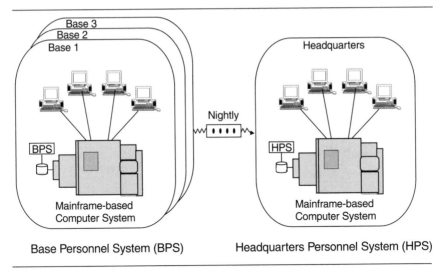

Figure B-1   Existing Air Force military personnel information system architecture

inconsistent edits between the two systems. Part of this was attributable to the base-level system's requiring very loose edits, while the headquarters system was much more constrained. Consequently, there was a large rejection rate for data that was uploaded to the headquarters system, and data was often lost in the transaction process.

To access data at the base level from the headquarters database, users had to log in and connect to the system over standard phone lines. This access approach had proven to be unreliable and added to the problems associated with transferring data.

B.1.4.2   Military Automated Personnel System

The hardware architecture for MAPS is shown in Figure B-2. MAPS is designed as a single integrated personnel system that incorporates real-time data updates and access between the base- and headquarters-level systems. The headquarters portion of the system incorporates a mainframe computer that is used only for data storage. It is part of the headquarters local area network (LAN). MAPS incorporates a client/server design at both the base and headquarters levels. Data transfer between the levels is provided by a designated military network (MILNET) interface.

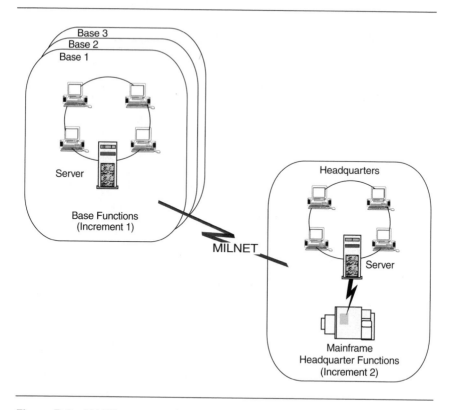

Figure B-2 MAPS system architecture

The MAPS client/server architecture integrates GUI and display functions on individual PCs, while the shared application functions reside on a UNIX-based server. This design is applicable at both the base and head-quarters levels.

When MAPS is initially fielded at each Air Force base, it will be required to interface with the existing base-level information systems. These systems will gradually disappear as the Business Process Modernization Initiative progresses. As each existing information system is reengineered and integrated into the overall information system structure, all base-level applications will transition to a common enterprise architecture with access to a common database. As with MAPS, all interaction between applications will then occur through the shared database.

The MAPS design incorporates two functional subsystems: the base-level functional subsystem and the headquarters-level functional subsystem. The base-level subsystem includes those standard functions that support the military personnel assigned to individual bases or to commands that are resident on base, such as individual aircraft squadrons. The type of personnel data that must be available from MAPS at the base level includes individual information on each officer and enlisted person assigned to the base. This data includes age, rank, skill level, training history, individual personnel assignment and promotion history, and information pertinent to past performance evaluations. The base-level MAPS subsystem also contains personnel information at the command level, such as squadron mobilization personnel requirements, casualty data, skill profiles, and personnel replacement priority information.

The MAPS headquarters subsystem includes military personnel functions that generally support higher-level information requirements than those needed at the base level. The headquarters subsystem provides information that supports overall force mobilization, strategic planning, and analysis of force manpower requirements. For example, if a senior Air Force commander wants to deploy an offensive air superiority fighter, such as the F15-E, the headquarters subsystem can provide information about the location of each F15-E squadron and the availability and training history of the pilots, maintenance personnel, and other support crew. If the Air Force needed to plan for night air sorties into mountainous terrain, MAPS would help identify those squadrons with the appropriate qualifications.

The overall MAPS development plan called for the subsystems to be developed and delivered in separate increments. Increment 1 would include the base-level functions, and Increment 2 would include the headquarters functions. In addition to development of the respective increment functionality, MAPS required that the data from the current military personnel information system be converted and entered into the redesigned MAPS data structures. As such, the MAPS software development effort included the development of data conversion software for both the base-level and the headquarters-level databases.

B.2

Getting the Project under Control

After his review of the MAPS development effort, Lt. Col. Thompson knew that he was facing a big challenge. A detailed review of the development and management processes revealed that the project was essentially managed with milestone schedules and viewgraphs. By mid-1998, the software development schedule milestones had begun to slip on a regular basis. Although this was evident in the milestone charts, no action was being taken to identify and correct the underlying causes. An analysis of the problem report data in the configuration management database showed that many more problem reports were being opened than were being closed. All of the available personnel were assigned to implementing and testing the code to meet the defined schedule for Increment 1. There wasn't enough time to keep up with the problem fixes at this stage of the development.

To gain control over the MAPS project, Lt. Col. Thompson had to address two key issues. The primary one was the schedule and progress. Lt. Col. Thompson had to assess the feasibility of the current schedule and determine why performance against the schedule was lagging. Second, he had to address the overall product quality of the developed products. Based on past experience, Lt. Col. Thompson knew that the software defects represented in the open problem report backlog had a lot to do with the schedule pressures. The schedule had limited the time spent resolving and closing problems. Given the increased visibility of the project after the results of the oversight committee review, Lt. Col. Thompson knew that the system had to work correctly when it was initially fielded.

By this time, it was clear to Lt. Col. Thompson that he needed better and more detailed information to manage the critical software information needs. To help him get the information, he assigned one of the members of his project staff, Jennifer Cooper, as the MAPS measurement lead. Ms. Cooper had previous experience with implementing a measurement process, but this would be the first time she had to plan and perform measurement for an existing project. Ms. Cooper met with Lt. Col. Thompson to identify and prioritize the major software information needs to be addressed by the measurement effort.

From the discussion, it was clear that Lt. Col. Thompson would give the measurement activities a high priority. He intended to use the measurement results to help get the project back on track and also to show senior management how the project was progressing.

Lt. Col. Thompson and Ms. Cooper discussed the potential problems related to implementing measurement on an existing program. Although all of the measurement data they wanted would not be immediately available, they had enough basic information to start to address the key information needs. They both decided that it would be a good idea to review the measurement results on a weekly basis.

As one major step in gaining control of the MAPS development, Lt. Col. Thompson put together an Integrated Product Team (IPT) consisting of representatives of a number of organizations associated with MAPS. These included the base-level and headquarters user communities, the designers, the test and integration organization, quality assurance, and installation personnel. Ms. Cooper was also a member of the IPT. The IPT's task was to identify and prioritize the risks and problems on the project. The major risk they identified was in converting the existing databases to the shared relational database that would be accessed not only by MAPS but by future applications as well. Their concerns were twofold. First, they were concerned that the existing data would be so error-prone that it would make the conversion process labor-intensive and would result in a schedule slippage. They estimated the probability that this risk would occur at

50 percent. If this did occur, the impact would be to increase the effort as well as schedule. Without more information, they viewed their probability estimate as a guess more than anything else. They also could not come up with a precise impact estimate. Their second concern was that the process of data standardization needed to make the shared data concept a reality would get bogged down in organizational battles. They estimated the probability that this risk would happen at 70 percent. There was currently high-level support within the Air Force and within DISA for data standardization. Their concern was that this might change with future personnel changes. They estimated the impact on MAPS as minor. The real impact would be on the Air Force vision of data sharing and interoperability.

The IPT met with Lt. Col. Thompson and recommended two risk-mitigation strategies. To handle the error-prone data, they suggested that very close attention be paid to the first few data conversion efforts. The IPT members felt that this would give them a much better sense of the extent of the problem and would allow them to replan a more manual effort in the conversion phase if necessary. For the data standardization effort, they suggested that the MAPS project be proactive in working with other Air Force organizations and DISA to identify shared data and reach a consensus on the data model and data elements. They also identified a middleware package that could probably be used to translate data between MAPS and the other databases.

Lt. Col. Thompson gave the IPT the go-ahead to implement these recommendations. He asked Ms. Cooper to develop a means to quantify the extent of any problems related to data conversion. This quantitative data would be used as an objective basis to change the plan, if that proved to be necessary.

B.2.1   Evaluating the Project Management Plan

When Lt. Col. Thompson reviewed the MAPS development plan, he tried to identify how the original schedules and staffing requirements had been established. The most detailed schedule information available was in the form of Gantt charts showing major project milestones and dates. There was little detail with respect to the low-level MAPS software development activities and associated CI development tasks. There was a project work breakdown structure (WBS), but it seemed to apply only loosely to the current tasks. It appeared that the overall development schedule was driven by the required delivery date of the system. Key development activities were scheduled very optimistically to meet the delivery date.

There was no MAPS staffing plan that allocated personnel resources to specific development tasks. A total of 40 software personnel were assigned full time to the MAPS project. All were available through the planned delivery date for Increment 2. The people were being applied to the project on a level-of-effort basis.

The first question Lt. Col. Thompson had to answer was whether or not the original MAPS project schedule was realistic, given the projected level of staffing and the overall performance of the development team to date.

Lt. Col. Thompson asked Ms. Cooper to generate an independent schedule estimate based on the software size and the expected productivity. Although this sounded like a straightforward request, Ms. Cooper understood that the characteristics of the project required two separate sets of analysis. There were two different types of development taking place, each described by distinct development approaches:

- Development of the application software for both incremental deliveries. This development effort was based on the use of a commercial database, SQL, Ada, and GUI-generation and report-generation tools.

- Development of the data conversion software. This development effort could best be described as a typical support software development effort using a high-order language with minimal process requirements.

Ms. Cooper needed to estimate the size of the software to be developed in order to generate a new estimate of the MAPS development schedule. She decided to use function points as the basic size measure for the Increment 1 and 2 application software because of the mix of language (Ada, SQL, code generators). Ms. Cooper used two methods to calculate the required productivity figures. In addition to a simple functional size to effort ratio, Ms. Cooper used a software cost model that accepted function points as input data. The model also took into account the productivity impact of language type and reused code.

For the data conversion software, Ms. Cooper used lines of code to estimate the software size. In this case, lines of code seemed a better choice
because she was not readily able to convert the sizing information to function points.

Ms. Cooper spent several weeks with the development team to arrive at
the function point counts and the lines-of-code estimates. The function
point counts were based on the methodology defined in the *Function Point
Counting Practices Manual* from the International Function Point Users
Group (IFPUG). The responsible team leaders generated estimates
of source lines of code for each of the application functions. Ms. Cooper
summarized the sizing results for Lt. Col. Thompson as shown in Figure B-3.

The figure shows the estimated size for each of the CIs in Increments 1 and
2. The figure also shows the primary language and the projected number of
low-level design units.

The relational database and the Ada-to-SQL bindings inherent in the
MAPS design were relatively new COTS software products. Input screens
and reports were generated by fourth generation languages (4GLs).

Ms. Cooper's projections indicated the following:

- The minimum schedule to develop both functional increments would
  be four months longer than the planned development schedule.

- In order to meet even the extended schedule, the MAPS development
  staffing levels would have to be significantly increased.

Although these analysis results were expected, they indicated that Lt. Col.
Thompson would have to replan the remainder of the MAPS project to
define a more realistic development plan.

B.2.2   Revising the Project Management Plan

Lt. Col. Thompson used the cost model estimates as the basis for a revised
project management plan. He asked Ms. Cooper to show the new schedule
in the form of a Gantt chart. This revised schedule is shown in Figure B-4.

Configuration Item	Abbr.	Language	Number of Units	Size (Function Points)
Increment 1—Base Level Functions				
1. Personal Information	BPI		58	429
2. Assignments	BAS		36	227
3. Availability	BAV		12	71
4. Unit Training	BUT		20	114
5. Unit Skills Inventory	BUS		34	223
6. Security Clearances	BSC	Ada, SQL, and code generation	15	138
7. Performance Evaluations	BPE		41	252
8. Promotions	BPR		37	154
9. Unit Mobilization	BUM		51	390
10. Unit Reenlistments	BUR		17	92
11. Casualty Reporting	BCR		23	109
12. Unit Replacement Priorities	BUP		27	147
13. Personnel Database (Base-level Entities)	BPD	COTS		450
Increment 1 Total			371	2,796

Configuration Item	Abbr.	Language	Number of Units	Size (Function Points)
Increment 2—HQ Functions				
1. Organization Master	HOM		33	189
2. Force Training	HFT		28	141
3. Force Skills	HFS	Ada, SQL, and code generation	22	123
4. Manpower Requirements	HMP		55	375
5. Manpower Authorization	HMA		21	115
6. Force Replacement Priorities	HFP		30	170
7. Strategic Planning	HSP		47	320
8. Force Mobilization	HFM		65	392
9. Personnel Database (HQ-level Entities)	HPD	COTS		210
Increment 2 Total			301	2,035

Configuration Item	Abbr.	Language	Number of Units	Size (SLOC)
Data Conversion Programs				
1. Base-level	BDC	C	10	9,500
2. HQ-level	HDC	C	7	6,000
Conversion Total			17	15,500

Ridgway AFB: MAPS   Data as of 31 Dec 98

Figure B-3   The MAPS software size estimates

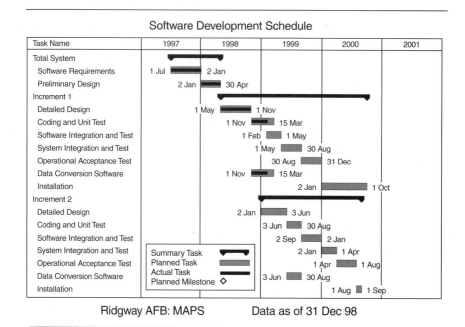

Software Development Schedule

Task Name	1997	1998	1999	2000	2001
Total System					
Software Requirements	1 Jul ▓▓ 2 Jan				
Preliminary Design	2 Jan ▓▓ 30 Apr				
Increment 1					
Detailed Design	1 May ▓▓ 1 Nov				
Coding and Unit Test	1 Nov ▓▓ 15 Mar				
Software Integration and Test	1 Feb ▓ 1 May				
System Integration and Test	1 May ▓▓ 30 Aug				
Operational Acceptance Test	30 Aug ▓▓ 31 Dec				
Data Conversion Software	1 Nov ▓▓ 15 Mar				
Installation	2 Jan ▓▓▓ 1 Oct				
Increment 2					
Detailed Design	2 Jan ▓▓ 3 Jun				
Coding and Unit Test	3 Jun ▓ 30 Aug				
Software Integration and Test	2 Sep ▓▓ 2 Jan				
System Integration and Test	2 Jan ▓ 1 Apr				
Operational Acceptance Test	1 Apr ▓▓ 1 Aug				
Data Conversion Software	3 Jun ▓ 30 Aug				
Installation	1 Aug ▓ 1 Sep				

Legend (inset box):
- Summary Task ▬▬
- Planned Task ▓▓
- Actual Task ▬▬
- Planned Milestone ◇

Ridgway AFB: MAPS   Data as of 31 Dec 98

Figure B-4 The MAPS development schedule

The revised schedule began with the completed activities. The system requirements and high-level design activities were accomplished from July 1997 through May 1998.

Top-level requirements and design were completed early in the development effort for the entire system. With these activities complete, the revised schedule called for the independent development of the application software in two parallel increments as previously defined. The development of each increment included detailed design, coding, and integration and test.

The detailed design for Increment 1 was completed in November of 1998. Increment 1 was to be fielded by the end of 2000. Detailed design for Increment 2 was scheduled to begin in early 1999. Increment 2 was scheduled for delivery in mid-2000. The data conversion software was scheduled for parallel development with the respective functional increments. Data conversion and installation was scheduled to occur over a 10-month period for Increment 1 and a 1-month period for Increment 2.

Lt. Col. Thompson identified two major development activities on the critical path: the personnel information CI for the base-level subsystem and the data conversion software for both functional increments. The personnel information CI was critical because it had to be completed before the other CIs could be integrated and tested. The data conversion software was critical because it was needed to convert the existing databases at each base and at headquarters. The data conversion effort had already been identified as a high-risk item by the IPT. The data conversion software had to be completed—and had to work properly—before the MAPS increments could be fielded. Lt. Col. Thompson decided to track these critical-path items closely.

The results of the productivity analysis were also used as the basis for the revised MAPS staffing plan. The projected effort allocations for Increment 1 and Increment 2 were graphed as shown in Figure B-5. When Lt. Col. Thompson reviewed the incremental effort allocation, he noted that the peak, full-time staffing requirement for any increment did not exceed 35 people. Since the schedule called for the MAPS increments to be developed in parallel, Lt. Col. Thompson asked Ms. Cooper to generate a system-level effort allocation graph. This graph is depicted in Figure B-6.

When Lt. Col. Thompson looked at the total system effort profile that aggregated the individual effort requirements, several things became apparent. It was clear that the number of people currently assigned to the development team was not adequate to meet the peak staffing requirements that would occur in 1999. Even more important, the level staffing profile of 40 people did not meet the needs of the project. The development had been inefficiently overstaffed through 1998 and was then projected to experience shortfalls in 1999.

Lt. Col. Thompson used the measurement results to brief senior management about some of the issues impacting the development of MAPS. They agreed with his overall assessment and added four months to the development schedule. They also agreed to allocate additional funding to support the 1999 staffing requirements. The plan was to use qualified Air Force personnel from other projects and to hire outside contractors to help with detailed design, coding, and software integration and test for the MAPS Increment 2 development.

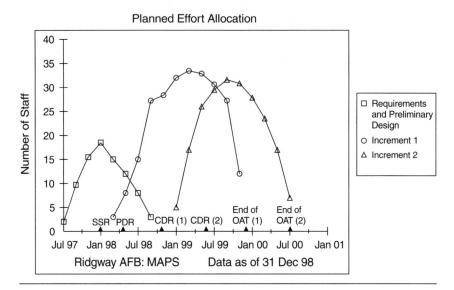

Figure B-5   Total Required Effort for the MAPS Project

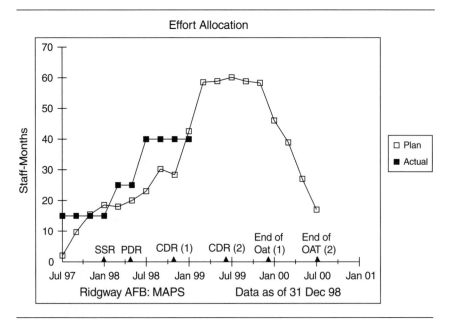

Figure B-6   The effort allocation indicator showing that additional funding must be allocated to meet the 1999 staffing requirements

B.2.3   Tracking Performance against the Revised Plan

Once the new schedule and staffing plans were in place, Lt. Col. Thompson's concerns shifted from evaluating the feasibility of the plans to assessing performance against the plans. Although the milestone data continued to be useful in addressing the schedule and progress issues, more detailed information was required to track the degree of completion of the key development activities and products. The need for this information was clear as Lt. Col. Thompson reviewed the Gantt chart that represented the revised project schedule. The milestone schedule indicated that detailed design for Increment 1 had been completed and software implementation was well underway. Based on the schedule, about two-thirds of the time allocated for coding had already elapsed. This didn't mean, however, that two-thirds of the Increment 1 software had been coded. To get information about the degree of activity and product completion that they needed, Lt. Col. Thompson and Ms. Cooper decided to implement several work unit progress measures.

Work unit progress measures compare the actual completion of associated work units for software products and activities against an established plan. If objective completion criteria for each type of work unit are defined and adhered to, work unit progress measures provide for a clear determination of development progress. For each of the MAPS CIs, Ms. Cooper recommended that the project use counts of the number of design units implemented as the work unit progress measure. The design units represented the lowest practical level of measurement, and the data could be collected easily from the configuration management system. In this case, an implemented design unit was defined as one passing unit test and entered into the project library.

To generate the CI work unit progress indicators, Ms. Cooper first defined the planned rate of unit completion. Without detailed planning data available, Ms. Cooper generated a straight-line completion plan beginning with the Critical Design Review (CDR) and ending with the scheduled completion of the Increment 1 coding activity. In Ms. Cooper's previous experience with work unit progress measures, she had found that the more accurate plans for the cumulative number of work units completed over time often looked more like an S-shaped curve than a straight line. This was due to the fact that the first few units tended to be completed slowly, followed by a faster rate of completion as the activity progressed. Nearing the end of the software activity, the completion rates tended to slow again as the more difficult units were completed. For the MAPS work unit progress measures, the straight-line plan was not perfect, but was seen as a useful approximation. Everyone understood that they would not be too alarmed if progress lagged behind the straight-line plan at the beginning of the development activity.

Once Ms. Cooper had established the plan, she accessed the configuration management library to obtain a count of units completed to date. Specifically, she counted the number of units that had been entered into the library each week over the course of Increment 1 implementation. The resulting graph is shown in Figure B-7. The graph indicates that the CI implementation was progressing in accordance with the revised development plan.

Ms. Cooper knew that Lt. Col. Thompson wanted to emphasize software measures related to the schedule progress issue. As such, she decided to

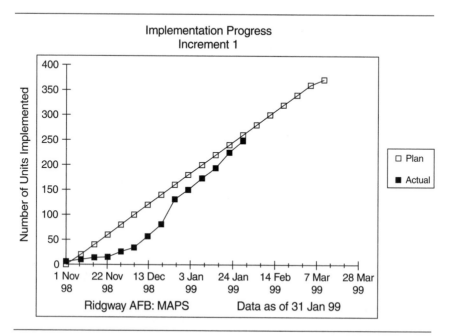

Figure B-7   The CI implementation progress indicator showing that increment progress was in accordance with the revised plan

track progress for the two items on the critical path very closely: the development of the personnel information CI and the development of the data conversion software. The personnel information CI was scheduled for completion by March 1999. Ms. Cooper constructed a plan to track work unit progress for the single CI the same way she did for the aggregate of the CIs in Increment 1. Again, the plan was derived by drawing a straight line between CDR and the scheduled end of the coding activity. The resulting indicator was graphed and is depicted in Figure B-8. When the actual number of design units were compared to the plan, it became immediately clear that progress on this critical CI was lagging.

Ms. Cooper then decided to try to identify the source of the progress problem in the personnel information CI. She defined two new work unit progress indicators using a somewhat different perspective. She graphed the development progress data for the screens and reports separately from the units that performed internal processing. The screens and reports were being implemented using a 4GL, while the internal processing code was being written in Ada.

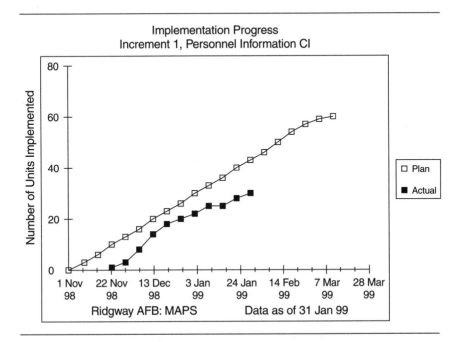

Figure B-8   An indicator comparing the actual number of design units to the plan and showing the personnel information CI to be lagging

The results are shown, respectively, in Figures B-9 and B-10. The measurement data showed that the screen and report development was on track and indicated that the problem was confined to the Ada code. When Lt. Col. Thompson investigated, he found out that the Ada developers were having difficulty interfacing their respective CIs to the COTS relational database. The problem was not critical from a technical perspective, but the workarounds were taking quite a bit of time to implement using SQL. Lt. Col. Thompson did several things to correct the interface problems. First, he brought in representatives from the COTS vendors to work on-site with the Ada developers to provide real-time support in resolving interface problems. Second, he had the development team conduct a one-time in-depth inspection of the CI's design and completed code. This inspection identified some design structures that were inefficient but could be corrected. Lt. Col. Thompson also assigned several of his most experienced Ada programmers to work on the personnel information CI in an attempt to correct the problem.

The other portion of Increment 1 that was on the critical path was the data conversion software for the base-level databases. In tracking work unit

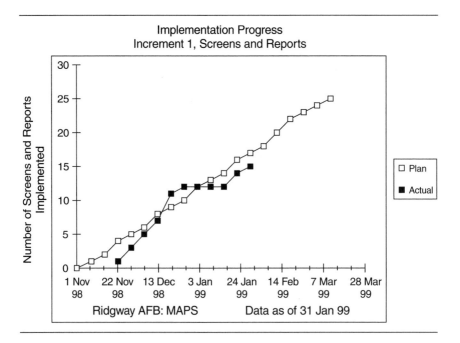

Figure B-9 The development progress indicator for screens and reports showing no major problem

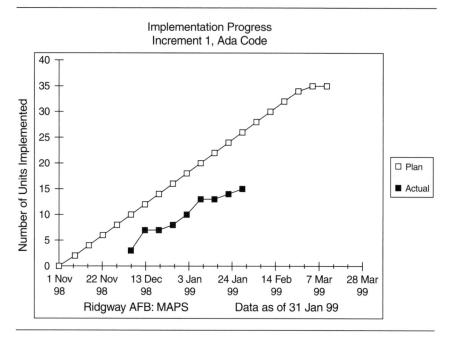

Figure B-10   The development progress indicator showing a significant problem in production of Ada code

progress for this software, Ms. Cooper decided to count the lines of code that had been entered into the configuration management library, rather than counting the number of completed units. She decided that completed lines of code was a better measure of progress than a count of units because the data conversion software was divided up into relatively few units, and they varied drastically in size. The units were not equivalent, and using them to track progress would have been misleading. Ms. Cooper generated the plan and actuals for the data conversion software and graphed the indicator as shown in Figure B-11.

The results showed that the data conversion software development progress was on track.

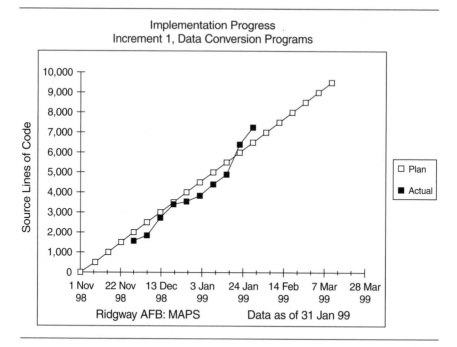

Figure B-11   The implementation progress indicator for data conversion showing no problem

B.3

Evaluating Readiness for Test

During 1999, the MAPS measurement process was effective in helping to manage the software development effort. Progress against the revised plan was sufficient enough to allow for the resolution of the problem reports previously backlogged. Additional personnel that were added to the development team allowed for the concurrent development of both the base- and headquarters-level MAPS increments. The progress measures showed that Increment 1 was nearing the completion of integration and test, and some system-level testing had already been conducted. The primary issue had shifted from schedule and progress to the quality of the software. The key concern was the readiness of the software for operational test and evaluation.

B.3.1   Increment 1

As the initial 2000 delivery dates grew closer, Lt. Col. Thompson wanted to know if Increment 1 was ready to begin operational test. To help answer this question, Ms. Cooper defined a set of related indicators and graphed them, as shown in Figures B-12 through B-15. On each of these indicators, the dates for the Start of Software and Systems Integration and Test and for the Operational Acceptance Test (OAT) were marked.

When Ms. Cooper first joined the MAPS project, the project had not been collecting effort data at the level of detail required to show how much effort was being applied to software rework. As an organic development

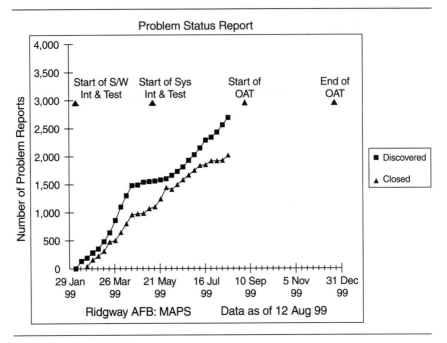

Figure B-12   Increment 1 readiness for test—problem report status

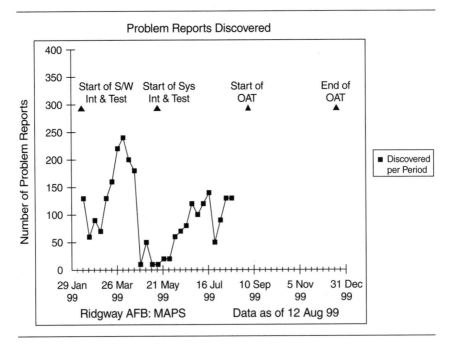

Figure B-13   Increment 1 readiness for test—problem reports discovered

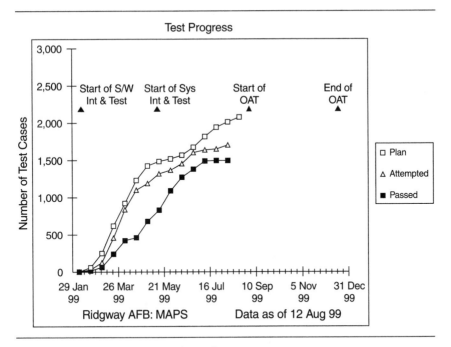

Figure B-14   Increment 1 readiness for test—test progress

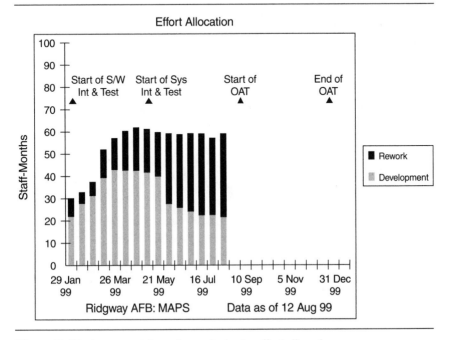

Figure B-15   Increment 1 readiness for test—effort allocation

activity, it was difficult to get the staff to record on their timecards how they actually applied their effort during the week. Since the emphasis had been on generating new code to meet the existing schedule, the development team didn't see a need for the information anyway. As such, only development effort was collected as part of the time-reporting system. To get the data she needed, Ms. Cooper asked one of the programmers to modify the problem reporting system to collect the redevelopment and retesting effort data related to software rework on a problem-by-problem basis.

The change in the process was briefed to the suppliers, and Ms. Cooper began to collect the data she needed to compare the amount of effort spent in rework versus new development. The data was graphed and is presented in Figure B-15.

Ms. Cooper combined the rework effort data (Figure B-15) with a work unit progress graph for cumulative problem reports (Figure B-12) and a graph of the number of problem reports being opened on a weekly basis (Figure B-13). She also included a graph of test case progress (Figure B-14). This combination of indicators suggested that Increment 1 was not yet ready to begin operational test. Lt. Col. Thompson wanted to see (1) the open and closed problem report trends converging; (2) the number of new problems being discovered declining; (3) the number of test cases passed equal to the number planned; and (4) the amount of effort being applied for rework decreasing. The results indicated that the development staff was spending an increasing amount of time correcting new Increment 1 problems. This was a concern because they should have been transitioning to the development of code for Increment 2. Lt. Col. Thompson met with Ms. Cooper and asked her for more information in order to identify what needed to be done to improve the situation. Specifically, he wanted information about the types of problems being reported. He was hoping that there was a common type of problem that could be effectively managed.

Ms. Cooper spent the better part of a week with several of the testing personnel reviewing the problem reports and classifying them as being related to performance, logic, interfaces, or other. She decided to implement this classification scheme as a permanent part of the problem reporting system so that the information would be readily available to support future analysis. The results of the classification effort were graphed and are depicted in

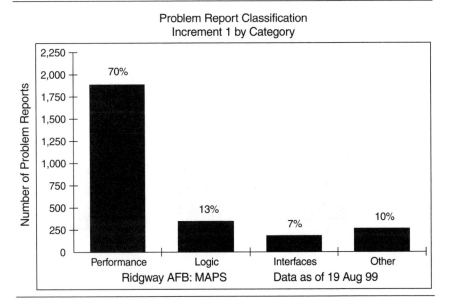

Problem Report Classification
Increment 1 by Category

Figure B-16   The problem report classification indicator showing that the
Increment 1 problems were related to performance deficiencies

Figure B-16. By far, the greatest number of Increment 1 problems were related to performance deficiencies.

Ms. Cooper further classified the performance problems according to their sources. The results are shown in Figure B-17. The most common type of performance problem was due to the incorrect use of SQL by the developers.

Ms. Cooper discussed the results of her analysis with Lt. Col. Thompson and pointed out that the MAPS development represented the first time that many of the people on the development team had used a relational database and SQL. The staff's previous experience had been with hierarchical databases and COBOL. This probably should not have been a surprise, since the SQL issue was part of the reason for the previous personnel information CI development problems. Lt. Col. Thompson again decided to bring in some additional expertise to address the SQL issue. Although to bring in new people, the problems needed to be fixed quickly.

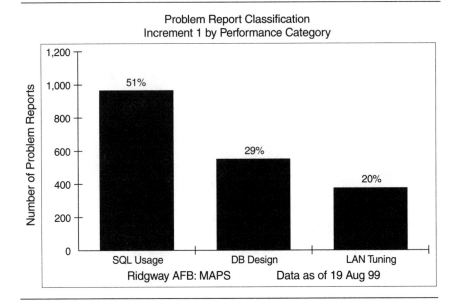

Figure B-17 The problem report classification indicator showing the cause of performance problems was the incorrect use of SQL by the developers

B.3.2 Increment 2

Increment 2 was scheduled for delivery early in 2000. According to the development schedule, Increment 2 should have been nearing the completion of system test by the 1st of April 2000. To assess the Increment 2 readiness for test status, Ms. Cooper generated the same combination of graphs using the same indicators as she had done for Increment 1. The results are shown in Figures B-18 through B-21.

This time the situation was much more encouraging. The trends for open and closed problem reports were converging, the discovery rate for new problems was declining rapidly, and the amount of rework was relatively low and stable. In addition, a comparison between the number of test cases planned, executed, and passed provided further evidence that testing was being completed in accordance with the schedule. Ms. Cooper wondered why the number of newly discovered problems was declining so rapidly.

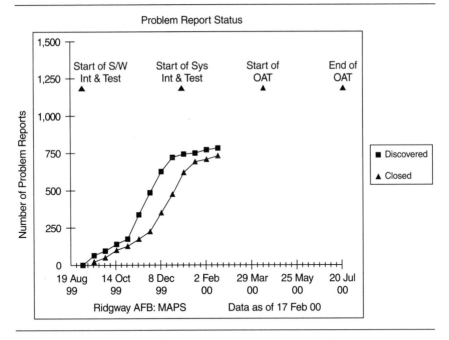

Figure B-18   Increment 2, readiness for test—problem report status

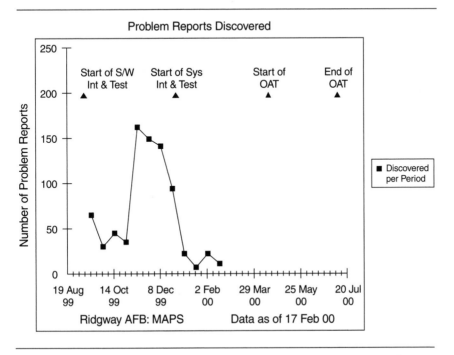

Figure B-19   Increment 2, readiness for test—problem reports discovered

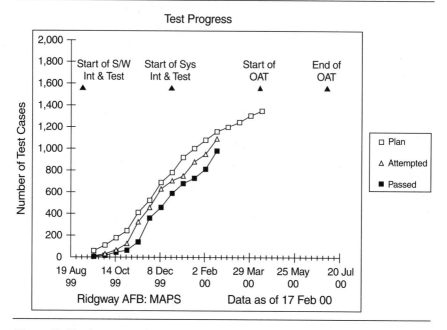

Figure B-20   Increment 2, readiness for test—test progress

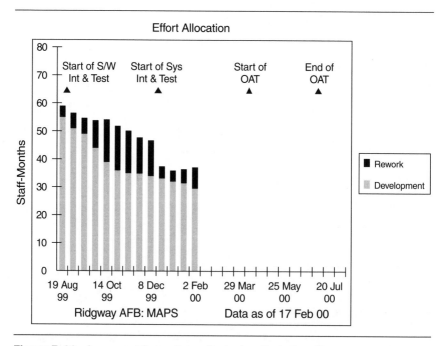

Figure B-21   Increment 2, readiness for test—effort allocation

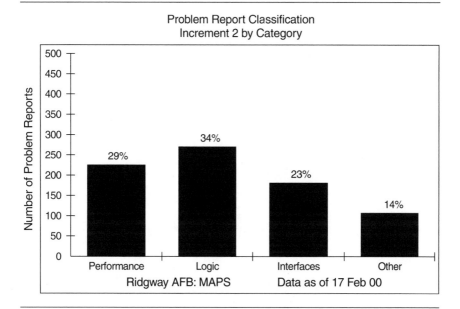

Figure B-22   The problem report classification indicator verifying that the issues and problems experienced in Increment 1 had been addressed

Was the software that much better? Were discovered problems not being reported? Had the testing stopped? The test progress results helped Ms. Cooper answer part of her question. Since testing was proceeding as scheduled, the lower number of new problem reports were not a result of reduced testing efforts. Ms. Cooper looked into the reporting process and found that the identified problems were still being consistently documented.

Ms. Cooper continued to track the classes of reported problems, as shown in Figure B-22. In contrast to the results for Increment 1, which had a high proportion of problems related to performance, the problems for Increment 2 were much more evenly distributed. The measurement data for Increment 2 indicated that the issues that were experienced in Increment 1 had been successfully addressed. Lt. Col. Thompson's decisions had helped to focus the right resources where they were needed.

B.4

Installation and
Software Support

With the development of MAPS proceeding according to plan, Lt. Col. Thompson asked Ms. Cooper to extend the measurement process to the fielding of the Increment 1 base-level systems. This was scheduled to occur from January through October 2000, with delivery of the systems occurring at a relatively constant rate.

To support the installation process, a total of ten people were assigned and divided into five teams. Each team was scheduled to spend two weeks installing MAPS at each of the 100 base-level sites. The work during the two-week installation period included data conversion, software installation, user training, and user support. After installation, the MAPS development team would provide support via a 24-hour help line. The plan called for each site to run the existing military personnel system concurrently with the newly installed MAPS for one week before shutting down the old system completely. The 100 base-level sites included all Air Force bases in the United States and overseas, Air Force Reserve commands, and selected Air National Guard units.

B.4.1   Increment 1 Installation

To track the installation progress, Ms. Cooper defined and graphed a simple work unit progress indicator as depicted in Figure B-23. Since data conversion was one of the major risks identified by the IPT, she wanted to have the earliest possible warning of any problems.

It is clear from the graph that the installations were behind schedule almost from the start. Ms. Cooper investigated and contacted each of the installation teams to identify the causes for the delays. She heard a consistent story. The old base-level system that MAPS was replacing had very loose edit requirements. It would accept almost any personnel data that was entered. The result was that the data conversion software written to the MAPS data specifications kept rejecting data that was in a different format from what was expected. This was not an easy problem to fix because each of the existing base-level databases was different.

Ms. Cooper showed Lt. Col. Thompson a linear extrapolation of the actual installation data points. This is shown in Figure B-24. Based on the actual

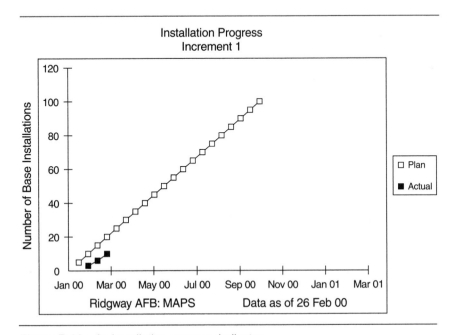

Figure B-23   An installation progress indicator

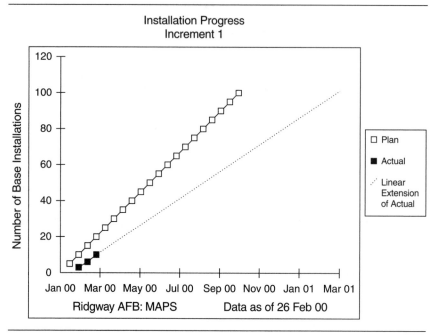

Figure B-24 An installation progress indicator showing a linear extrapolation of the actual data points in Figure B-23

rate of progress, a total of fifteen months would be required to complete the installations, not ten months as originally planned. The rate of base installation was limited by the availability of teams. Based on the projection, Lt. Col. Thompson decided to extend the installation schedule. He also asked Ms. Cooper to provide an update to the projection as more data became available.

B.4.2 Software Support

By November 2000, MAPS had been installed at 68 of the 100 base-level sites. As part of the measurement process, Ms. Cooper had been tracking and categorizing problem reports from the field. Given the previous problems on the project, it was important to Lt. Col. Thompson to address the users' concerns.

At the highest level, Ms. Cooper classified the problem reports as being related to hardware, software, or user error. She analyzed the software-related problem reports in more detail by focusing on those that were the result of defects in the design or the code. She classified the problems as related to performance, logic, interfaces with other systems, and other. The data coming in from the field showed that the most frequent type of problem was related to logic defects. This is shown in Figure B-25.

Ms. Cooper also decided to classify the problems according to their source by identifying the CI that had to be changed in order to correct each problem. She graphed the ratio of problem reports to function points for each CI. The results were graphed as shown in Figure B-26. Ms. Cooper found that the unit mobilization (BUM) CI accounted for a disproportionate number of defects. Clearly there was a problem with this particular CI.

Lt. Col. Thompson asked Ms. Cooper to compare how much effort was being applied to correcting the problems with what it would cost to redesign and redevelop the unit mobilization CI. Ms. Cooper generated the graph shown in Figure B-27 to reflect the effort that was applied over a two-month period.

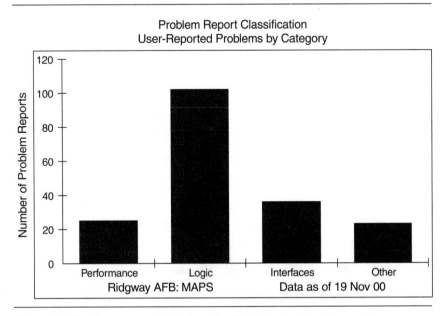

Figure B-25 Measurement data from the field showing that the most frequent problems were related to logic defects

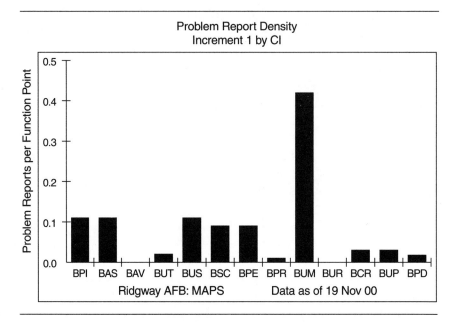

Figure B-26 A comparison of problem reports to function points showing that the unit mobilization (BUM) CI accounted for most of the defects

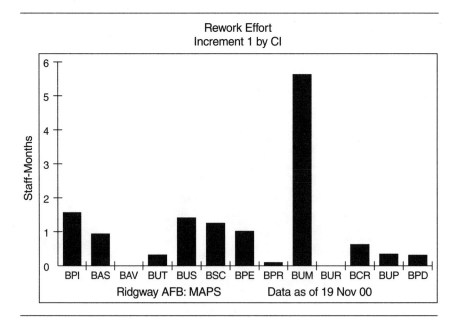

Figure B-27 The rework effort indicator, identifying the unit mobilization (BUM) CI as the major cause of problems

Ms. Cooper noted that the Unit Mobilization CI required the equivalent of three full-time staff members to support problem resolution. She was surprised that there continued to be such a high rate of newly discovered problems, particularly considering that the unit mobilization CI had been in operational use for almost a year. In talking with the lead programmer responsible for maintaining the CI, she found that as existing problems were corrected, new ones were being introduced. She decided to compare the cost of continuing to maintain the CI as currently implemented over a projected ten-year period with the cost of reengineering and maintaining a more reliable version of the CI. The screen and report generation functions did not need to be changed.

Ms. Cooper estimated that the cost of reengineering would be $1.2 million over a ten-month period, with estimated software support costs of $800,000 over the remaining nine-year period. This $2.0 million was compared to an estimated $3.0 million cost to maintain the existing CI over the same ten-year time frame. This comparison was based on an average $100,000 cost per person-year.

Lt. Col. Thompson decided to redesign the unit mobilization CI and planned to release it in the next MAPS update scheduled for late 2001.

Of course, budget factors needed to be considered in the redesign decision. Given the development funding constraints, it would have been easy to defer the changes. By including the maintenance organization in the decision, funds were made available from several sources to support redesign of the CI during the life-cycle phase.

B.4.3 Epilogue

The MAPS development turned out to be a good example of implementing a measurement process on an existing project. As the project progressed, the data required to manage the key issues was identified, collected, and analyzed. The measurement activity focused on addressing the primary software information needs related to schedule and progress, and product quality.

The measurement process was adapted to the specific characteristics of the MAPS project. Measures suited to information system software, such as function points, were implemented. New measures were also defined to support the installation process. By the end of the MAPS development, the entire project team realized that measurement was useful in identifying and resolving both management and technical problems.

APPENDIX C

Synergy Integrated Copier Case Study

This case study describes the development of a new line of integrated office copiers and printers requiring a significant amount of embedded software. This family of products is designed to take advantage of networking and Internet technologies by combining standard copier capabilities with network and remote printing capabilities. This product will increase the convenience and speed of printing while reducing the overall costs of having different hardware devices for copying, printing, scanning, and faxing. The concept is an innovative departure from traditional offerings in the copier industry, providing significant opportunities for new business by replacing noncopier devices such as network printers and fax machines. Executive management views the new product line as a strategic opportunity to increase market share in a highly competitive industry if the product can be brought to market ahead of the competition.

Product and Project Overview

The Doppel Corporation (DopCorp) has a well-deserved international reputation as a major producer of high-quality office copiers. This business has become increasingly competitive, offering limited growth opportunities. Market research recently identified a potential opportunity in producing a single document-processing device that would replace the entire suite of scanners, printers, copiers, and fax machines that populate the typical office. In addition to integrating scanning, copying, faxing, and printing capabilities, the product concept requires an extensive set of document-production options such as binding and collating that would be configurable remotely from workstations. This product would provide new and powerful marketing opportunities in these two areas:

- Capturing business from existing competitors in the copier market by offering increased functionality

- Providing a platform for entering the markets for networked printers, remote printers, scanners, and fax equipment

The window for a successful introduction of the new copier products into the market was estimated to be 18 to 24 months. Competitors were expected to require two years to respond to an aggressive initial marketing campaign and product roll-out. Executive management quickly committed to developing the proposed system. The project was code-named Synergy (Figure C-1). In order to ensure that this product would get to market before any competitor's products, project completion was set for 18 months after start. Rapid time to market was established as a high-priority objective for the Synergy project. At the same time, executive management made it clear that DopCorp wanted to protect its reputation for quality.

Product Description

As the product concept evolved into system requirements, marketing requested that two versions of Synergy be developed. The low-end model (S1) was intended for small offices where a single system could be expected to service all needs. The high-capacity, high-end model (S2) was targeted at businesses with larger document-processing needs. In this environment, multiple S2s in different locations would be networked to share the workload and offer more document-processing options (e.g., glue binding, electronic storage and retrieval). Marketing agreed to initial delivery of the S1 model in 18 months, to be followed by delivery of the S2 model 6 months later. The key requirements for the two models were as follows:

Basic Model S1 Features

- Color output

- Copy from feeder or manual

- Print as an attachment to a computer or network

- Convert paper images to electronic form

- Send and receive faxes

- Allow selection of options at control panel or from remote terminal

- Provide standard setups for making reports and brochures

- Handle multiple paper sizes, colors, thickness, as well as transparencies

- Print 30 pages per minute

- Provide error handling and help diagnostics for users

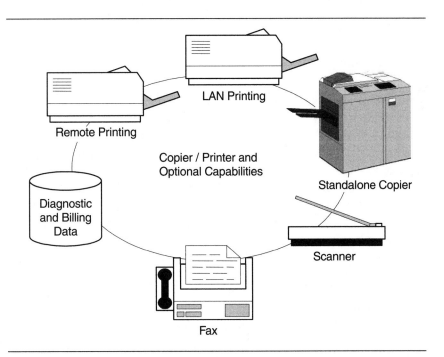

Figure C-1   Basic capabilities of the Synergy product

Additional Model S2 Features

- Double the printing speed

- Workload management for multiple devices

- Configuration management for stored documents using network resources

- Binding options, including glue, up to 250 pages

- Recognize and assimilate front and back covers, report pages, and section separators

- New hardware components to be interchangeable with standard plug-in interfaces

- Remote upgrades to software components for software maintenance or support of new hardware components

- E-mail collection and reporting of internal diagnostics for preventive or just-in-time maintenance

- Collection and reporting of billing information via e-mail for leased equipment

Project Organization

The Synergy project adopted the typical structure used within DopCorp. Each product is developed by an integrated product team reporting to the product manager. This team includes the lead system engineer, subsystem managers for software and hardware (equipment), and representatives from the manufacturing, purchasing, support (documentation), and marketing departments. Each team is charged with the measurement responsibilities of creating estimates and plans and then of tracking progress against the plans. Figure C-2 shows the organization put into place to develop and manage Synergy.

The lead systems engineer develops the product architecture and coordinates the development of subsystem requirements based on the product concept. The lead systems engineer also develops and coordinates final testing prior to the hand-off to manufacturing.

Historically, DopCorp acquired many critical components for its products from external sources, so the purchasing manager was a key member of

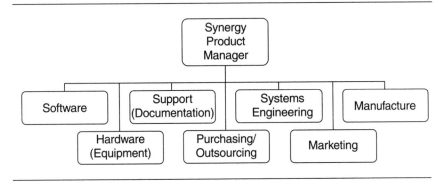

Figure C-2   Project organization

the team. Two key Synergy components were intended to be outsourced. First, the paper handling component and associated software were designed to be a family of components that were interchangeable based on the sorting, collating, and other options desired. The vendor chosen for outsourcing this component was selected because this company had the following features.

- A long, established relationship with DopCorp

- Fully integrated into the project team

- Used many of DopCorp's standard processes

- Participated in routine subcontract status meetings, milestone reviews, and change control board or cross-functional team meetings whenever the agenda included changes to standard interfaces or to the finished component

Second, the communications chip was being produced by an outside vendor. Custom logic in the chip would eliminate the need for some of the software development necessary to handle networking and Internet communications. The supplier was a relatively new company. DopCorp selected this vendor because they were the only ones who promised quick design and delivery of the needed chip.

Development Approach

Time to market was a key consideration for the Synergy project. The product manager decided to implement a strategy for rapid application development. This strategy entailed the following actions to reduce product development time:

- Maximize reuse of software components by utilizing a proven, product line architecture

- Streamline the development process

- Assign the most senior and experienced staff to the project

Maximum software reuse was possible because for the past five years DopCorp had managed their copiers as a product line. As part of their product-line strategy, they had written key architectural components as generically as possible to facilitate future reuse. The product-line architecture is shown in Figure C-3.

The primary components that required modification for the Synergy project were those labeled "Raster Image Processing" and "Image Format Conversion" in Figure C-3. These were key to Synergy's capability. Once an image was digitized as a raster image, it was possible to process and greatly improve the quality of that image through DopCorp's image-processing software. Thus, regardless of the source of an image (fax, workstation, paper scan), the image could be enhanced, stored,

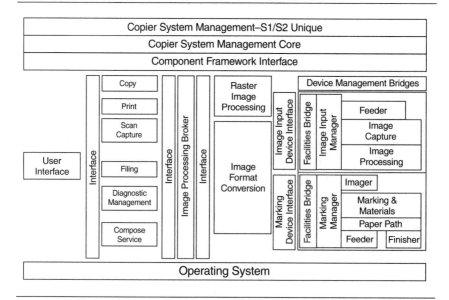

Figure C-3   Product-line architecture

retrieved, and printed from the copier, from the local-area network, or from the Internet.

A robust and mature commercial package was found that supported many of the network management functions including resource monitoring and diagnostic reporting. The package also allowed for reconfiguring the network to allow multiple S2 models to share the workload.

The project was planned as two incremental builds. The first build would support the S1 (low-end) capabilities, while the second would support the high-end S2. The project team established a system of regular reviews and meetings to monitor progress against the project plan and address problems as they arose. The technical leads for each subsystem, together with the lead engineer, met weekly to resolve technical issues, such as interfaces and shared resources. The product manager reviewed project status weekly with the project team, using measures that addressed technical and management performance issues. In addition, the product manager identified synchronization points between marketing, hardware, and software. At each of these points, there was to be a major review with DopCorp's CEO and senior management to evaluate hardware, software, and marketing progress to date. Four synchronization points were defined, as shown in Figure C-4.

These reviews acted as development gates. At each review, a "go / no-go" decision was made based on progress up to that point. In addition to time to market, product quality was a key issue. Not only was it important to protect DopCorp's reputation for high-quality products, but excessive rework needed to correct defects would negatively impact schedule. The

Month from Project Start	Marketing Milestones	Hardware Milestones	Software Milestones
2	Define market strategy and product concept	Define supporting technology	Define high-level software requirements
5	Define product features	Hardware design	Software architecture
11	Product announcement, marketing plan ready	Prototype ready for software integration	Detailed design, code, and unit test completed
15	Demonstrate product	Working prototype	System integration completed

Figure C-4   Product synchronization points

project was planned with emphasis on formal inspections as an essential component of the development process. Analysis of historical data from two recent projects indicated that introducing inspections on requirements documents and providing more rigor in the design and code inspections could yield significant reductions in rework. Inspections were required for all requirements documents, design documents, code units, and test cases. Results of the inspections were to be tracked to closure, and the number of defects was tracked against historical data trends.

Estimation and Feasibility Analysis

Due to the importance of getting to the market as soon as possible, most of the planning effort was focused on the S1 model. This section describes how estimates were developed that formed the basis for project plans for S1.

Estimating Software Size

The marketing motivation for undertaking the project meant that schedule was a key constraint. Within fairly broad limits, cost could vary. The challenge was to develop a feasible project plan to meet the schedule while also meeting quality and product performance requirements. DopCorp has a relatively mature estimation process in place. They use a combination of parametric modeling and activity-based costing to arrive at their estimates. The models used had previously been calibrated to the DopCorp environment, using data from historical data on completed projects.

The size estimates for the two critical components, Raster Image Processing (RIP) and Image Format Conversion (IFC), are shown in Figure C-5.

The number of lines of new and modified code was estimated by team engineering consensus. Both RIP and IFC were written in C++. Individual team members independently assessed the requirements for each software component and then discussed the size of the changes required with the group in order to arrive at a consensus. Once they had their size estimates, the project office used a parametric cost model that allowed them to enter time as a constraint to observe the impact on staffing requirements and total effort.

Component Name	Component Abbreviation	Number of Units	New plus Modified Source Lines of Code
Raster Image Processing	**RIP**	**524**	**77,500**
- Input Signature Correction	- ISC	128	18,900
- Input Structure Analysis	- ISA	95	14,100
- Image Coding	- ICD	83	12,300
- Image Compression	- ICM	218	32,200
Image Format Conversion	**IFC**	**453**	**66,970**
- Image Expand	- IEX	25	3,750
- Gray-Scale Processing	- GPR	78	11,500
- Color Processing	- CPR	270	39,920
- Output Rendering	- ORE	80	11,800

Figure C-5   Estimated size of software components

Estimating Software Schedule

One of the model outputs was a high-level Gantt chart, shown in Figure C-6. The development was scheduled to begin January 2 with detailed requirements analysis. Increment I was scheduled for completion in mid-January of the following year, followed by three months of system test. This schedule was evaluated for feasibility, using historical data from several completed projects as a basis for comparison.

Since time to market was critical, the product manager wanted to plan and track progress at a detailed level so that any deviations would be flagged early, allowing appropriate action. Therefore, a project measurement process was established and appropriate measures were defined. A software lead was assigned to each of the software components shown in

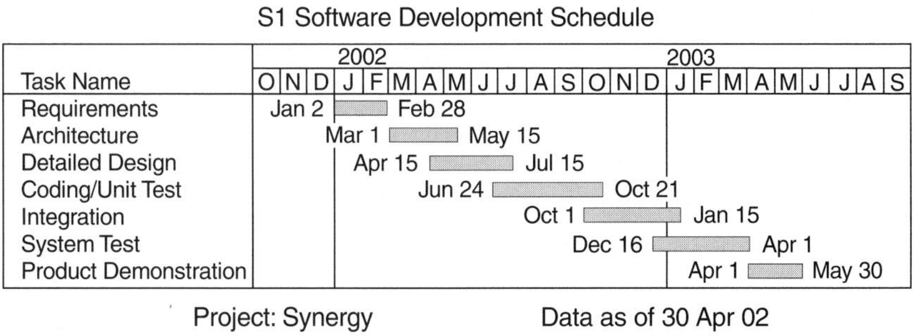

S1 Software Development Schedule

Task Name	2002 O N D J F M A M J J A S	2003 O N D J F M A M J J A S
Requirements	Jan 2 ▨ Feb 28	
Architecture	Mar 1 ▨ May 15	
Detailed Design	Apr 15 ▨ Jul 15	
Coding/Unit Test	Jun 24 ▨ Oct 21	
Integration	Oct 1 ▨ Jan 15	
System Test	Dec 16 ▨ Apr 1	
Product Demonstration		Apr 1 ▨ May 30

Project: Synergy   Data as of 30 Apr 02

Figure C-6   Gantt chart for S1 software

Figure C-5. Each lead was responsible for constructing a detailed plan for design and implementation and then monitoring and reporting progress against their approved plan, in accordance with the project measurement process.

Planning Activities, Work Products, and Staffing

Progress was to be monitored using measures that compared plans and actuals for work products completed. Each team leader constructed a detailed design, code, and unit test plan for the configuration item. Detailed plans were generated from the estimated number of labor hours required to complete each low-level unit. Once the labor hours were estimated, planned start and end dates were assigned. From these dates, work unit progress plans were constructed. For example, an indicator containing the base measure of planned detailed design progress for the Input Signature Correction component, consisting of 128 units, is shown in Figure C-7. A unit could not be counted as "designed" until the design peer review had been held and signed off by the team leader and by Software Quality Assurance (SQA). Similar plans with associated measures and indicators were created for code and for unit test progress.

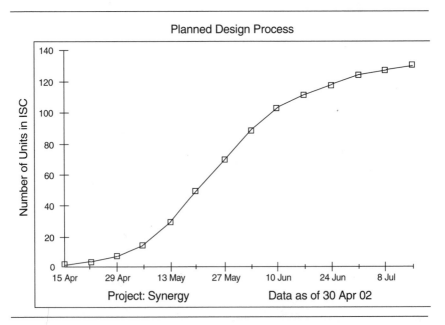

Figure C-7   Planned design progress for input signature correction

The Test Team also constructed a set of plans. Figure C-8 shows an indicator based on the integration test plan for the Raster Image Processing CI in terms of the units integrated. Figure C-9 shows an indicator based on the plan for test procedures executed.

Once the detailed plans were in place, individual project members were given specific assignments. The staffing plan, visually presented by the indicator in Figure C-10, peaked at 42 people. This peak occurs during software integration test.

An integrated analysis of all plans was conducted to ensure that the detailed plans were feasible and consistent with each other. The design, code, and integration plans were checked to ensure that all units were represented. In addition, the rate of completion of these activities was evaluated, based on historical trends, effort availability, and other schedules. The various plans were then compared to one another to evaluate the amount of overlap and to ensure that adequate effort would be available as needed. The plans were evaluated to be feasible with medium risk. The project manager decided that the defined amount of risk was acceptable given the importance of this new product.

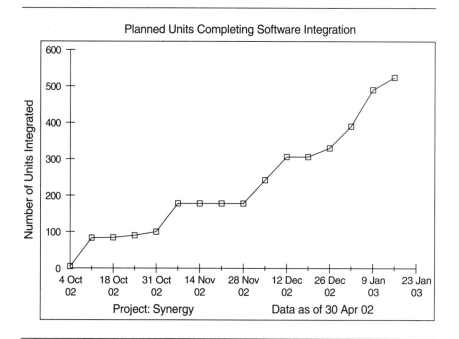

Figure C-8 Planned units completing software integration

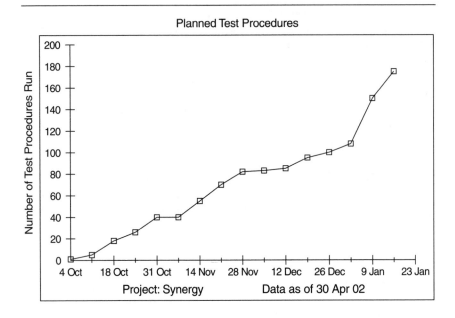

Figure C-9   Planned test procedures

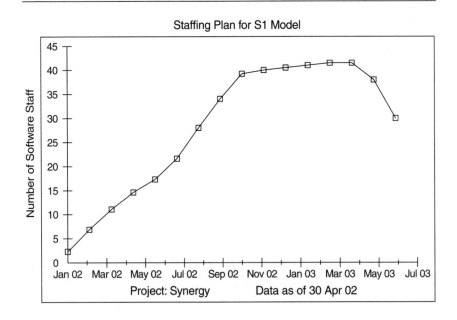

Figure C-10   Staffing plan for S1 model

Performance Analysis

The project progressed smoothly through the planning and design phases. Teams had settled into a routine of using measures to assess their progress against the plan, and inspections were catching errors in the requirements and design phases. Size estimates were proving to be reasonably accurate. Software design progress was closely following the plan, as demonstrated by the indicator in Figure C-11. Parallel activities in manufacturing, supplier ramp-up, marketing, training, documentation, advertising, logistics, and warehousing were all well under way. The company had also recently committed to two international trade shows and had contracted for several expensive commercial spots during the Super Bowl. Because time to market for the product was a critical competitive concern, senior management tracked the product schedule weekly and met monthly with the product manager for in-depth reviews of the measurement analysis results and project status.

DopCorp had collected defect measures from each development phase of their projects for several years and was able to draw upper and lower bounds on expectations for defects discovered during the Synergy devel-

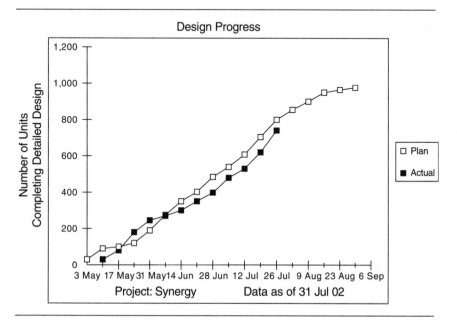

Figure C-11   Design progress

opment. They tracked the number of defects found during code inspections on a weekly basis, normalized by product size to obtain a derived measure of defect density. Each inspection package contained about 500 lines of code. They plotted the density of design defects they expected to find based on their historical data along with upper and lower control limits (see the indicator in Figure C-12). The project manager was particularly interested in making sure that people were not cutting corners in the inspections and failing to discover defects. The associated decision criteria for this indicator was a discovery rate that was below the lower control limit. In fact, this occurred during the thirteenth and fourteenth week of coding. Since the decision criteria was breached, further analysis was required to understand the cause of the out-of-control situations.

The development team also compared defect densities across configuration items. This derived measure is calculated by dividing the base measure of number of defects by the base measure of lines of code for each CI. The associated indicator is shown in Figure C-13. ISC had a considerably higher density than the other components, indicating that, for whatever reason, it was more error-prone. Reinspections were prescribed for all. The two drastic situations in Figure C-12 occurred during weeks when there were no inspections of ISC code. A process action team was organized to investigate the higher ISC defect rate.

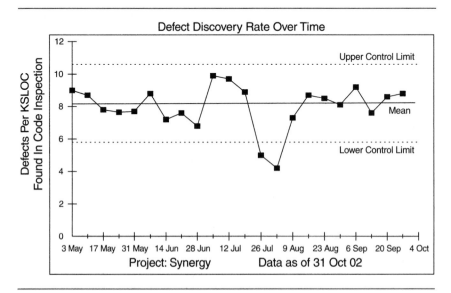

Figure C-12 Defect discovery rate over time

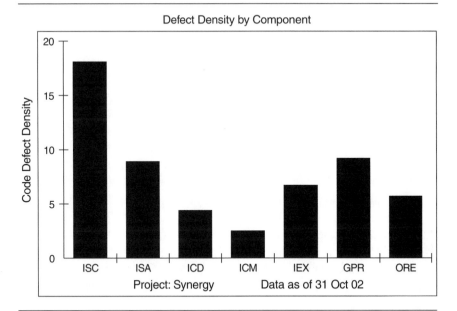

Figure C-13   Tracking defect density by component

Redesign and Replanning

In order to bring the product to market as early as possible, the systems engineer decided to use standard communications chips for dial-up protocols and to limit the size of the system memory. This was clearly stated in all of the requirements and design reviews and was approved at each level. These limitations were to be evaluated closely after initial production for possible upgrades at a later time.

Several weeks after software coding was under way, manufacturing and suppliers were tooling up. Memory and communications chips had been purchased and were being installed on the motherboard. At that point, the lead engineer discovered that the wrong model had been specified for the purchased communications chips. The fax logic was not designed to share printing tasks with a local area network. This effectively prohibited incoming fax or remote printing transactions any time a local network print job was running, and local printing jobs would be delayed during long fax transmissions. Marketing's assessment of the impact of this constraint was that it could lower sales projections of the entry-level model by as much as 20 percent and would be a potential cause of significant customer dissatisfaction. Neither was acceptable for the initial offering of a major new family of products.

A hardware solution was simply not possible. A quick assessment by the lead engineer indicated that the replacement chips would not easily fit onto the motherboard and estimated that it would require an additional seven months or more to rework the hardware and manufacturing elements.

The product manager called together a cross-functional team of engineers from software, hardware, and communications disciplines to address the chip logic problem. The ideal solution would have minimal impact on both project schedule and product performance. The team was directed to focus on a software solution and to make recommendations based on three options: reduced functionality, technical trade-offs, and adding additional resources. Rejecting the change or slipping the schedule were deemed to be against the best interest of the company and would be considered only in the extreme circumstance that the team could find no reasonable solution in any of the three directed areas.

In deciding on an approach to the problem, the team focused their efforts in these three associated areas:

- Size of the software change

- Staff availability, knowledge, and productivity

- Availability of memory

Having identified the major areas of concern, the team formulated the following strategy.

1. They directed software engineering to perform a quick search to determine whether an existing component could be found within DopCorp that would solve the chip problem.

2. An architecture design group was chartered to estimate the size and complexity of the code needed and the potential effort required to develop it. They were to consider both the effort required to modify existing code (if such code could be found) and the effort required to develop new code.

3. Product engineering was to examine memory usage and to determine whether sufficient memory would be available for the additional code.

4. Another task was organized to conduct a feasibility analysis to analyze the impact of the change on existing staffing and effort requirements to understand whether the project could absorb the change with existing resources or whether additional staffing would be required. If new resources were required, they were to develop contingency plans for acquiring them quickly.

The team was able to locate a reusable component for the change rather quickly. The company had developed a prototype fax/printer about 18 months earlier and had developed the code in the lab to save the time and cost of incorporating a chip for the prototype. The code had been successfully used in demonstrating the product, but it was abandoned when the project was canceled. The prototype was 8,000 lines of C++ code. Based on the similarity of the communications requirements, the software engineering team estimated that 80 percent of the logic could be reused. This meant that an additional 1,600 lines would have to be added or modified. Using productivity data from actual experience on the project's other components, they projected an effort of approximately six staff months to accomplish the new work. This estimate was further stated as three engineers over a two-month period. The project office estimated that this would add another month to the schedule due to the overhead of having to bring new members on board late in the project. The project office also estimated that the impact on schedule could be minimized if experienced programmers could be found who were already familiar with the prototype code.

One member of the Synergy project had worked on the prototype code, and two additional people were located within DopCorp who had been part of the prototype effort but who were now assigned to other projects. The only possibility of making the schedule was to reassign the two programmers to the Synergy project to work on the additional code. However, this would require action from the highest management level. The product manager asked his staff to put together the indicator shown in Figure C-14.

The line labeled Δ represents the projected completion date for coding with the benefit of the three experienced programmers. The line labeled +

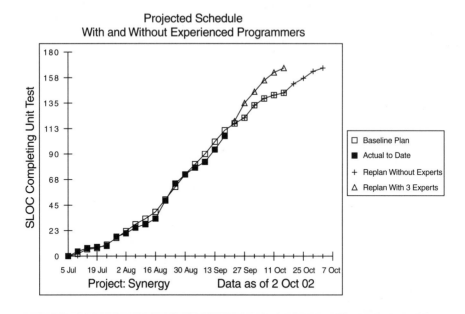

Figure C-14   Projected impact on schedule with and without programmers experienced with prototype

represents the projection based on the addition of two new members (along with the one experienced person who was already a member of the team).

Beside the impact on schedule, the other concern was the impact on product performance. The initial estimates of the new program logic were in the range of 4 megabytes of storage. While not large, adding the change to memory would exceed the maximum 80 percent utilization window needed to ensure response time requirements. Without that window, response time would degrade dramatically.

Further analysis revealed that the fax buffer was designed to hold up to 99 pages of data and that 8 megabytes of storage were allocated to the buffer. If the buffer could be reduced to 50 pages, 4 megabytes could be made available for the new code—enough for a basic set of logic to allow simultaneous operations. Development agreed to monitor the size estimates closely and to advise marketing at the earliest possible moment if estimates appeared to be threatening the existing buffer size allocation.

A small amount of new logic would also be required in the application code to complete the handshaking routine. The network printing application would be required to check the fax buffer routinely for incoming data and to establish connection to the multiplexing logic. This additional handshaking logic would slow the throughput rates for printing and for fax reception, but they were expected to remain within acceptable limits, and the proposed solution was accepted.

A project review at the executive level was held to decide whether to commit additional resources to the Synergy project. The project manager was able to make a convincing case that a software solution could be implemented without negatively affecting performance or schedule if the two experienced programmers could be reassigned to the Synergy project. The CEO was impressed by this argument and also by the fact that the project's performance to date had been on track. She directed a reassignment of priorities so that the two experienced people could be put on the Synergy project for two months. The Synergy project was allowed to continue.

Conclusion

The Synergy project was not trouble-free, but problems were identified while there was still time to handle them. The new S1 model was available within the 18-month window and proved to be a commercial success. As a result of the S1 and S2 models, DopCorp increased its market share by 14 percent in the 24 months following product introduction.

GLOSSARY

Accuracy An evaluation criterion that determines whether the implementation of a measure conforms to its definition as specified in a measurement procedure.

Aggregation Structure A structure that captures the relationships among the measured software entities so that data can be combined and decomposed as appropriate to the question being considered. There are three basic types of aggregation structures: component, functional, and activity.

Analysis The process of integrating measures, decision criteria, and project context information to evaluate a defined information need. Analysis also includes the derivation of cause-and-effect relationships across project issues. There are three types of analysis: **estimation,** which produces estimates of software size, effort, schedule, and quality; **feasibility analysis,** which assesses the feasibility of project plans during initial planning and replanning activities; and **performance analysis,** which assesses the project's actual performance against plans throughout the project.

Analysis Model An algorithm or calculation combining one or more base and/or derived measures with associated decision criteria. It is based on an understanding of or assumptions about the expected relationship between the component measures and their behavior over time.

Attribute A property or characteristic of an entity that can be distinguished quantitatively or qualitatively by human or automated means. An attribute is the property or characteristic of an entity that is quantified to obtain a base measure.

Base Measure A measure of a single attribute defined by a specified measurement method. A base measure is functionally independent of other measures.

Build An iterative release of a software product that is placed under formal configuration control as the current, approved product baseline, during either software development or operations and maintenance.

Component (of Software) An element in the design of a software product, for example, a major subdivision of a product, an element of that subdivision, a class, object, module, function, routine, or database. The terms *software component* and *software unit* have the same meaning.

Customer An individual or organization that procures a system, software product, or software service from a supplier.

Data A collection of values assigned to base measures, derived measures, and/or indicators.

Data Provider An individual or organization that is a source of data.

Data Store An organized and persistent collection of data that allows for its retrieval.

Decision Criteria Numerical thresholds, targets, and limits used to determine the need for action or further investigation or to describe the level of confidence in a given result. Decision criteria help to interpret the measurement results.

Derived Measure A quantity that is defined as a function of two or more values of base and/or derived measures.

Developer An organization that builds the software products. See also **Supplier.**

Entity An object (for example, a process, product, project, or resource) that is to be characterized by measuring its attributes.

Estimation See **Analysis.**

Estimator A type of indicator that uses one measure to predict the value of another. The measures used to produce estimators are typically composed of historical data from past projects. The analysis model specifies the predictive relationship that exists between two measures.

Experience Base   A data store that contains the evaluation of the information products and the measurement process as well as any lessons learned during the measurement process.

Feasibility Analysis   See **Analysis.**

Indicator   A measure that provides an estimate or evaluation of specified attributes derived from an analysis model with respect to defined information needs. Indicators support the user with respect to decision making.

Indicator Value   A numerical or categorical result assigned to an indicator.

Information Need   An insight necessary to manage objectives, goals, issues, risks, and problems. What the measurement user needs to know.

Information Category   Common categories of information used in the PSM process to help identify and prioritize project-specific information needs. The PSM common information categories represent broad areas of software concern that must be managed in most projects.

Information Product   One or more indicators and their associated interpretations that address an information need (for example, a comparison of a measured defect rate with a planned defect rate along with an assessment of whether or not the difference indicates a problem). Information products are the collection of indicators, interpretations, and recommendations provided to the decision maker as an output of the measurement process.

Integrated Analysis Model   A model that relates project information needs and issues in terms of cause and effect.

Issue   Areas of concern that may impact the achievement of project objectives. There are three types of issues: **problems,** which are areas of concern that a project is currently experiencing or is relatively certain to experience; **risks,** which are areas of concern that could occur, but are not certain; and **lack of information,** which includes areas of concern where the available information is inadequate to reliably predict project impact.

Lack of Information   See **Issue.**

Measure (n.)   A variable to which a value is assigned to represent one or more attributes. The term **measures** is used to refer collectively to base measures, derived measures, and indicators.

Measure (v.)   To make a measurement.

Measurable Concept   An abstract relationship between attributes of entities and information needs.

Measurement   A set of operations having the object of determining a value of a measure.

Measurement Analyst   An individual or organization responsible for the planning, performance, evaluation, and improvement of measurement.

Measurement Construct   A mechanism that specifies exactly what will be measured and how the resultant data will be combined to produce results that satisfy a defined information need.

Measurement Function   An algorithm or calculation performed to combine two or more base and/or derived measures.

Measurement Information Model   A formal mechanism for linking defined information needs to the software processes and products that can actually be measured. The Measurement Information Model establishes a defined structure for relating measurement concepts and terms.

Measurement Librarian   An individual or organization responsible for managing the measurement data store(s).

Measurement Method   A logical sequence of operations, described generically and used in quantifying an attribute with respect to a specified scale. The type of measurement method depends on the nature of the operations used to quantify an attribute. The method may be **subjective** (involving human judgment) or **objective** (using only established rules to determine numerical values).

Measurement Plan   A virtual or tangible product that documents applicable project information needs, measurable concepts, measurement constructs, and measurement procedures. It also documents how the project measurement process and resources will be managed.

Measurement Procedure   A set of operations, described specifically and used in the performance of a particular measurement according to a given method. A measurement procedure defines the mechanics of collecting and organizing the data required to instantiate a measurement construct.

Measurement Process Model   The process framework for establishing, planning, performing, and evaluating software within an overall project or organizational structure. The measurement process comprises activities and tasks.

Measurement Process Owner   An individual or organization responsible for the measurement process.

Measurement User   Any individual or organization that makes use of the measurement information products.

Observation   An instance of applying a measurement procedure to produce a value for a base measure.

Operator   An individual or organization that operates the system.

Organizational Unit   The part of an organization that is the subject of measurement.

Performance Analysis   See **Analysis.**

Problems   See **Issue.**

Process   A set of interrelated activities that transform inputs into outputs.

Project Context   The unique characteristics and environment of a software project that impact interpretation of the measurement results. Project context is defined, in part, by the assumptions and constraints, and the technical and management processes of the project.

Reliability   An evaluation criterion that determines the extent to which the repeated application of the measurement method yields consistent results.

Risks   See **Issue.**

Scale   An ordered set of values, continuous or discrete, or a set of categories to which an attribute is mapped. The type of scale defines the nature of the relationship between values on the scale. Four types of scales are commonly defined: **ratio,** in which the measurement values have equal distances corresponding to equal quantities of the attribute where the value of 0 corresponds to none of the attribute (e.g., the size of a software component in terms of Lines of Code (LOC)); **interval,** in which the measurement values have equal distances corresponding to equal quantities of the attribute (e.g., cyclomatic complexity has the minimum value of 1, but each increment represents an additional path); **ordinal,** in which the measurement values are rankings (e.g., the assignment of defects to a severity level); and **nominal,** in which the measurement values are categorical (e.g., the classification of defects by their type).

Software Process   A set of interrelated activities implemented by an organization to develop software.

Software Product   A set of computer programs, procedures, and associated documentation and data.

Software Service   Performance of activities, work, or duties connected with a software product, such as its development, maintenance, and operation.

Stakeholder   An individual or organization that sponsors measurement, provides data, is a user of the measurement results, or otherwise participates in the measurement process.

Supplier   An organization that enters into an agreement with the acquirer for the supply of a system, software product, or software service under the terms of that agreement.

System   An integrated composite consisting of one or more of the processes, hardware, software, facilities, and people that provide a capability to satisfy a stated need or objective.

Unit (of software)   An element in the design of a software product, for example, a major subdivision of a product, an element of that subdivision, a class, object, module, function, routine, or database. The terms *software unit* and *software component* have the same meaning.

Unit of Measurement   The standardized quantitative amount that will be counted to derive the value of the base measure, such as an hour or line of code. A unit is a particular quantity, defined and adopted by convention, with which other quantities of the same kind are compared in order to express their magnitude relative to that quantity.

User   An individual or organization that uses the system to perform a specific function.

Value   A numerical or categorical result assigned to a base measure, derived measure, or indicator.

Bibliography

Abts, Chris, Barry W. Boehm, A. Winsor Brown, Sunita Chulani, Bradford K. Clark, Ellis Horowitz, Ray Madachy, Donald J. Reifer, and Bert Steece. *Software Cost Estimation with COCOMO II.* Upper Saddle River, NJ: Prentice Hall, 2000.

Austin, Robert D. *Measuring and Managing Performance in Organizations.* New York: Dorset House, 1996.

Bache, R., and G. Bazzana. *Software Metrics for Product Assurance.* London: McGraw-Hill, 1994.

Bailey, Elizabeth K., Mary B. Busby, Wolfhart B. Goethert, et al. *Software Effort and Schedule Measurement: A Framework for Counting Staff-Hours and Reporting Schedule Information.* CMU/SEI-92-TR-21, ESC-TR-92-021. Pittsburgh, PA: Software Engineering Institute, Carnegie Mellon University.

Bailey, Elizabeth K., Anita D. Carleton, William A. Florac, Wolfhart B. Goethert, Robert E. Park, and Shari Lawrence Pfleeger. *Software Measurement for DoD Systems: Recommendations for Initial Core Measures.* CMU/SEI-92-TR-19, ESC-TR-92-019. Pittsburgh, PA: Software Engineering Institute, Carnegie Mellon University, September 1992.

Basili, V., and D. M. Weiss. "A Methodology for Collecting Valid Software Engineering Data." *IEEE Transactions on Software Engineering,* pages 728–738. November 1984.

Baumert, John H., and Mark S. McWhinney. *Software Measures and the Capability Maturity Model*. CMU/SEI-92-TR-25, ESC-TR-92-025. Pittsburgh, PA: Software Engineering Institute, Carnegie Mellon University, September 1992.

Boehm, B. W. *Software Engineering Economics*. New York: Prentice-Hall, 1981.

CMMI Development Team. *Capability Maturity Model—Integrated Systems/Software Engineering (Version 1)*. Software Engineering Institute, Carnegie Mellon University. 2000.

Deming, W. E. *Out of the Crisis*. Cambridge, MA: MIT Center for Advanced Engineering. 1986.

Fenton, N. E. *Software Metrics: A Rigorous Approach*. Chapman & Hall, London, 1991.

Florac, William A., et al. *Software Quality Measurement: A Framework for Counting Problems and Defects*. CMU/SEI-92-TR-22, ESC-TR-92-022. Pittsburgh, PA: Software Engineering Institute, Carnegie Mellon University, September 1992.

Grady, Robert B. *Practical Software Metrics for Project Management and Process Improvement*. Englewood Cliffs, NJ: Prentice Hall, 1992.

Grady, Robert B. *Successful Software Process Improvement*. Englewood Cliffs, NJ: Prentice Hall, 1997.

International Vocabulary of Basic and General Terms in Metrology. Geneva, Switzerland: International Standards Organization, 1993.

ISO TR 10017: 1999, "Guidance on Statistical Techniques for ISO 9000:1994." Geneva, Switzerland, 1999.

ISO/IEC 14143: 1998, "Information Technology—Software Measurement: Definition of Functional Size Measurement." Geneva, Switzerland, 1998.

ISO/IEC 14598-1: 1999, "Information Technology—Software Product Evaluation, Part 1, General Overview." Geneva, Switzerland, 1999.

ISO/IEC Draft Standard 15939, "Software Measurement Process." Edited by K. El Eman and D. Card. International Organization for Standardization. Geneva, Switzerland, January 2001 (final coordination draft).

ISO/IEC TR 15504-1:1998, "Information Technology—Software Process Assessment, Part 1, General Overview." Geneva, Switzerland, 1998.

Kan, S. H. *Metrics and Models in Software Quality Engineering.* Reading, MA: Addison-Wesley, 1995.

Kitchenham, B., et al. "Towards a Framework for Software Measurement Validation." *IEEE Transactions on Software Engineering,* pages 929–944. December 1995.

Lyu, M., ed. *Handbook of Software Reliability Engineering.* New York: McGraw-Hill, 1996.

McCabe, Thomas J., and Watson, Arthur H. *Structured Testing: A Testing Methodology Using the Cyclomatic Complexity Metric.* National Institute of Standards and Technology (NIST) Special Publication 500-235, August 1996.

McGarry, J., et al. *Practical Software Measurement.* Joint Logistics Commanders and Office of the Undersecretary of Defense for Acquisition. 1997.

Park, Robert E., et al. *Software Size Measurement: A Framework for Counting Source Statements.* CMU/SEI-92-TR-20, ESC-TR-92-020. Pittsburgh, PA: Software Engineering Institute, Carnegie Mellon University, 1992.

Putnam, Lawrence H., and Ware Myers. *Measures for Excellence: Reliable Software on Time, within Budget.* Englewood Cliffs, NJ: Prentice Hall, 1992.

Rozum, J. A., and S. Iyer. *A Data Definition Framework for Defining Software Measurements*. (technical report) Pittsburgh, PA: Software Engineering Institute, Carnegie Mellon University, 1996.

Walters, G., and J. McCall. *Factors in Software Quality*. Rome Air Development Center, Rome, NY, 1977.

Weinberg, Gerald M. *Quality Software Management Vol. 2: First-Order Measurement*. New York, NY: Dorset House Publishing, 1993.

Index

Other Titles of Interest from Addison-Wesley

Measuring the Software Process

Statistical Process Control for Software Process Improvement

William A. Florac and Anita D. Carleton

This book shows how to use measurements to manage and improve software processes within your organization. It explains specifically how quality characteristics of software products and processes can be quantified, plotted, and analyzed, so that the performance of software development activities can be predicted, controlled, and guided to achieve both business and technical goals.

0-201-60444-2 • Hardcover • 272 pages • ©1999

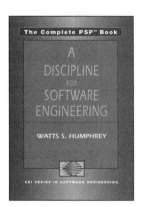

A Discipline for Software Engineering

The Complete PSP Book

By Watts S. Humphrey

This book scales down to a personal level the successful methods developed by the author to help managers and organizations evaluate and improve their software capabilities—methods comprising the Personal Software Process (PSP). The author's aim with PSP is to help individual software practitioners develop the skills and habits needed to plan, track, and analyze large and complex projects, and to develop high-quality products.

0-201-54610-8 • Hardcover • 816 pages • ©1995

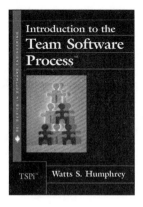

Introduction to the Team Software Process℠

Watts S. Humphrey

The Team Software Process (TSP) provides software engineers with a framework designed to build and maintain more effective teams. This book, particularly useful for engineers and students trained in the Personal Software Process (PSP), introduces TSP and the concrete steps needed to improve software teamwork.

0-201-47719-X • Hardcover • 496 pages • ©2000

CMMI℠ Distilled

A Practical Introduction to Integrated Process Improvement
Dennis M. Ahern, Aaron Clouse, and Richard Turner

The Capability Maturity Model Integration (CMMI) is the latest
version of the popular CMM framework, designed specifically
to integrate an organization's process improvement activities
across disciplines. This book provides a concise introduction
to the CMMI, highlighting the benefits of integrated process
improvement, explaining key features of the new framework,
and suggesting how to choose appropriate models and representations for your organization.

0-201-73500-8 • Paperback • 336 pages • ©2001

CMM in Practice

Processes for Executing Software Projects at Infosys
Pankaj Jalote

This book describes the implementation of CMM at Infosys
Technologies, and illustrates in detail how software projects
are executed at this highly mature software development organization. The book examines the various stages in the life cycle
of an actual Infosys project as a running example throughout
the book, describing the technical and management processes
used to initiate, plan, and execute it.

0-201-61626-2 • Hardcover • 400 pages • ©2000

CMM Implementation Guide

Choreographing Software Process Improvement
by Kim Caputo

This book provides detailed instruction on how to put the
Capability Maturity Model (CMM) into practice and, thereby,
on how to raise an organization to the next higher level of
maturity. Drawing on her first-hand experience leading software
process improvement groups in a large corporation, the author
provides invaluable advice and information for anyone charged
specifically with implementing the CMM.

0-201-37938-4 • Hardcover • 336 pages • ©1998

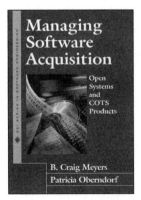

Managing Software Acquisition
Open Systems and COTS Products
B. Craig Meyers and Patricia Oberndorf

The acquisition of open systems and commercial off-the-shelf (COTS) products is an increasingly vital part of large-scale software development, offering significant savings in time and money. This book presents fundamental principles and best practices for successful acquisition and utilization of open systems and COTS products.

0-201-70454-4 • Hardcover • 400 pages • ©2001

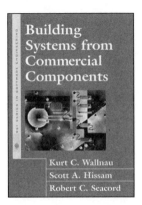

Building Systems from Commercial Components
Kurt C. Wallnau, Scott A. Hissam, and Robert C. Seacord

Commercial components are increasingly seen as an effective means to save time and money in building large software systems. However, integrating pre-existing components, with pre-existing specifications, is a delicate and difficult task. This book describes specific engineering practices needed to accomplish that task successfully, illustrating the techniques described with case studies and examples.

0-201-70064-6 • Hardcover • 432 pages • ©2002

Component-Based Software Engineering
Putting the Pieces Together
By George T. Heineman and William T. Councill

This book provides a comprehensive overview of, and current perspectives on, component-based software engineering (CBSE). With contributions from well-known luminaries in the field, it defines what CBSE really is, details CBSE's benefits and pitfalls, describes CBSE experiences from around the world, and ultimately reveals CBSE's considerable potential for engineering reliable and cost-effective software.

0-201-70485-4 • Hardcover • 880 pages • ©2001

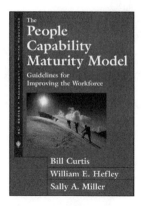

The People Capability Maturity Model
Guidelines for Improving the Workforce
Bill Curtis, William E. Hefley, and Sally A. Miller

Employing the process maturity framework of the Software CMM, the People Capability Maturity Model (People CMM) describes best practices for managing and developing an organization's workforce. This book describes the People CMM and the key practices that comprise each of its maturity levels, and shows how to apply the model in guiding organizational improvements. Includes case studies.

0-201-60445-0 • Hardback • 448 Pages • ©2002

Software Product Lines
Practices and Patterns
Paul Clements and Linda Northrop

Building product lines from common assets can yield remarkable improvements in productivity, time to market, product quality, and customer satisfaction. This book provides a framework of specific practices, with detailed case studies, to guide the implementation of product lines in your own organization.

0-201-70332-7 • Hardcover • 608 Pages • ©2002

Making the Software Business Case
Improvement by the Numbers
By Donald J. Reifer

This book shows software engineers and managers how to prepare the *business* case for change and improvement. It presents the tricks of the trade developed by this well-known author over many years, tricks that have repeatedly helped his clients win the battle of the budget. The first part of the book addresses the fundamentals associated with creating a business case; the second part uses case studies to illustrate cases made for different types of software improvement initiatives.

0-201-72887-7 • Paperback • 304 pages • ©2002

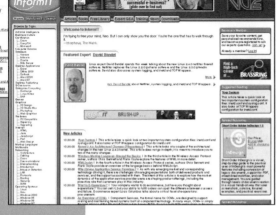

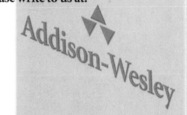